A Journey Into Depression

An Intimate Odyssey Towards Hope

Christopher Gajewski

A Journey Into Depression

An Intimate Odyssey Towards Hope

A collection of podcast transcripts that can be found at

https://friendsofgina.com/

Cover Art by Maria Sakharova

DEDICATION

To Rachel and Justine

Who saved my life

CONTENTS

Live Aloha

"Aloha is the Hawaiian word for love, affection, peace, compassion and mercy, that is commonly used as a simple greeting but has a deeper cultural and spiritual significance to native Hawaiians."

The literal translation of aloha is taken from two words, "Alo," meaning "presence," and "Ha," meaning "breath." Together, it translates to "The Presence of Life" or "Breath of Life."

Foreword

I thought I had things managed, until I realized they were about as far from managed as they could possibly get.

In 2000, I was diagnosed with Major Depression, PTSD and Anxiety Disorder. I started counseling, was put on meds, and got on with my life. I thought I had things under control. I mean, I was taking my Zoloft regularly, working, living, and doing all of the things you were supposed to do. I was okay.

But I was not okay. I would later realize that I lived a life of quiet desperation as a highly functional depressive. It finally caught up to me in 2018.

I still had no idea what was going on, only that the depression that I thought I was handling struck like a sledgehammer. From the outside looking in, I had everything. Inside, I was empty and exhausted beyond anything I had ever known.

At 47, I put a plan in motion to end my life.

It was a good plan! A great plan: one last adventure and then I would call it a day. In 2019, I sold my business, asked my wife for a divorce, put my house up for sale, and planned on going overseas where I would travel a bit and then find a nice, quiet beach to kill myself.

The pandemic screwed up everything.

In 2020, I finally put a different plan into motion and set off across the United States, chronicled in my book, "Disconnected: An Odyssey Through Covid America."

Something happened on the highways and byways of America. I didn't find hope, but I found pieces of things that I might be able to put together to form a new life, a healthier life. First though, I needed to get through the next few months.

Aye, it was a good plan. A great plan. When I did not follow through with it, I knew I was completely and totally screwed. I found myself in Texas, almost out of money with no job. The depression that I had been able to escape from on the roads caught up to me when I settled down.

It was sort of like being hit by a truck. Night after night.

I struggled through, sitting in my garage, thinking of turning on the car to allow the carbon monoxide to sweep me away.

The suicidal feelings finally began to pass but I knew that I still had a lot of work to do. I stayed there for 14 months and then took another job opportunity in Tijuana.

That's when I really got to work.

In June of 2022, I launched a podcast, "Let's Get Naked About Mental Health!"

Weekly, I would strip down and talk openly and authentically about my journey from suicide to...well, to where I am. I'm still on the journey.

It was my 12th step, reaching out to people, talking to them, explaining what I had a figured out and encouraging them to begin talking about it as well, begin their journey.

I was also reaching out to the loved ones of people struggling, to help them to understand what we with depression barely understand.

This book is the combined transcripts of the podcast. It is a journey into depression and an intimate odyssey towards hope.

You are welcome to join me.

Introduction

I begin each episode a certain way. Instead of repeating it in the book and annoying the living hell out of you, I will have it here just once. It is important.

...Before getting into the episode: the important stuff. I just want to remind everybody that I am not a psychologist, psychiatrist, therapist, or any kind of professional with an --ist at the end of their title. I am just a guy who has been there.

If you are in crisis, or know somebody who is, I implore you to reach out to a professional. There is now a national hotline in the United States you can call or text. 988. I'll repeat that because it bears repeating. If you or someone you know is in crisis, I implore you to reach out to a professional. Dialing or texting 988 in the US will put you in touch with a crisis counselor instantly.

Now, let's unmask mental illness...

***

A word about the first few episodes. I was struggling. I wanted to do it, was doing it, but I was struggling to find my voice. And a title. It may get a bit confusing at first. The "podcast for the Coffee Chronicles" would eventually become "Let's Get Naked About Mental Health!" Then, it would later become, "Let's Unmask Mental Illness." It was a process. And still is.

If you listen to the original episodes, I struggled to find my voice there as well. I can always improve but I think that by the fifth episode or so I began to hit my stride.

Me? As I say, I am just a guy who has been there.

I've been many places in my 51 years. I get into it in episodes, but, before diving in, I thought I would write a little bit about myself. There is so much stigma attached to discussing mental health, so many misconceptions, and, I think, more so for men.

Depression is seen as lying in bed all day unable to move or do anything.

The supposed rules of being a man include never crying and being strong.

They are both total crap.

I'm a man. Some may even call me a manly man, with the hairy chest that I beat on occasion. I was a scrappy, scrawny, SW Philly kid, worked in most of the trades, and learned to stay away from electrical work because I always seemed to end up electrocuting myself.

I joined the Army Reserves, Infantry, when I was 17 and became one of the youngest non-commissioned officers at 20. Then, I went off to college to earn my degree in Communications (Journalism) from the University of Miami, Coral Gables. I did a semester abroad at the University of Glasgow and backpacked through Europe.

I have a speech impediment, a stutter, and my two favorite sayings are, "I don't give a rat's ass," and "I'm too old for this shit." The stutter has been lifelong, the sayings since I was 30 or so. I have a bad attitude. You can take the boy out of Philly, but you can't take the Philly out of the boy.

I am a business owner and became one of the first orthodontic labs in the country, if not the first small lab, that offered 100% digital workflow.

With the technology threatening many in my industry, I formed a national association to help--including my closest competitors. I became a leader and educator and was recognized as such in an industry publication.

During the pandemic, I added a few more things to my resume including scavenger and bootlegger.

I've traveled to more than a dozen countries and did a 152-day road trip across the United States. I went to all 50 states and racked up close to 40,000 miles.

I suffer from depression. It is something I have struggled with all my life, but it was when I was 30 that I was diagnosed with what I call the trifecta: Major Depression, PTSD and Anxiety Disorder.

I cry. I bawled like a baby when my cat died, my best friend for 18 years, with the snot and swollen eyes almost making it impossible for me to drive home from the vet where I just needed to be held.

I find no shame in it. I've been weak and sometimes not as strong as I needed to be.

In my 51 years, I've been human.

I know and understand that depression is an illness.
It is real.
It is treatable.
I am not alone.
There is hope.

Episode 1: Diving In

Welcome to the first official podcast for The Coffee Chronicles. Thank you for joining me.

The Coffee Chronicles is old, older than podcasts. I started writing columns a few decades ago and publishing them on my website.

I have recently switched the focus of my website. It was focused on the book I was working but is now focused on an idea I had a long time ago, Friends of Gina, or Gentler Insanities Anonymous. It is a pretty simple idea.

If I have a $1,000 a day cocaine habit or am a fall down drunk, there are a dozen meetings I can go to each night. But what if I suffer from depression, anxiety, PTSD or any of the other mental health issues that can be having a serious impact on my life?

Friends of GInA is a place to go for support, information, and really just someone to say, "I've been there, I might be there now, and I understand in a way your closest family and friends may not."

Depression is hard to explain. It can even be difficult to understand it ourselves. I have spent a lifetime trying to figure out what were "bad decisions" and what were decisions that my depression influenced me to make. --I do own all of them though.

The memes and quotes you see on Facebook and Instagram are nice enough, but I wanted to do something more, do something that goes beyond the superficial and dive deep into my world. You are welcome to join me. I am trying to be open, honest, authentic and articulate. That is why this podcast could just as easily be renamed, "Let's Get Naked and Talk about Depression."

Friends of Gina was inspired by a story I once heard on the television show, "The West Wing." Leo, a recovering alcoholic, was talking to Josh, who was in crisis following a traumatic event. The story goes something like this:

The Pit

A person falls down a deep hole and starts yelling for help.

An engineer comes along, looks down, sizes up the situation, and yells back: "I'll devise a way out and then I'll be back." And he walks away.

A priest walks up, looks down at the man, and yells, "I will pray for you." Then, he walks away.

A friend walks up, sees the man in the pit, and, without a word, jumps down into the hole.

In the deep, dark place, the man says with bewilderment to his friend that had just jumped down, "What the hell did you do that for? Now we're both stuck down here."

The friend replies, "Yes, but I've been here before. I know the way out."

***

Do I know the way out? At times. But the pit is someplace I know well. I realize now that my battle with depression has gone on my entire 50 years. Sometimes it is just a skirmish here and there and sometimes it is an all-out war. There are also lulls in the battle that can go on for years.

So, I invite you to come down with me. Or maybe you are already there? Or maybe you know someone who is and can't reach or understand them?

But who am I?

First, who I am not: I am not a therapist, psychologist, psychiatrist or any kind of professional with an --ist at the end of their title.

I am just a guy who has been there, am there now at times, and I am willing to be vulnerable and talk about my experiences. I promise to be authentic. I'll be serious, maybe funny at times, and will explore other aspects of mental health.

As I have mentioned, I have a lifetime of experience with it. I have been diagnosed with what I call the trifecta: Major Depression, PTSD and Anxiety Disorder. Somehow or another, I managed to sidestep Mom's Manic Depression--now called Bi-Polar Disorder.

I am also a former journalist. In my travels, I have experienced a lot and spoken with many different types of people in various professions. I have spoken with the true mental health care professionals, the people with the --ists at the end of their job titles.

This particular episode, and the motivation to begin my own podcast, came from a recent interview that I did on a professional's podcast.

"Before You Kill Yourself" is hosted by Leo Flowers, a TEDx speaker, stand-up comedian, personal coach and has a Masters in Counseling/Psychology. He had invited me to be on his podcast to promote my upcoming book, "Disconnected: An Odyssey Through Covid America."

The experience was not what I was expecting. Not that it was a bad experience, but it went very differently than what I had imagined.

Though I was a hundred miles away, this is kind of what it felt like:

I walk in all spiffy, freshly shaved, in a collared shirt, slacks, my expensive--but very comfortable--shoes and holding a copy of my book under my arm. Leo, a large man, greets me, shakes my hand with a firm grip and we start to chat. He knows I have a speech impediment, a stutter, so he is making me comfortable with small talk before we start the interview.

Small talk was over. He seizes me, rips off my clothes and tosses me into the deep of the end of the pool where the secrets behind the book are waiting.

What did I expect? It's a suicide prevention podcast. It's called, "Before You Kill Yourself." And I had revealed to Leo the motivation behind the book, behind my odyssey through Covid America.

He jumped into the pool with me, kept me afloat, and we started doing laps.

The big reveal came first. I had hinted at it throughout the book, slipped in bits and pieces that some few had figured out, but Leo brought it out front and center.

Yes, I had planned on killing myself. It was a well thought out plan that had evolved over a couple years. It is a much longer story, but I was just so damn exhausted I just didn't see any point in going on any longer.

So, I got rid of everything, disconnected from everything and everybody, and went on one final adventure. At the end of the adventure, the plan was to find some nice, quiet place to end my life.

In the back of my head, I also played the lottery. It was sort of like if you are down to your last dollar and you know the collection guy is coming the following day, you use the dollar to buy a lottery ticket. I figured that my odds were about the same. By posting and sharing my journey on social media, I had hoped to find something or somebody to ease the exhaustion.

It was ironic, I told Leo, because family members thought I was manic. I didn't blame them. As I mentioned: it's in the genes. I could see exactly how they saw it. But it was actually the opposite. I found that interesting: a violent reaction to a depressive episode that could be perceived as a manic episode.

The exhaustion did ease while I was on the road, the depression eased. I also found tools, teachers, and glimpses of the extraordinary.

When I finally settled down in Texas after the journey, that is when things got really ugly.

Leo and I would go on to talk about depression, suicide, suicidal idealization, being parentified, boundaries (or lack thereof), my inner child, and other things as we did laps in the deep end of the pool. He kept me from slipping under.

It was an exhilarating experience.

Then, Leo got out of the pool.

As he was toweling off, he asked me the final question, the final question he asks every guest: what would you say to someone who is about to kill themself?

That's when the demon came up, grabbed me by the ankles and pulled me under. Leo had his back turned so didn't see me sputtering and gasping.

The question triggered me because I am still on that particular doorstep. I really didn't have an answer, or at least not one that would do anybody any good.

I was still suicidal.

As I had explained to Leo in the interview, suicidal thoughts are nothing new to me. I have had them on and off all my life. They are like a swarm of gnats on a summer evening. I brush them aside and move on. My recent crisis, and a previous one, had turned the gnats into a swarm of hornets. The swarm of hornets had transformed back to gnats on a summer evening, but they fill my mind and choke me at times.

Leo's question, "What would I say to someone that was about to commit suicide?" had me looking into a mirror and asking, "What would I say to myself? What should I be saying to myself?"

The demon relaxed his grip, and I made my way to the shallow end of the pool to find more solid footing. I stumbled through an answer based upon this, a column I wrote in 2014 following the death of Robin Williams.

In Memory of Robin Williams…and Others Who Lost the Battle Against Depression

The doorstep to suicide is the loneliest place in the universe. I've been there, so understand. Many people don't, and that is understandable. How can someone be expected to comprehend such a distortion of reality? I've stood in a room full of people who loved and cared about me--and felt completely alone. While friends and family were giving me hugs, all I could feel was a vile self-loathing for being such a burden on these wonderful people.

The doorstep to suicide is a very cold place. I had always thought differently. When thinking about it, it was a passionate event. A climatic ending. But when I was there, it was a very cold and serene place, like an arctic field. Suicide becomes a rational decision, the only option that makes any sense. It can't/won't get any better, so what's the point? You are standing in that arctic field, alone and bitterly cold. There is no place to go, no shelter, no warmth, no hope.

The doorstep to suicide is a timeless place. Imagine if you will an agony so terrible that it becomes your existence. The pain so awful that it fades into a numbness that encompasses your every breath, until your breaths are a burden. There is just a "now," bereft of a joyful past and a hopeful future. I was 29 years old, and my life was over. I could not remember the 28 years of love and joy behind me and could not imagine the 15 years of happiness that awaited me.

The doorstep to suicide is a selfless place. I would have never of thought that. The opposite really. I had always considered suicide the most selfish thing a person could do. How could they do that to their friends and family? I had been there, been a witness as a person tried to go through that door and had to clean up afterwards. Selfish, self-centered damnable...but perception distorts as badly as reality on that doorstep.

What many consider selfish distorts into selfless. The question, "how can you do that to your family and friends" becomes "how can you NOT do that FOR your family and friends?" How can you continue to exist and allow your existence to drag them down, and do them harm?

I sat on that doorstep for a cold, timeless moment, got up, put my hand on that doorknob...and I am not quite sure what happened. An internal whimper. An upwelling of passion that escaped like a gasp through the ice that made me think, "something is not right here."

I called Rachel. An old friend. Two thousand miles away. She would understand. But she didn't. It still made sense to me, to step through that doorway. I hurt so bad. How could she not understand?

"Just one year," she said. "Give me one year. Put it aside for one year." If I could make it through 29, then what was one more? Give her one more year. That didn't make any sense, but, for her, I could do it.

The doorstep to suicide is a place I never went back to, but I still can remember it. I wonder if it was the same for Robin?

The path to the doorstep is a cluttered place, filled with misconceptions and burdened by the stigma of mental illness.

Depression is a disease.
Depression is real.
Depression can be treated.
You are not alone.
There is hope.

***

Finally, now, I can give Leo, and you, the clearer answer that I could not give then.

What would I say to someone that was about to commit suicide? I would ask them for more time, as Rachel did for me. I wouldn't try to argue with them or talk them down. I would just ask for one more month, one more year.

I know. I understand. That distortion of reality will pass if you give it time. There is help, through meds, counseling, and other ways that I will get into in further episodes. But, at the moment, I would ask the person to give me more of their time.

You can find my appearance on Leo's podcast here:

And that is a wrap for this initial episode of the Coffee Chronicles.

If you are in crisis, or think someone you love may be, I implore you to reach out. A new hotline just went live. Dial or text 988.

I want to repeat that. If you are currently in crisis, I implore you to call or text 988. Take that first step to get yourself more time.

I am now mentally and metaphorically putting my clothes back on. I need to get back to work. There is editing and writing to be done. There is a job hunt to continue and there is finally a podcast to prepare to upload on something or another.

Next week, I will be exploring how depression is misunderstood by us and those around us.

Thanks for joining me!

Episode 2: Into the Deep

The title, and the podcast, are still a work in progress. Bear with me. I listened to my first podcast again and realized I was about as monotone as that actor, Ben Stein, from Ferris Buehler's Day Off.

Anybody? Anybody? Buehler?

I need to work on it. I figure by the 8th or 9th episode, I'll work my way from Ben Stein to Robin Williams in "Good Morning Vietnam."

The title? Getting naked about mental health? I have always been lousy with titles unless they pop into my head. I'm still waiting for one to pop. Anybody? Anybody? Buehler?

Anyway...

How do you know if a loved one is in crisis? How do we know we are in crisis? It is something we hide well, not wanting to reveal our secret world to others or even to ourselves.

There is still a lot of stigma attached to depression--and mental illness in general. There is also a lot of misunderstanding. There can be shame, not wanting to show weakness. For my part, I did not want to share because I did not want to burden the people I love. I also did not know how to explain it. When I did try to explain it, something that I understood, it was difficult for them to understand.

And I could hide myself from it, escape it by ignoring it. For a while.

So, let's get into my secret world, and then travel into the deep. The mental clothes and defensives are coming off as I make my way to the surf. A soundtrack begins to play as I recall one of the oddest conversations I ever had with my brother.

One of my favorite albums is Peter Gabriel's "Secret World Live." I would start playing it here in the background, but I seem to get myself into enough trouble without even trying so why wade into copyright and fair use law?

The conversation with my brother started out normal enough, just two brothers chatting as I drove him to pick up his motorcycle. Then, my big brother started being my big brother and we started talking about financial stability, the future, retirement and safety nets. The conversation then turned to disability insurance.

"No, I can't get that," I said

"Why not," he asked.

"I don't know why but my diagnosis from 15 years back is still in my file: Depression, PTSD and Anxiety Disorder. No insurance company will touch me with that in my file."

Joe stopped, looked at me, and said, "Why would you have PTSD?"

If he had taken a crowbar and cracked me on my jaw--or maybe a human sized fly swatter--the effect would have been the same. I stopped, and for the briefest of moments, I disengaged from the present and tumbled through my past. A part of me screamed though 15 years, and then I was back in myself, complete, whole, and the only thing I could do was shrug.

He jumped on his motorcycle and drove off and I sat in my car for a moment or two. Then, I drove off. When I pulled up alongside of him on the highway, I almost ran him off the road. Just a quick swerve into his Harley. Instead, I made my way home with all of the "almost responses" percolating in my head.

Why would I have PTSD? Really?

For every action, there is a reaction. When my mind screamed through the last 15 years and hit the far wall, it came back with an echo of anger. The memories were softer and diffused, the anger softer and diffused. The knowledge of my present, where I was, steadied me.

But really?

He was aware of most of what I went through. Hell, one of the potential triggers made national headlines. January 4th, 1987: the largest train accident in the history of Amtrak that left many dead. Did I not communicate it well? And if I did communicate it, was he listening?

He's been a good big brother. He's of the old school, and, at times, can be cut from the cloth of the caricatures of the 50's man. Emotionally stunted but prepared to do whatever he must, whatever he thought was right. He even mentioned to me once, in another conversation, something to the effect that he has the emotional intelligence of a shrub.

I will always be eternally grateful to him. There are many things he has done for me. He once even gave me a home when I moved back up to Philly, when I was trapped someplace else in a bad situation. It would become the stepping off point, the foundation, for all else that came.

You know: the good stuff.

In that moment, though, I was angry at him. How could he not know about my PTSD?

Echoes of echoes. When the anger hit the far wall of the last 15 years, it came back with a soundtrack, the opening chords of the album, "Secret World Live." In the rising tide of the audience's applause, the anger diffuses. In the opening percussions, the anger dissipates. And then Peter sings to me:

"Come talk to me."

Oh, my brother, where do I begin? It was my secret world, my private world, known only to a few. But how can I explain it now without writing yet another lengthy introduction to my Coffee Chronicles?

The great play took place on stage, and that is what everybody saw. I was the adventurer and traveler, the college student and the Army Reservist. I was the romantic and the lover, the friend and brother and son and nephew and cousin. I was the dreamer and doer and spender and chef and writer.

To this day, I am not sure if it was all a lie.

"Please, come talk to me."

On a side stage is where another play was taking place, the secret world, the private world. It was where the depressive lived, and the savior, the writer, and the lost one and the broken thing. It is where the cast was populated by demons and imps and devils. It is where I struggled to keep a tenuous grip on sanity while I arrogantly tried to force the first stage to become the only reality, the only world. It is where I lived the lie.

"Just like it used to be, come on and talk to me."

The truth was the struggle between the two stages is what I never wanted anybody to see. It is the nature of depression, my depression, to isolate myself, to not reach out, to keep the battle contained from spilling over into the "real" world. To hide it, whether out of shame or fear of the reaction of others.

To not contaminate others with my own failures?

The struggle was titanic at times, and I lost many battles. But I became pretty damn good at keeping the mask on so that nobody, even you my brother, would never know.

More anger dissipates as the echo of the echo of the echo comes back to me. People saw what I wanted them to see. But when the mask that you wear does not fit with the actions on display--or the inactions in my case--people make their own assumptions. And without further evidence, without further communication…

"We can unlock this misery, come on, come talk to me…"

That all took place about five years ago. He still doesn't get it at times, but the more I open up about it, the more supportive he is. Like I said: he is a good big brother.

But let's get beyond brothers and cousins and best friends. I've made my way to the beach, and it is time for me to start stripping down to enter the surf.

I have been procrastinating. Aye, you would too. A couple years ago, a friend, a psychiatrist, told me to step away from this project.

It was an especially difficult time. I wanted to write a book explaining depression but, after decades, my depression introduced something new into the equation: depressive attacks. I didn't even know what the hell they were until I talked to my therapist about it.

A depressive attack is like a panic attack, but depression instead of panic. Instead of a lightning strike of panic coming from nowhere, it was like a sledgehammer of depression being swung by the universe to crash into my skull.

I would be having a fairly good day. Then, always around the same time of the day, about six at night, the sledgehammer would hit.

It would always start with a very small and inconsequential thing. A normal thing.

In one attack, it began because I did not get a reply from a friend who I had texted. It was stupid. We would text constantly at times and then not text for days or even weeks. Our lives would get busy, and the conversation would pause to be picked back up at a later time. That was normal.

I texted, she did not reply, and the sledgehammer hit. The spiral downward from having a good day to being on the floor in tears happened within seconds.

How absurd is that? Because I did not get a reply from someone that I knew would reply when she had time became this awesome and terrifying event. The depression slammed into me, and I wanted to kill myself to end the pain.

It passed. I went through it for a couple weeks until I finally talked to my therapist about it. It was a depressive attack, she explained.

"It happens at night at about the same time," she asked.

"Yes."

"The clozapam you take at night for anxiety? You are taking one and a half pills? Take the half at dinner time and then the one at night before bed like regular."

At that was that.

So, between the increased frequency of the sessions with my therapist, and on the advice from my friend the psychiatrist, I stepped away from the project. It was too close, too present, and they were afraid the experience of writing would pull me under.

Now, it is time to stop procrastinating. It has been a while. I need to get back to that book.

In the podcast, it is time to wade into the surf. Start swimming out so I can dive deep.

I had a funny conversation with another friend a few years back. For some reason, she always imagined me as the archetype tortured writer, typing away in the middle of the night, dredging the depths of my soul.

Nope, I told her, that's not me. Midnight was my time to fly and revel in the writing. I'd sip coffee, sometimes play music, and have fun.

With the book, it is different. The working title is, "Broken Thing: An Odyssey into Depression."

How do you remember things? For me, when I choose, it is like diving into a pool. I submerge in the memory and relive it, all the senses reactivating: sounds, smells, feelings, sights, and tastes.

It is what I need to do to write the book to try and explain depression.

I recently read an article on LinkedIn. "Five Tips to Cope with Double Discrimination" by Ashley Nester, MSW. The poster wrote: "I have learned that I am not responsible for another's misunderstanding of my experience. But I can use my perspective to help and educate others."

I added a reply:

"I love this, but I'd add something else: be understanding of their misunderstanding.

One of the things I've learned is I need to be an educator, especially to the people who love and care about me.

I think it is human nature for us to try to identify with another person by basing it upon what we know. It's hard for people to grasp that my clinical depression is so much beyond what they understand as depression. It is hard for them to grasp such a distortion of reality."

People suffering from depression get frustrated and hurt by the reaction of their loved ones, like me with my brother. The loved ones get hurt because they cannot help, or do not even know. I have been on both sides.

The thing I have come closest to that explains the struggle is from a science fiction show, "Star Trek: Deep Space Nine." Benjamin Cisco, the lead character, encounters a species that does not understand linear time, they exist in all time at all moments. He had to explain linear time to them.

Think about that on for a second. How would you explain linear time? Give it a second. I'll wait.

...

How would you explain linear time to somebody? Hint: Cisco would end up using baseball.

But that is what explaining my depression can be like. As I said, it is natural for a person to try to identify and empathize by basing it upon their own experiences. I have learned, though, that for many, their depression is not like mine. They reach for feelings, like the death of a loved one, to identify with me. But that cannot come close. I have lost loved ones so understand.

Clinical depression, to me, at its heart, is a powerful illusion. It is a distortion of reality so profound that it cannot exist in normal reality. Worse, as we are experiencing that depression, we see that distortion of reality as normal.

Just as an example, I was in my therapist's office for a session. We were discussing various things and in an aside, I mentioned my suicidal thoughts. Then, I moved on with the conversation.

"Wait, wait, wait," my therapist said. "Let's talk about the suicidal thoughts."

"Why," I asked.

I wanted to move on with the session. The suicidal thoughts were unimportant to me.

"How long have you been experiencing them," he asked. "Don't you want to talk about them? Do you have any plans to hurt yourself?"

I was puzzled. Confused. I was about 33 and suicidal thoughts had been a part of my entire life. I wrote that they were like gnats on a summer evening. I can have them for days at a time, weeks, or even months. They pop up in my mind a few times, or a dozen times, per day. I brush them aside and do what I have to do. Bringing them up in a therapy session was like going to my family doctor and discussing the pain in my back I've had since I was 14.

"Aren't they normal," I asked him. "Doesn't everybody have them?"

"No."

"Oh," I said. "Well, I'll bring them up the next time they are here."

I must be "here" now to discuss my depression.

I talked about the doorstep to suicide in my previous episode. I need to set up camp here to write the book. Maybe just off the doorstep a little way. I forget the altered reality, but to explain it and write my book, I need to remember. I need to dive into that pool and allow the demon to grasp my ankle and pull me down.

It is scary, but also therapeutic. I'll be overthinking the hell out of this one. I need to tell my story. Maybe, by sharing, and helping people to understand themselves and their loved ones better, I will be able to find some peace. Find a purpose for going through what I have gone through. I may even be able to find some mercy that I seem to be able to offer freely to others but am unable to grant myself.

Shall we dance into the darkness? Do not worry. I know the steps, I know the tunes, and I understand the halls of midnight. We shall not go astray.

And that is a wrap for this week's episode. If anybody knows Mr. Gabriel, can you ask him if I can use some of his music? I'd appreciate it.

Thanks for joining me.

Be kind to each other. Be kind to yourself.

Aloha.

Episode 3: A Lie of Omission

I lied in my previous episode after promising to be authentic. It was a lie of omission, but a lie is still a lie, so I wanted to rectify it, come clean.

I mentioned that I hide my secret world. I explained that I do this for various reasons, but I omitted the main reason: fear.

I was taught lessons in life--and perhaps they were the wrong lessons to learn. The lesson I learned was to hide my depression. I am still terrified each time I post something or upload a new episode.

Some lessons are very hard to unlearn.

The first major depressive episode I had was when I was 30. Things had happened to trigger it that I will not get into now. It was bad, though. I rocked in my rocking chair and listened to the water pump through the radiator in an apartment outside of Philly for weeks. I knew what was coming. I had already lost my first real job as a journalist because I could not function anymore. I was spiraling downward.

Later, I would be told that I had entered a period call decompensation. Basically, my mind was shredding.

Friends in Florida knew what had happened and started asking me to move there to recover and regroup. I refused. I knew what was coming and knew they had no experience with this kind of thing. They kept insisting so I finally packed up and moved to Florida to stay with them. The decompensation paused for a while but then picked up where it left off.

That is when I almost took my life the first time.

My friends never knew.

What they did know is what they saw: I was not doing what they asked me to do. Find a job, start a career, and start getting out more. I was simply unable to, and I was starting to get into my old bad coping mechanisms, my escapes. What money I did earn went to the strip club.

They did not understand, and I never explained. The therapist I finally started seeing was surprised I was not hospitalized, that I was even able to function.

They would eventually ask me to leave, and I lost all contact with them.

The big lesson I learned, though, was from my mother. She was bipolar with manic episodes and depressive episodes that were awful.

Because of the experience with my friends, I used to say that there was a part of me that wished I was like mother. When I was going through a rough time, it could be passed off or interpreted as me being lazy, a piece of shit. When she had her episodes, there was no mistaking it: people could point and say, "there is something very, very wrong here."

I was angry at a lot of people for a long time for my mother's sake. The anger, and the lesson I learned, can be encapsulated by the time I spent with her at the hospital while she lay dying, the cancer finally catching up to her.

I come from a huge family. On my mom's side alone, I was grandchild #35 or so when I was born. My mom was the youngest of nine. I am the middle child of three. Many times throughout her life, I felt like the only child of an only child.

My one uncle was there in the hospital, the baby boy of the family and closest to my mom in age. He would pop in and out of her life as his own issues permitted. His ex-wife and his two daughters were there as well. It was the most I had seen of my mom's family in one room in decades.

Another uncle showed up. I had not seen him in 40 years or so. The anger returned as he started to cry at my mother's side, telling her how much he loved her. I kept my mouth shut because it made her happy.

My brother was there. It was only the second time he had seen her in over 20 years, the first being when she was on another death bed.

--that is a story in and of itself. My mother was about to die on so many occasions, it was commonplace, but this time, the doctors assured me before I flew down, that this was really it. She was only waiting for her children to arrive before she allowed hospice to do their thing.

So, I brought my stepfather and called my brother. He flew down and got us a hotel room.

The anger is no longer there but a memory of the lesson is.

Hide! Don't let people see it!

Hell, I don't blame people. My mother's bipolar disorder could be terrifying. I remember one time when I was in Miami and Hurricane Andrew crushed the city. I thought to myself, "You should see what my mom can do."

I wanted to run like hell away from my mom on a few occasions. More than a few. That's what you do if a hurricane is bearing down on your city. But that will all be in another book I am working on, Mother & Son.

So, yeah, fear is the main reason for hiding my depression. Fear of losing those I love and those who love me. Aye, I understand. From both sides.

For me, with posting and the podcast, I guess the cat is out of the bag and running free. I am still terrified every time I hit "post" or "publish." As I mentioned, though, it is therapeutic, and, I think, necessary. We have to keep communicating, sharing, and attack the stigmas and fears associated with mental illness.

As Pink Floyd says, "Keep Talking."

It has gotten much easier for me now.

The last place I always post, though, is LinkedIn. I'm job hunting. I think to myself, with no pun intended, am I committing career suicide by posting about this? Would any company touch me if they knew? But I also feel that LinkedIn is where it needs to be posted the most.

Too many people are suffering in silence, from interns to CEO's. In Thoreau's words, "they are living a life of quiet desperation."

We don't know how to talk about this thing. We isolate ourselves and feel completely alone. Many people don't understand. How do we explain it to them? How do we get beyond the fear of rejection? How do we move past the fear of being perceived as weak?

I don't know. I don't have all of the answers. As always, you are welcome to come along on my journey as I attempt to figure them out.

I am here. I understand. I am listening. I am talking.

As always, if you or someone you know is in crisis, I urge you to dial 988, the new national crisis hotline. It is a good first step, to start talking.

Aloha

Episode 4: Deeper into Aloha

Let's get naked about mental health! --it's the title I am going with for now.

In this episode, I'll be stepping back in time to the pandemic to discuss aloha, a state of being, the warped perception of memory & time that depression brings, and I'll even bring Rob Thomas into the equation, the lead singer for Matchbox 20--though I like his solo work better. Bilbo Baggins will even be along.

Now, let's dive deeper into aloha.

I use the word aloha often. As I am not Hawaiian, I sometimes feel like a fake. But I love the word, and the meaning behind the word.

Like most people, I thought aloha as a simple Hawaiian greeting, a way to say hello and goodbye. There is a deeper meaning behind it, though. When you say it to someone, you are offering them something.

From Wikipedia: "Aloha is the Hawaiian word for love, affection, peace, compassion and mercy, that is commonly used as a simple greeting but has a deeper cultural and spiritual significance to native Hawaiians."

Seeing the word "Aloha" is very common in Hawaii. You constantly see signs like "Live Aloha" and "Drive Aloha." Hawai'i's nickname is The Aloha State.

Then, we can go even deeper into aloha.

The literal translation is taken from two words, Alo, meaning "presence" and "Ha," meaning breath. Together, it translates to "The presence of life" or "Breath of Life."

Aloha is a state of being. It is a force that binds the universe and all of us together. It is something that I have tried to integrate into my life to help with the depression.

One of the most important tools I learned in dealing with my depression was the idea of the net. As I traveled almost 40,000 miles across the United States, I highlighted my journey in markers using a road atlas. My travels became the strands and the stops the places where the strands connect.

On the west coast, I found a teacher, Sara, that taught me to do the same thing with my personal connections. Form a net. The paths between us and the people in our lives becomes the strands of the net and the people become the connection points. The more people we allow in, and recognize as being there for us, the stronger the net becomes.

Especially for me, nights can be like a highwire act across the chasm of depression. The fall can be awful, terrible. When I allow myself to realize the net is there, though, move beyond the perception of isolation, it becomes less terrible. There is a safety net if I do fall.

In the spring of 2020, before learning about the safety net, it was just me, isolated in an empty house during Covid, at night, contemplating aloha in front of the fireplace. A song was playing, Peter Gabriel's "Mercy Street" from his album "So." The song is about depression and suicide.

I tried singing in my last episode and that went about as well as it always does: awful. So, I'll just stick with reciting the opening verse.

Let's take the boat out
Wait until darkness
Let's take the boat out
Wait until darkness comes

Let's take the boat out and contemplate the one word in the translation of "aloha" that never seemed to fit, but it seems more and more to encompass the definition.

Aloha has five "foundational" concepts. I get the first four: love, affection, peace, and compassion. When I say "Aloha" to you, it is what I am offering you. The more I think about it though, the fifth foundation, mercy, is what I am offering myself. And it is what I refuse.

Supplicant. Criminal. Just a broken man. On the floor, with arms outstretched to the universe. Tears coursing down my face. Pain compressed into a tight ball in my chest. Expanding. Searing along every nerve ending. Until it feels as if I am in that old torture device, an iron maiden, where I am in the body shaped tomb lined with nails and it closes upon me.

"Just a break," I scream. "Just some peace."

But it could just as well be, "Mercy!"

I've been there on the floor, and then huddled into my ball. Waiting for the waves of the depressive attack to wash over and through me, waiting for them to ebb, so I could stand again. Waiting for mercy.

But am I waiting for the universe to grant me mercy? Or am I waiting for myself to grant me mercy?

Let's take the boat out
Wait until darkness
Let's take the boat out
Wait until darkness comes

And the darkness has come. More nights than not now. Aye, I was expecting it. The darkness is like a vortex pulling me into the halls of midnight, a dark place, with the demons and imps and the regrets of 49 years. I was trying to run from it, was doing a damn good job of it, but it's hard to run anywhere in lockdown. I was isolated and isolating myself.

The word, "mercy"? It is a noun that mean, "compassion or forgiveness shown toward someone whom it is within one's power to punish or harm."

I'm beating the hell out of myself these days. The big three no-no's of therapy, "should have," "could have," and "would have," are standing behind me with their cat of nine tails, lashing me as I go about my day. Every time I sit still. 16 hours a day to myself, to do anything and everything I always wanted to do and yet?

Let's take the boat out
Wait until darkness
Let's take the boat out
Wait until darkness comes

I need to think about this some more, as the boat rocks in the cool night air on the waves of depression. Contemplate the unthinkable: forgiving myself. Being compassionate to myself. Showing myself mercy.

****

Fast forward just a little bit. It was still the spring of 2020. My thoughts of running away to Europe were shot to hell. Europe was closed. So, I was turning my thoughts to traveling across America.

I fell into the Covid hibernation along with the rest of the world. Staying still, but not really, filling my days. In the absence of mercy, being in motion helps. Peter Gabriel was singing to me most nights. Then, one night, Rob Thomas took the stage...

***

Welcome to the new spring. I don't where you are, but here in PA the land just can't seem to shake out of winter. We see spring weather for a few days and then freeze warnings the next. Flowers and plants are struggling to figure out if it is time to grow or not. My koi are wondering whether to hibernate or not. There was some funky looking alien thing popping out of the ground that I was about to rip out—only to be told it is a fern and to leave it the hell alone.

Have you ever seen a fern popping out of the ground? It really does look like something from the movie, "Alien." But I digress...

Is America doing the same, struggling with an awakening they are not sure about? Trying to shake free of a winter that won't let go of its grasp? Awakening into what?

I thought I would reread Travels with Charlie by John Steinbeck. And the commentary. It's pretty interesting. I am picking stuff up that I missed before. --Maybe because I am not being forced to read it this time and just skimming the Cliff Notes before class? [My apologies to all of my former English teachers.]

Steinbeck hated what he found as he traveled the byways of America. In 1960, it was a nation on the cusp of a great change: the Civil Rights Movement. As a Nobel Prize winning author, he had taken to himself, removing himself from his roots in California and moved to New York. He had spent the last 10 years traveling abroad so wanted to try and rediscover the America that had inspired "Grapes of Wrath" and "Of Mice and Men." An old man searching for remnants of his youth.

He found a nation in the grip of impending turmoil. I wonder what I'll find. Will the soup kitchens reopen? What will America reawaken to as this long spring dogs us?

[I have no idea why, but The Metamorphosis by Franz Kafka keeps popping into my head. Will I awaken one morning in my Subaru Outback as a giant cockroach? A question for English teachers: why the hell did you make me read that?]

But then the lights dim and the spotlight shines down on me on the karaoke stage. In Alabama—the one state that has not made it illegal for me to sing. And to a quickly emptying, running, crowd, we

21

hear the opening bars of what I always felt was an underrated freshman solo effort by Rob Thomas, Something to Be.

"Hey man
I don't want to hear about love no more
I don't want to talk about how I feel
I don't really don't want to be me no more"

The winter of my discontent? Restless. Staring back at myself in a mirror. I need a shave, but I think I look pretty damn good for 49.

"Dress down now I look a little too
Boy next door
Maybe I should find a downtown whore
That'll make me look hardcore
I need you to tell me what to stand for."

Standing at my fireplace. My naked back arched as I grip the mantle. It's nighttime in this winter of discontent. Restlessness plus lockdown brings back the three big no no's of any therapy session: should have, could have, would have.

"I've been looking for something
Something I've never seen
We're all looking for something
Something to be"

But I have seen it. Experienced it. And like catching a fish in the stream with your hands, it wriggles, slips and leaps back into the stream, zipping away as you stare at the distorted reflection of yourself in the water.

I hear the rustling of whips being unrolled behind me. The scratchity skritch of the iron tips rustling against each other. I don't know why, but it is something I invite.

The lashes fall, crisscrossing my back. No big deal. I've been here before. Been here for a long, long time this time around. The red welts rising, the blossoming pain dripping with blood, knowing that all I have to do is turn around and they'll be gone. But I stare into the fire, the gas flame never touching the fake logs. Wondering, as the whips crack.

It was a good day. I met my stepfather and his club at Governor Printz Park in Tinicum. They rotate between there and North Avenue. Stories upon stories. Once the "breakfast club," it has now become the "social distancing" club. Barred from meeting at McDonalds for their coffee, they now bring their coffee and lawn chairs on nice days to form a circle and chat about the old days and current days and the new days to come.

My stepfather is a pain in the ass. He taught me everything I know about being a pain in the ass and I excelled under his tutelage. Him and my mom fought with me for over 10 years about allowing me to buy them a computer. After my mom passed, I was worried for him. Worried about his isolation, so I pushed harder. He finally relented.

Now, I'm jealous. He has more of a social life than me, uses the computer far more than I ever did. His forays into Facebook put him in touch with many of his old friends from high school and his breakfast club expanded. He's learning piano and Spanish as well.

But with the tide coming in at Tinicum, and the cold wind alternating with the warm sun, they wondered if this was the new norm. Just guys talking about who the virus has touched and where. I got after Rich a few weeks ago because he gets rides to the club in Tinicum. As a liver transplant recipient, and older, he's in the highest risk category.

He received his new liver the day my nephew was born, who is now 21.

"Christopher," he said to me in that tone only an old man from West Philly can take, "I should have been dead 21 years ago. I was down to 5% liver functioning and knew I was about to die. I'm living now. Leave me alone. And come join us."

Other conversations with other people. Talk of surges and spikes and flattening the curve, of border openings and how other countries are doing. Of people barricaded inside of their homes against an unseen agent. Of articles about spread and vaccines and tracing. Of a reality that we must awaken into, hearing again and again, "when this is over, we'll…"

I especially love my house in the spring, the house I have to try and sell. I like the colors. My wife did an incredible job with the perennials to blend them with the existing landscaping. I particularly like the blue/purple ground cover at the base of the fiery red tree. But I also just enjoy the simple green slowly replacing the browns. All emerging at different rates to flower at different times.

"Hey man
Play another one of those heartbreak songs
Tell another story of how things go wrong
And they never get back
My pain is a platinum stack
Take that shit back
You don't want to be me when it all goes wrong
You don't want to see me with the houselights on
I'm a little too headstrong
Stand tall
I don't want to get walked on"

And the house lights come on and I turn away from staring into the fireplace. A little too headstrong is an understatement. Something to be is something I know. It's about staring down the should haves, could haves, and would haves. With a towering, fiery arrogance that can only be born of SW Philly, Infantry, and 49 hard years: "Piss off."

It's all about the now. What will I find out there with the music playing and the high winds wrapped around me urging me onward and outward? Will I find an America that I never really knew? Will I find a me that I knew so long ago?

***

And then back to the present day...

That's another one of the tricks I learned about dealing with depression: the memories. I need to remember. Peter Gabriel helps sooth me into memories of myself, the side stage, where I need to write my book on depression. Rob Thomas helps me to remember the main stage: life and living.

I spoke about it in the previous episode: the timeless moment, the existing in only the here and now. In the depression, it is the hunched shoulders, the listlessness, a reality of depression. The illusion.

I am 51. I know for a fact that my entire life has not been depression. I know, rationally, that the depression has only come in chunks. Weeks, months, and sometimes years as with this last episode. But it still only remains a small percentage.

I'll hazard a guess at 5% of my life?

So, where the hell does the other 95% go? I struggle for it in the depression.

It can be like Bilbo Baggins in the Hobbit. When he and Thorin Oakenshield and Company are wandering for what seems forever in the Mirkwood forest. The dense and depressing forest is all that they come to know. It is all that Bilbo comes to know.

Then, being the smallest, Bilbo climbs to the roof of the forest. He struggles but is finally able to break through and stick his head out above the foliage. He is greeted with sunshine and a cool breeze. He sits in awe, but then has to return.

It is easy to forget who and what I am. It is easy to forget that I am not a depressive but only a person suffering with an illness, going through a depressive period. It is so easy to forget the 95% of my life filled with friends and family and happiness and love.

It is easy to forget the normal times, where it is just the day to day.

The reality becomes the moment, the 5% becoming the entirety of my life.

I am reminded, though, of the 95%, by the oddest things. Like a Rob Thomas song, that makes me turn from the fireplace and look at the depression and say, "Piss off!"

I just need to remember! We just need to remember.

Depression is such a powerful illusion. It twists reality and makes us believe it is the reality. The only reality.

And that's a wrap for this episode. In next week's episode, I'll be getting into...

...oh hell, I don't know. I was supposed to get into professional burnout in this episode, but things seemed to take me down other paths. I'll know when I get there. There really is a logical progression for all of this but my tangents are well known and can be epic.

Thanks for joining me.

Remember:
Depression is an illusion.
It is an illness.
It is treatable.
There is hope.
I am here.
I am listening.
And I will keep talking.
Aloha.

Episode 5: The Mental Health Triangle

In this episode, I'll be discussing an idea I had regarding mental health treatment: The Mental Health Triangle. It is going to invariably lead to where I screwed up. It is based upon a conversation I had with a friend at a business conference, and he explained a book he read a long time ago. We can't remember or find the book so I have still have a reward offered to anybody who can find it.

Now, let's get into the episode.

How do you approach mental health treatment? I, well, approach it wrong. Even now, I am just applying two sides of the triangle.

The mental health triangle is based upon a conversation I had with a friend at a business conference. Lance and I were discussing business models. He was telling me about a book he had read a long time ago, sometime in the 80's, about a production triangle. If you google "Production Triangle," you'll find hundreds. We can't find this particular one.

Lance is a very successful businessman. He found that this model can be applied to any business. Each side has to be equal or else the triangle collapses. For a visual, think of taking away one side of a triangle. It collapses in on itself, flatlines. The business doesn't go under necessarily, but it is operating in an unhealthy manor. It can't reach its full potential and struggles more than grows. The sides of the triangle need to be equal, with equal attention given to them.

The sides of the production triangle are products or goods, marketing, and finance. I won't get into that, but I will remind everybody that there is a reward to anybody that might recall the book from a business class they may have taken in the late 80's. Anyway...

Our conversation turned to other things, but the triangle stayed in my head. Lance had mentioned he could apply it to almost anything and does. He even applies it to sex when teaching about love and intimacy in his church classes.

I went back to my hotel room that night and continued thinking about the triangle. I was already in the midst of my depressive episode and the production triangle began to merge with it. It gave me a lot to think about.

I had thought I had gotten past the depression. I was taking my meds regularly and things seemed to be going well. I was living a fantastic life. I had a good job, a beautiful home, a wonderful wife. Then, I hit a wall. I was still in the early stages of the episode and wondering what the hell had happened. What triggered it?

Professional burnout was definitely a part of it--or maybe professional burnout was a symptom of it?

Then, while lying in bed in a hotel room in Chicago, the mental health triangle began to form.

On one side of the triangle is meds, or psychiatry. It had taken me a few years to find the right one, but Zoloft had been helping a lot.

Wait. Halt. Pause.

I really need to repeat myself here. I am not a doctor or specialist, so all of the following is conjecture and based upon personal experience.

Back to the Zoloft.

I had been through a few different meds and only later realized that you need patience. There is no such thing as a magic pill. I think I read that each med has only a 40% chance of working well and you need to give it a couple months to see if it will work.

I swore by my Zoloft though. I had been on it for a long time, and it helped. Until it wasn't helping anymore. --I would later discuss it with my psychiatrist, and she felt that I had been on it for so long that my body had become resistant. She switched me to a fairly new drug on the market, Viibryd.

There was still something very wrong though. Another side of the triangle came into focus: psychology, or therapy. Talk therapy. For me, that side of the triangle was weak at best.

Though I knew I needed it and had known I needed it for decades to work through past issues and current ones, I had only toyed with therapy. A couple sessions here and a couple sessions there.

I grew up during what I consider the dark ages of mental health care. Due to cutbacks and insurance issues, talk therapy had been regulated to pure crisis intervention--unless you had the cash to pay for it.

But that was one of my problems. I had the cash. I was doing well. I knew I should be in therapy. As a student of systems theory, one of my soapbox issues (I won't get started into it for now), I knew that just taking meds was not the entire solution. It was only a part of it.

That has always been one of my problems. I take the path of least resistance. The easiest path. I had been doing well, the pills were helping, I was feeling good, so why spend the extra time and money for therapy?

Therapy, for me, is like meds. You need to experiment to find the right one. It takes time and patience. You need to have a healthy, therapeutic relationship with your therapist and connect in the right way. The only times I had even attempted that particular journey was when I was in crisis mode and forced to react to a situation instead of acting on my own behalf.

Then, it hit me. The third leg of the triangle. The flatline. My business was doing well but, according to Lance--though he never said it out loud, was flatlining.

The third leg of the Mental Health Triangle is personal care. I had completely ignored it all my life. I tell people that I did worse than burn the candle at both ends; I took a flamethrower to the entire candle. I burned myself out, poured out all of myself, without doing anything to replenish myself.

Oh, I lied to myself. I'm pretty good at that. I told myself the vacations, the meets with friends, and my cat were enough. It wasn't. I had developed unhealthy coping mechanisms at a young age.

I knew the answers, but I never pursued them.

A part of me, the petulant child, wants to scream and throw a tantrum. "It's not fair! I shouldn't have to do this crap. Other people don't and they are perfectly fine!" (They are not, but that is another story).

But isn't that the lesson we all learn at a very young age? Life isn't fair. Ignoring the unfairness, ignoring the things we should be doing, doesn't help.

My mental health triangle came into focus, and I fell asleep. It gave me a lot to think about over the coming months as the depression got worse and my life fell apart.

Crisis intervention versus personal care.

Acting versus reacting.

The deeper I got into the depressive episode, the worse the depression got, the harder it was to do anything. I think about all of the things I should have been doing, all of the things I knew would help, but that, for me, is the nature of depression.

This is where friends and loved ones really pissed me off. I would get all of the normal advice. It was all of the normal, simple things. The things I knew. They can all be summed up in the sentence, "stop being depressed."

I can't!

It might seem simple from the outside looking in, but from the inside looking out, it is a much different perspective. It is like trying to function with layers of blankets wrapped around me. The deeper into the depression I get, the more layers get added.

I remember one incident when I was in tears because I couldn't put on my socks. I have been in situations before when I couldn't put on socks and needed help, but they were because I had thrown out my back or had surgery. This wasn't that. Physically, I felt perfectly fine.

I could reach for the sock. After struggling, I could get it on a few toes, but I couldn't get the one sock on my foot. I gave up and went barefoot that day. Which made me feel like an even bigger piece of shit.

How did I get there? How did a very accomplished man get to the point where he couldn't put on his socks? It goes back to the triangle. And where I screwed up. So, let's go back and take a look at the triangle from a personal perspective.

Psychiatry. Meds.

I didn't like them. I hear that repeated a lot. The first med I was put on was when I was in college was Prozac. The pills got tossed all over my apartment one night. I didn't like the way they made me feel. --that's something else I hear a lot.

I still don't like them. Without insurance these days, my choices are limited. Very limited. I don't have access to the new drugs that are coming to market, so I am sticking with a tried and true one: Lexapro. With the med comes the tried-and-true side effects. I really don't like those.

TMI? Too much information? Is there such a thing in this podcast? One of the reasons why my doctor switched me to Viibryd was she felt I had become resistant to the Zoloft. The other reason was it was known to have less of a particular side effect. Sexual dysfunction.

Nope, it doesn't work. I am unmanned. I'm becalmed on the sea of manhood, without even a breeze to stir my sail. The desire has even gone away as well for the most part. I tell myself this is a good thing as my penis has gotten me into almost as much trouble as my mouth.

I am lying to myself.

Not that I get many opportunities, but it would be nice to have dirty thoughts once in a while. I remember the feelings of sexual attraction, I remember sexual fantasies, I remember the feeling of waking up with...well, you know. But they are all just memories, distant ones. And getting more distant.

At first, I thought it was just a natural part of getting older. Then, I was talking about it with a nurse, my aunt.

"No," she said.

I think I was 48 at the time. She said maybe, maybe, after a couple more decades, but now it definitely was not natural. So, I went to a specialist and went through all of the tests. Some were very uncomfortable. From testing my testosterone levels to some poking and prodding with needles in very sensitive areas. There was nothing physically wrong with me. It was all in my head, and in my meds.

I know a lot of people struggle with the side effects. I've reached a point in my life where I am like, "what else can I do? What's the alternative?"

At one point in early 2021, with the depression hitting me harder, I thought the meds--Viibryd and Clonazepam at the time-- weren't working anymore. So, I said the hell with it. I did do it the smart way: I weaned myself off them, taking smaller doses until I was off them completely.

That turned into a complete and utter disaster.

It took a few weeks, but I realized that the meds had been working. They had been helping. I went from being depressed into falling into an abyss that took me months to get out of.

But what can you do, I do, about dealing better with that first side of the pyramid?

Well, first, don't be stupid like me and stop taking your meds.

You really need to talk to a psychiatrist and have some patience. Remember what I said about the meds: each one has a 40% chance of being effective and takes time to see if it will be effective. Now, there is even a genetic test that can point towards what type of drug should be most effective.

Also, there are new drugs coming to market, the first in decades. Viibryd is fairly new. If you have not spoken with a doctor about meds in a while, it might be time to stop in and have a discussion.

Finally, there are also new therapies getting a lot of exposure. If you are like me, and Google is keeping track of your every move, you are seeing a lot of ads on Instagram and Facebook about new kinds of therapy. Psychedelics, ketamine, and magnetic resonance therapy (MRT) are a few. I am working on an article now about these new treatments that I have heard have good outcomes, especially for those who have become resistant to traditional meds.

The second side of the pyramid, psychology or talk therapy, is an entire other article.

There is now unprecedented access with the new technology being integrated. A great example is Better Help, at www.betterhelp.com. It offers consumers a way to find a therapist and connect with them for online or phone sessions. The website matches you with a therapist based upon criteria you input.

I am excited about things like this. In my opinion, therapy devolved into a "triage" type mindset. If a person is in crisis, you would get help to get you get past the crisis.

It can be much more than just a crisis though. With me, it has been a lifelong struggle. It is not whether or not I would have another crisis, it was when I would have another crisis.

Talk therapy can, and should be, getting to the roots of the problems. I don't think anything magically disappears. Trauma, depression, PTSD, Anxiety Disorder and everything else has roots somewhere. Now, maybe I will have depression for the rest of my life, along with the PTSD and Anxiety Disorder, but that doesn't mean I can't do anything about it. There are healthier coping mechanisms to learn and even sometimes learning the causes of what is happening to us can open better paths to recovery.

It was like one time I was tested for ADHD. I was excited! I had taken the online tests, matched up perfectly, answered everything to have the ADHD diagnosis, and then went to a specialist for their diagnosis. Finally! I would get the directed help I needed to at least work on one aspect of what was wrong with me.

While waiting for the diagnosis, it was like a cross between the Maury Povich Show, waiting for the DNA test results, and the NFL draft, waiting to put on that coveted professional jersey.

Then, Maury made the big reveal. "I am sorry, but you do not have ADHD."

Wait. What? I was crushed. I answered all of the questions! I had taken the online test and it said I had ADHD. I wanted to have ADHD! It was an answer. A path.

There was no ADHD professional jersey for me. I was not part of the team.

The doctor offered to put me on a medication just to see if it would have any effect but explained that it wouldn't. I didn't bother. I just went back to searching for answers.

About a month or two later, I was talking to a friend of mine, a psychiatrist that specializes in PTSD. I mentioned the test and the results.

"Didn't anybody mention to you," he replied, "that PTSD can present itself as ADHD?"

I was about 48 at the time. My initial PTSD diagnosis came when I was 30.

Talking to a professional can help.

And as I mentioned in other episodes, just talking can help. Which leads to the third side of the triangle, for me, the base, the foundation. This is the one that should have been the strongest to support the other two sides, but it was the one I failed at miserably my entire life.

Self-care.

A part of the reason why I am doing this podcast is it is a journey along my path to healing and recovery. Another page on my website is Friends of GInA, Gentler Insanities Anonymous. I would eventually like to see meetings for people who suffer from what I call the "Gentler Insanities." Friends of GInA is taken directly from the 12-step program and modified for people like me.

It is a pretty simple idea. I believe that talking about our problems with people who understand is a healthy step. It gets us away from the isolation, makes us feel not so alone.

Another recent discovery I have made, this year, was through a friend of mine whose life was saved by Alcoholics Anonymous. I won't get into his story as that is his to share, but we discussed it. We were talking about AA and my idea. He liked it.

The 12-step program is an awesome support system. You can find meetings at multiple places and multiple times any day of the week. My friend shared with me something interesting that I didn't know: anybody can go to open meetings.

There are closed meetings, just for those suffering from an addiction, but there are open meetings available to anybody that walks in the door. My friend suggested that I try out a few of the open meetings until I can get my own program up and running.

I had thought about it a bunch of times. Hundreds. Maybe thousands. When the depression hits, especially at night, I withdraw into a tight ball. It can become a battle. In Philly, I would heave a sigh of relief at 2 am, when I knew the strip clubs closed, one of my unhealthy coping mechanisms. Or I would be there being chased out by the lights.

But what if there was some place I could go, just to listen, and maybe talk, grab a cup of coffee, and be there with people who might not understand my particular issues--but "issues" can be a very big boat. I don't have to isolate myself. I don't have to battle this alone.

Another step I have taken is yoga. I have been hearing about it for years and they offer classes at night, during my witching hours. I had always thought of yoga as just stretching and exercise. There is a lot more to it.

I finally started going a few years back when the professional burnout and the depressive episode was really starting to kick in. I was looking for a lifeline so grabbed one, a yoga studio not too far from where I worked.

It was transformative.

At first, it was exactly what I assumed it to be: 45 minutes of stretching and exercise followed by a cool down period. That alone was helpful. I found that after the sessions, I was invigorated and feeling better. I had more energy. Then, I got deeper into yoga, into mindfulness.

To me, yoga is a "fake it till you make it" activity. Some of the benefits are there immediately. The stretching, poses, and exercise can help with all manner of issues. The real benefit of yoga, to me, is on a deeper level, a mental level.

I would say a "spiritual level" here, but I don't want to scare anybody away that might be considering it. Get all mystical. So, let's stick with mental.

After a couple months of practice, I was in the middle of a session, assuming the half pigeon pose. I couldn't do it right. One leg is supposed to be stretched out behind you with the other leg tucked up under you, perpendicular to your body. I could do the stretched-out leg, but my body just wouldn't do the perpendicular part.

"That's perfectly fine," my instructor encouraged me after a previous class when I asked her about it. She would always talk about how this was our practice, our yoga, and to just allow our bodies to do what it was comfortable doing.

So, I reached into the pose. My one leg was stretched out fully behind me and the other mostly just tucked underneath me. But that was perfectly fine. I leaned more into it, with my head finally touching the ground and my arms outstretched in front of me. I found...something. A quiet, a peacefulness, a stillness of my mind where the depression and other issues could not touch.

"You got it now," my yogi whispered to me, and then walked on to the next student.

And it was about then that the pandemic shut down everything, including yoga studios. I still can't seem to do yoga from home. I just can't get into it. Maybe if I had had a few more months of practice?

And then there is the gym about 15 steps from the door of my apartment that I stare at each day. And the two mile walk I was doing until I threw out my back.

I know, I know: it is hard. Remember: this is the guy who couldn't put on a sock. The differences in me then and now, however, make me wonder. What would my life have been like if I had started some of these healthier habits before, years ago, built them into my life?

...I hear a rustle of whips being unleashed me, the steel heads of the cat of nine tails going scritchity sckritch. The three big no no's of therapy: "should have," "could have" and "would have." I mentally turn around.

Oh, c'mon guys. Put away the whips and let's sit down and chat. Have some coffee. C'mon. Take a seat. Get comfortable. Cream and sugar?

I do agree that "should have, could have and would have" are useless. For the most part. We can beat ourselves all day with regrets. But I also believe they are useful in learning from the past to create a better tomorrow for us.

I really don't know. I've never been here before. A lot of this all came together for me a few years ago, while the depression was starting to hit. There were also a lot of other things occurring in my life. I'm guessing, though, that a strong pyramid may have insulated me more, protected me more from the effects of the depression.

I've heard of a bunch of different things. One person I know makes it a point to go to the animal shelter once a week to play with puppies. Puppy therapy?

And with the thought of diving into a room full of puppies, that is a wrap for the episode.

Thanks for joining me!

Aloha

Episode 6: Triggers, Stuttering and Coping

In this episode, I'll be discussing triggers, a particular incident, and how my mental health journey had many parallels to my journey as a person who stutters. I wish I had learned a few lessons from myself but that is not my way. I typically see the writing on the wall but ...oh look, a shiny thing!

Now, let's get into the episode.

Yes, I did stutter.

You may have picked up on it in previous episodes, my videos, or you may know me personally. I have a speech impediment. A stutter. I call myself a PWS, a person who stutters.

On a rooftop bar in Chicago, a few years back, I was chatting with an old friend of mine. We were talking about life and various things. Regina got this look on her face, the look that told me I was in for something. She asks the best questions.

She asked, "Why do you refer to yourself as a PWS, but also as a depressive."

It would be over a year before I had answer to for her. I only knew at the time that it was not a matter of semantics. It was a deliberate choice of words. Somewhere during my odyssey across the United States, the answer finally hit me.

I always say I am a lousy advocate for people who stutter. I don't give a rat's ass what people think of the way I talk. I never did. Despite a very severe stutter when I was younger, I was one of the kids that always got the dreaded "talks too much" on their report card.

Each year, on October 22, International Stuttering Awareness Day, I repost something across the various groups I am a part of on social media. Aptly titled, "Yes, I did Stutter," it talks about how though I couldn't give a rat's ass about what people think of the way I talk, for others, it can be a true disability that robs them of hope and a full life. I then give advice on how to have a conversation with a person who stutters.

People can make a difference just by understanding the disability is there and by listening. --The full post is at the end of this chapter.

Was it a disability for me? Eh, I had my moments. Puberty was a bitch when I watched my friends and cousins talking to the pretty girls, an act that would trigger my stutter to new heights. Graduating college and applying for jobs, where the first contact was a phone interview, was pretty awful. For the most part, though, I return to the "rat's ass" phrase.

My stutter never hobbled me the way I've seen it do to others in the groups. Those who know me know that my mouth, and not being able to shut it, has gotten me into far more trouble than any single thing in my life.

Looking back, I think a huge part of that was my support system. Home was a "safe place." Anywhere with family was a safe place. I never did figure out if it was an unspoken rule or if word had been spread, but nobody ever said anything about my stutter. Ever. I was treated like every other kid in the family. I was given the opportunity to speak, and even told to shut up when I shouldn't be speaking--like every other kid in my family.

"This is not a carrot in my ear," is a phrase I remember often from mom when she was talking on the phone.

I was allowed to be me, and me is what I became.

Many people have wondered why I don't write a book about my experience. With my life experiences, they feel it would be a powerful book for people with disabilities. It is on my list of projects, but I really don't know how to approach it. Every time I think about my life, the stutter gets shoved far to the background, behind other things I had to battle to live the life I have had.

Life wasn't easy. Who's is? There was a lot going on and the stutter seemed like such a small thing compared to the events that triggered the depression, anxiety and PTSD. Only now am I learning about childhood trauma and the effects that it can have on an adult.

I wish I could find the damn thing, but I can't. I saw a post on Instagram where they listed seven signs in an adult that are manifestation of childhood trauma. I read through the list and thought, "aww, hell, that's me."

Like I said, with the stutter, I had a large, supportive family and network of friends. The depression was a different story.

Back to Regina's most excellent question and the answer: "Why do you refer to yourself as a person who stutters but also a depressive?"

I didn't have an answer for her on that rooftop bar in Chicago in the summer of 2019, but the question nagged me. The answer finally came to me as I made my odyssey across America during the summer of 2020.

To me, as a person who stutters, as opposed to a stutterer, I am not defined by my stutter. It does not make choices for me. There were bumps and snafus, but it never really determined my choices.

Aye, I'll never be an air traffic controller, but that still left a few million job choices.

A depressive, on the other hand, as opposed to a person who has depression, is controlled by their illness. On that rooftop bar, I was 48. I knew that the depression had controlled large parts of my life, made many decisions for me, and altered my course. Much of why I was traveling across America was to figure out how to stop it.

The depression, the stutter, and many other things are intertwined. Recently, I was triggered, making me fall back in time to a frightened 12-year-old who stuttered uncontrollably, without his family there to support him. Without my Mommy.

It was so much like a trigger for the depression. I was 12 years old again and I was a stutterer, not a person who stuttered. I had been attacked. I went into "protect the child" mode, which then triggered the depression in the 51-year-old man.

I shouldn't be here.

I retreated and processed. I realized I had been stupid. I really need to stop doing that.

With both stuttering and depression, there are triggers. I avoid them as best as I can. I've learned what can trigger both. Some can't be completely avoided and that is where therapy comes in, to learn better coping mechanisms. My mom was once told that because of her manic depression, she should give up her kids and move away to be on a farm.

With the stutter, I'm pretty good at seeing the triggers. I see those red flags from a mile away. A benefit of the stutter is that it has served as an "asshole detector" throughout my life. I'm a good judge of people and the stutter has made me a quick judge. When I first meet them, how do they react to my stutter? There are subtleties involved and everything is not black and white--I'll get into that later in the episode when I go through my annual stuttering awareness post. But, in short, certain red flags make me avoid certain people. I don't waste my time.

The depression can make me like a drunk driver, plowing through the red flags and orange cones, wondering what all of the bumps are. Then, total surprise when the cop pulls me over.

That's pretty much what happened.

Last year, I almost completely isolated myself. I would go out with friends once in a while, but mostly I stayed inside and kept to myself. I lied to myself, saying it was a healthy regrouping. It wasn't.

I then made changes in my life. When I moved, I refused to isolate. I start each morning, and spend most of the day, sitting outside of my apartment. There is this fantastic sitting area where I sip my coffee and type away. The interruptions to my work are more than compensated by the incredible connections I have made.

First, it was the staff. I know everybody and they have become like family. My coffee pot over floweth! And they started feeding me. I now have a few "mothers" who make sure I eat breakfast. Julio, in particular, makes sure I eat every bite.

Then, I started meeting my neighbors. And their puppies. I have met some truly incredible people: warm, friendly, and generous. We barbecue upstairs, chat and sip coffee here, and help each other out.

Then, along came...let's just call him Bob.

He seemed like a nice enough guy, smart with a wry humor. There were a couple red flags at first, but I ignored them as they were tiny ones. The humor had a bite to it, and he would continually talk over top of me. But he was engaging, and I engaged. He did try once, to be funny I guess, and mimicked my stutter. I called him on it, and he apologized and moved on. He was sober at the time.

The big red flags came out when he got drunk. The humor became more biting, more judgmental, angrier. Being stupid, I ignored them.

It's a problem I have with the depression. There is a pull to go outside my complex and drink. Mingle. Bob was an option as almost all of the people I met here are absolutely wonderful, but couples. Bob, like me, is single. He likes going out.

I own it, but the depression makes me stupid. I know better. I even lecture other people on it. By keeping unhealthy relationships in our life, it inhibits us from developing healthy ones. I was experiencing that here in my new home.

It was another red flag, a big one, flapping high above. When I first moved in, I met these two couples that live on my floor and across from each other. When I became friends with Bob, they started keeping their distance a bit. I would later find out that the one couple lived below Bob and had had multiple altercations with him when he was drunk.

The turning point --not the trigger yet-- occurred a few weeks ago. I went and knocked at Bob's door to tell him some news. Because we had become friends, I shared a lot with him. He was drunk.

Later that day, it became a "thing." Even more drunk, he approached me with a tirade about how nobody knocks at people's doors, they stand outside and text. The red flag was finally shoved into my face, and I finally stopped ignoring it. After a little back and forth, I told him he would never have to worry about me knocking at his door again.

I just went inside my apartment and ignored him. Later that night is when the attacks started, the trigger. I'm sitting outside and chatting with a neighbor when Bob starts texting me. Mean, angry, abusive. I blocked him.

Ever deal with an abusive drunk? I had driven through those orange cones with the big red flags and the cop was pulling me over.

Later that night, I'm sitting outside as usual, and, now even more drunk, he comes down to confront me. He wants a reaction, needs a reaction. I ignored him. All I really wanted to do was beat the hell out of him, but that does as much good as arguing, and I knew that would cause me problems.

He knew exactly what buttons to push. Like I said, I had thought him a friend, ignoring the red flags, and overshared. In the texts, he had brought up my stutter. Now, he started mimicking it. It was easy to push aside, though. It's not like I hadn't heard it before, but not since I was about 12.

When that didn't work, he got even nastier. He went deep into the things I had shared with a friend and tried to beat me with them. My marriage, my relationship with my daughter, my stutter, my employment, everything. Somehow, even my father got brought into it. That tipped me off. Abusive drunks are typically projecting.

Yeah, I got triggered. I started to make my way into my apartment, pissed off at myself that I was allowing him to chase me off, but I didn't want it to lead to a physical confrontation. It almost did anyway. As I was stepping into my apartment, he said something, and I had enough, lost control. I turned around and it was the wrong thing to do.

"Keep it up," I said. "You're about to get your ass kicked."

It was exactly what he wanted. What he needed.

I got a hold of myself, went into my apartment, and closed the door. The tirade continued outside. Louder, meaner, nastier. I cuddled up with the 12-year-old me.

The staff caught the entire thing, and other neighbors, but the damage was done, and I started the downward spiral.

I was 12 years old again with a man's body and pissed off at myself. Bob was throwing around the word, "coward," and the little boy, who had thrown himself at attackers no matter what their size, was thinking I was.

The 51-year-old me knew I was doing exactly what I should be doing. It's not about turning the other cheek or any kind of pacifist route, but about being smart. Ignore him and allow management to handle it.

I struggled. I had been triggered. Bob kept approaching me when I was with people that didn't know, mimicking my stutter and trying to provoke me in small ways, sneaky ways. I kept retreating to my apartment. Confused.

My complex had become a place of safety and health, a place where I could really heal. It wasn't anymore.

I guess this is really good example of where a therapist would help.

To top things off, I began stuttering badly again even when he wasn't around.

How do you stop the downward spiral?

I guess management spoke to him. For the most part, he kept his distance. That helped but wasn't really a solution. He'd still make passes and throw out the odd comments. Even sober now. I knew he was enjoying chasing me away, so I stopped. That just encouraged him. He wanted and needed more of a response from me, more of a reaction.

Embarrassed, though I shouldn't have been, I took to my stuttering support group on Facebook, where I am typically a mentor. I received a ton of positive reinforcement that I was doing the right thing. It started to help the 12-year-old me feel better though it had been a titanic struggle to hit the "post" button--I have issues reaching out for help.

I finally started to open up to my new friends in the complex, finding out that more people than I had had run ins with Bob, and they supported me. I slowly began building the healthy relationships that I had unknowingly inhibited because of my friendship with Bob.

I slowly began to feel safer again. But annoyed.

I told my one friend, who had had a run in, that I felt bad for Bob, that he obviously had problems.

"No," he replied, "he's just an asshole."

One night this past weekend, I was having a barbecue and drinks on the rooftop with the couples I had first met. Friends. It was a great night. I was really getting ready to leave, having had my two beers and knowing I needed to get some more work done. Bob showed up, drunk. He made some comments, "coward" was thrown out, and he even pulled up a chair. Like I said, I was getting ready to leave anyway and what he thinks of me returns me to the "rat's ass" phrase I am so fond of. Even the 12-year-old me was quiet.

A fresh, open beer was put in front of me. My one friend's wife, a lovely Brazilian woman, had become Momma Bear. "No, you are not leaving," she said very loudly. "You are welcome. You are wanted here. He is not."

He finally left. He had a few choice comments for me the following morning, but I just ignored him, and he finally left. I went back to management.

The spiral is slowing and even reversing. The stutter is back to normal. My safe place is my safe place again. Now, the 51-year-old me is just annoyed at management.

No, we can't avoid the triggers. I can't go live on a farm for the rest of my life and can't isolate myself. But I can get better at seeing the red flags and orange cones. I can find better, healthier coping mechanisms. And then, when I do screw up --and I invariably will-- I can learn how to recover faster. If I see myself driving through the orange cones, I don't have to make it a game to see how many I can take out before I get pulled over.

I can find and develop the healthy relationships that will help me on my journey, while maintaining the healthy relationships that I already have--that I typically isolate from when in the depression.

I'm mentally drawing the lines now. The interconnections between the depression and stuttering, how they are similar. They are actually both classified as "disabilities." There is a much, much larger picture here. It is something I need to talk to someone about, maybe a therapist?

But I STILL didn't make it onto my systems theory soap box. I'll climb on up eventually. But, for now, here is my annual post for International Stuttering Awareness Day.

While listening to it, can I suggest doing what I have ignored most of my life? Listen to it while thinking about how it could relate to other things. Depression and mental illness in general.

Yes, I Did Stutter

I'll be honest: I really don't give a rat's ass what people think of the way that I talk. In my fifth decade, I just don't have time for that nonsense anymore. But there are a lot of people who do, so I ask my friends, family, and other people that might get a hold of this thing to keep them in mind.

I am probably being a lousy advocate here. Many people who know me forget that I stutter or don't think very much of it because I have been so open about it and, well, let's be blunt: the stutter, drill sergeants, particularly mean nuns and everything else under the sun have never been able to shut me up. It has affected me, but in other ways, and I won't get into that now. I think my inability to keep my damn mouth shut has hindered me far more than my stutter ever did.

But, while remembering that I do stutter, forget about me…

You can make a difference in a person's life by listening to them, hearing what they have to say, and by simply being aware that they struggle with something that comes naturally to you, fluency.

First, how to have a conversation with someone who stutters:

1) Don't finish their sentences. I always hated that. Most of the time, they were wrong, and I would just have to start all over with the extra stress of having my stutter pointed out to me.

2) Don't tell them to relax. I realize you just want to help but it doesn't help. It does the opposite. Yes, relaxing would help, but putting a spotlight on the inability to relax just exacerbates the problem.

3) Don't talk over them. I know, I know: I've heard it a dozen times. I'm from Philly. "I do that to everybody!" You are not talking to everybody. You are talking to a person who stutters. I walk faster than everybody. When I was walking with my mom, though, I didn't drag her along at my pace. I walked slower, allowing her the respect and dignity she deserved.

For me, I just roll with it. And I reach out to others in groups and whenever I can to try to equip them with better tools for living with a stutter, trying to share my experiences and what has worked for me.

A lot of people stutter. It's more than you think. If you go by the numbers and do the math, about 77 1/2 million people in 2020. It is something that a lot of people hide but we are a large group.

For many, stuttering is a true disability that hobbles them, crushes their self-confidence and generally makes their lives hell. They crave the ability to engage the world but get slapped down so often it makes a simple task like ordering at a drive through a nightmarish experience.

Yeah, I think we make too much of our stutters, but that it neither here nor there.

Just by listening to them (while following the above rules), and being aware that people stutter, you can really make a difference in somebody's life. There is this expectation that our stutter is going to met with rudeness, laughter, ignorance, pity and that our conversations are going to become a battleground for fluency.

Confound the expectations! Help people that stutter learn that their voices are just as important as yours. It is really such a simple thing to do.

***

And that is a wrap for episode six. As usual, I have no idea where I'll be going with the next episode. Eh, I meander. I get lost. Tangents can take me into far away ...oh look! A shiny thing!

Thanks for joining me!

Until next week...

...but, before I go. One last thing. I reread the script for the episode. And then I looked at the last word that I end each episode with. It is right there below. Aloha, a Hawaiian word of greeting and parting, an offering of love, affection, peace, compassion and mercy.

Crap.

Aye, I'm still SW Philly. And I'm still a bit raw. But this podcast is as much for Bob as it is for anybody else. Alcoholism is a disease. Yeah, I agree with my friend and think that he is an asshole. But I also think he needs help. He needs aloha.

Management finally did their thing, and he is being evicted. As much as there is a huge part of me saying, "Bu-bye Felicia!" there is a tiny, small part of me that is offering him aloha. Aye, I have to teach that 12-year-old me better.

Maybe that will be my next podcast? Something about forgiveness.

Anyway, thanks again for joining me.

Aloha.

Episode 7: The Crazy Therapist

In this episode, I'll discuss the craziest advice I was ever given by a therapist. And how it worked. There was a bright shiny thing that was begging me to look at and go down a tangent, but I managed to stay on track, with a few twists and turns. There is also something about mirrors.

Now, let's get into the episode.

...but wait for a second. Pause. I am about to get into a story about someone who might be listening to this podcast. Karen seems to be popular these days, so let's call her Karen.

I've gotten into trouble before, hurt people unintentionally, hurt people I cared about, loved, because of miscommunication. When I explain to them how they helped me on my mental health journey, they took it the wrong way. They took it as a personal attack, only hearing "this is how I was triggered," and not the entire "what was wrong with me to be triggered," and how I then developed healthier coping mechanisms thanks to them.

But on to Karen. I met with Karen long past this incident occurred. The incident created a huge opening for a healthy change in me and, for that, I will be eternally grateful. It just took, well, me being me, to get there.

At the time, right after I graduated college, I hated Karen. I guess it is a very normal story, common even. We had started to date, began a relationship, I moved in with her, and we even moved into a second apartment together. Then, we broke up.

It was an ugly, nasty break up, filled with a lot of harsh words, vicious attacks and, well, I was angry with her.

Anger, though, does not do the feeling justice. Fury is more like it. Hatred. The anger came to dominate me.

In many ways, the anger was like the suicidal thoughts I experienced last year, when the swarm of gnats became a swarm of hornets. The anger made me impervious to the stings, but I was constantly in that swarm during every waking hour. I couldn't think or concentrate, couldn't get any work done, couldn't really function normally.

I was lucky enough at the time that my boss was my uncle. He rolled with it, allowing me to turn a normal eight-hour day into a 16-hour day with breaks and naps.

A thing you learn in therapy is that anger is a secondary emotion. It grows from something else, like hurt and pain. I knew this but I didn't give a shit. I wanted to be furious, allow myself that, and allow the anger just to be anger.

It wasn't healthy. I didn't care about that either.

With the way it was dominating me, I finally began one of my brief forays into therapy. That's when I heard one of the craziest pieces of advice I ever heard from a therapist. It almost made me walk out the door.

"Forgive her," the therapist said.

Are you kidding me?!? Forgive her?!? After all she did? After all I lost? After this, that and the other thing? Forgive her?!? Are you nuts?

I imagine she had seen this before. Many times. She calmed me down and got me to sit back in the chair. Then she explained.

"Look, Chris," she said, "I am not talking about reconciling with her. I am not talking about ever seeing her again, having any contact with her. That would be wrong as it was a very unhealthy relationship from what you have told me, and we can get into that. We are talking about you, not her. In this moment. In this time."

She went on to discuss the anger, not even bringing up the secondary emotion part. She knew I was furious, and the fury was dominating me. The fury was as unhealthy as the relationship had been. Maybe even more unhealthy. I was being completely controlled by it.

"You need to find a way to let the anger go," she explained. "The way to do that is by forgiving her."

I've never been a "forgive" kind of person. Aye, ya know, I'm from Philly. A baseball bat? Yes. Throwing fists? Yeah. Holding a grudge for a decade or two? You betcha. Forgiveness? Not a chance in hell.

But I was paying for therapy, trusted my therapist, so decided to give it a shot. This began a very long process. It was a "fake it till you make it" thing she explained. As part of the exercise, I had to verbalize it.

I found it all pretty ridiculous.

Thoughts of Karen would pop into my head often. Very often. I would be driving in my car, think of her, and the thought would release a flood of rage.

"I forgive you," I would say, out loud. Followed by, "You rotten, fricking bitch that ruined my life"...and a tirade that would last about 5-10 minutes. A phrase spoken in one second followed by at least five minutes of very bad words. I even came up with new ones and new ways to string them together. I can be very creative.

In my car, at home, in work: the "I forgive you," followed by the tirade.

The forgiveness wasn't genuine. It was just words. Empty. As my therapist knew they would be. The empty verbalization continued for about a month, followed by the tirade. My therapist said I was doing good and to keep it up.

It felt even more ridiculous.

The absurdity continued, the lie, but an interesting thing started to happen. The tirade became less and less over a few months. It got to the point where I was saying the empty words, "I forgive you," and then just moving on with my day, without the tirade.

This went on for another few months.

At some point in time, I realized two things. 1) the words weren't empty anymore. I had said them so many times, out loud, that I did finally begin to forgive Karen. And 2) The need to verbalize was becoming less and less as the thoughts of Karen, and the anger, were coming less often.

My life started to return to normal--or as normal as it ever got for me.

I don't really know how much time had passed, but it hit me one day. I hadn't thought of Karen in a long time, months. I hadn't had to verbalize or even think, "I forgive you" in a while because I hadn't thought of her in a long while. Karen, and the anger, had lost its control over me.

There were no thoughts of reconciliation or even contact. We were two young adults that weren't right for each other.

It all led to thoughts of the therapist and anger. You see the memes a lot on Facebook and Instagram these days, about how holding onto anger is like drinking poison to spite somebody else. No matter that anger is a secondary emotion, it's more than a useless emotion. I found out that it was a masochistic emotion.

It is not like Karen was affected by my anger. She never even knew about my constant struggle. But by being furious with her, I had given her far more power over me, after the relationship ended, than I ever had during the relationship.

I took the power back. Released her and, more importantly, released myself from the prison I had built around me.

This is not about being a pacifist or turning the other cheek kind of thing. Aye, you can take the boy out of Philly, but you can't take Philly out of the boy. There are still a few people I would like to "meet" one day, people who had hurt my daughter. Maybe she has forgiven them or forgotten them. I haven't. But I imagine that a therapist would say it is about her, and not me. They have no control over me, but they hurt my baby. I'd enjoy the opportunity to return the favor, tenfold.

There is a reputation to Philly, and we live up to it. It is home to cheesesteaks, hoagies, wader ice and the worst sports fans in the world, voted #1 in that category consistently many years running. I even have a shirt that says, "Philly: Nobody likes us, and we don't care."

A few years back, the "Peace Robot," or something like that, made its way from coast to coast as an experiment. Everywhere it went in the country, people would pose for pictures with it and send it on its way. Its trip came to an end in Philly, where it was mugged.

But let's get back to me, in my apartment. Far away from Philly...

I have since applied the "forgiveness principal" to many people in my life. Most recently, it was Bob from my previous episode. I've applied it equally to friends, family, acquaintances and strangers. It's gotten much easier over the years.

I have people that care about me angry about it. How ironic is that? They get angry that I'm not angry. But, then, most of them are from Philly.

I found that meme on Facebook is true, long before there was such a thing as Facebook. Holding onto anger really is like drinking poison to spite someone else.

Think about it. Whether you come into contact with the person every day or never see them again, they are never affected by your anger. Hell, if you come into contact with the person, they might be enjoying it. The only person it really affects is you.

Then, there is the other side of anger.

Maybe I am wrong, and maybe I really need to discuss this with a professional, but I still feel that anger can be a useful emotion, especially as a young child. Unable to do the adult calculations and processing, it was a simple and effective way to protect myself. It was a shield and sword, armor and protection against the things that were happening to me. It is a very simple coping mechanism.

I'll leave a lot of that until after I do discuss it with a professional, but I was a very angry child, that grew into an angry young man, that then grew into an angry adult. I sometimes wonder how that anger affected me and my relationships in my life. It would become something that people had to look beyond to get to know the real me. Maybe some people couldn't because the anger triggered them?

My anger, among other things, made me blind to certain solutions that have since become very important parts of my healthier life. In last week's episode, I talked about how I tend to ignore red flags in certain situations. How I can be like the drunk driver, plowing through the orange cones and red flags, wondering what the were, completely surprised when the cop pulled me over...or I ended up in a ditch. Maybe, in some cases, the anger was the poison that got me drunk in the first place?

Yeah, I was ignoring the true other side of anger. Anger as a child's defense? Like I said, I'll get into that another time. It was a tangent.

Look: a shiny thing!

But it is that shiny thing in the sand that you have to look at just right, at the right angle, to catch the sun so it blinds you.

Now, I want to be blinded. Aye, I got two more pages into this script. I was following that tangent towards other faraway places, away from the real issue. Important places, but I need to move out of the angle of the shiny thing and address the REAL other side of anger.

Anger at myself.

I was doing a damn good job of following that tangent when Lance called me, the friend from episode five. We started talking about what I had already prepared for this episode...and I find myself trying to angle my eyes to look at the shiny thing again, talk about Lance. So, instead of Lance, let's talk about Josh.

Josh is where I need to be right now.

It is 1996 or so and I am talking with Josh on the phone. It had been a bad week. I remember that. The stutter was getting the better of me at college. Josh had been my first roommate at college, and he was one of the people I could call when the stutter got bad...

No, Chris. Stop. Talk about it.

Josh, a few nights later. We got drunk with his girlfriend. I was hammered. Josh and his girlfriend were hammered. We were having a great time. I was a happy drunk. Josh passed out. His girlfriend and I continued having a wonderful time. Then, I made a pass at Josh's girlfriend.

She very nicely put me in my place, and I think she even smiled. Then, she went and joined Josh in his bed.

That's when the other side of anger took hold. Pure hatred, fury...at myself. I had just broken a friend's trust, a friend that meant the world to me. I had just turned an excellent evening, a celebration, into a total pile of crap.

Josh and his girlfriend eventually broke up and Josh never spoke of the incident to me. I never spoke of it to him. It hung there between us.

Decades later, I would find out that the only thing hanging between us was my anger at myself. I finally came clean to him, bared my soul, bared my anguish and crime.

It took him a long while to respond. He had to dig through memories and go back twenty years.

"Ohhhhhh. You mean so and so? Hell, Chris, I stole her from Jason. I am so sorry you beat yourself up about it all these years. There was no reason to. None. I can't even forgive you because there is nothing to forgive. But if it makes you feel better?"

Over the decades, I have gotten pretty good at forgiving other people. In terms of aloha, I can offer them and wish them mercy. Forgiving myself, offering myself mercy, is another story entirely.

It is the other side of anger, the flip side of forgiveness.

The depression, anxiety, PTSD, the unhealthy coping mechanisms, and just being what Lance referred to as merely being human, has led to many instances, many examples, of me being angry at myself...and then holding onto it to beat the hell out of myself for years and decades.

Another great example was with Karen herself. A couple years ago, so we are talking 20 years after our relationship ended, she reached out to me on Facebook. During my odyssey across America, I stopped by and saw her and her now grown sons.

We had spent 18 months together. There were many good times. One particular incident had eaten away at me for all those years. It would pop into my head once in a while and then dissipate, unforgiven.

Sitting with her on her patio in Florida, sipping coffee and sharing about our lives, I brought it up. Apologizing.

Like Josh, she had to work at remembering the incident. It took a while as she looked at me puzzled.

"Ohhhhhh. That. Chris, I appreciate you apologizing but there is nothing to apologize for. I was angry at the time, maybe for a few days, but? Don't even think about it anymore."

I could finally stop beating the hell out of myself. Over that thing. There is still a long way to go. A very long list. And perhaps a lot of counseling.

This is still very difficult for me to discuss. I have made a lot of progress though. I think it is safe to follow one of those tangents now.

Coffee first, coffee always.

Though coffee is the main part of my morning ritual, it is really the only thing I am able to do until after the caffeine kicks in.

But, after coffee.

When Covid hit, and the depression was really starting to hit hard, I realized that I had a choice to make each morning. Things were bad, I was isolated, I was depressed, I think my life got a bit more screwed up than other people's lives--though still not as bad as some.

I wrote then that I had to look at myself in the mirror each morning and make a choice, to be miserable or to be happy. I think it is a difficult choice to make at first and not as easy as some people may think.

Just like the "I forgive you," I had to reaffirm to myself to be happy and not miserable. It was an empty affirmation, another "fake it till you make it" kind of thing. And it took even longer than the process with forgiveness. I continued it though, knowing, hoping, it might click one day.

I forgot about it.

This was 2020 for those keeping track, about 2 1/2 years ago. Growing up, my stepfather, Rich, would annoy the living hell out of me. He would sing in the morning! Sing! What the hell was there to be that happy about? To get the coffee, though, I had to put up with the singing.

I think I finally figured out his secret.

It wasn't always the easiest times, but he chose to be happy each morning. He was awake, the sun was shining, the day was a new day full of possibilities. It made me even more miserable.

It was about a month ago now that it hit me. My sleep schedule had drastically changed. I was sleeping well but started finding myself waking up between 4:30 and 5:30--usually to crash and have to take a nap later in the afternoon. I had never been a morning person. Ever. What the hell was happening to me?

I figured it out. I was excited to be out of bed and get to work. My mind had chosen happiness and that translated to me being like a kid waking up on Christmas day, with the excitement of running down the stairs to open presents.

No, I do not sing. I've done karaoke (there's video) and I don't think I am allowed to sing in many states. But Rich would not annoy me these days. Possibly. There are still the endlessly repeated history lessons and stories while I am trying to have my coffee in peace.

There is that mirror in my mind, though, where I look at myself and make a choice. If I backslide, and have a previous bad night or day, sip one kind of poison or another, it may be empty words. But I'm human.

I think it is time to start doing something new. Maybe even before the coffee so my mind is not awake enough to reject it out of hand. Maybe it is time to look at myself in the mirror and say meaningless words.

"Chris, I forgive you. I grant you mercy."

Just saying that, reading that, made me squirm. This is going to be a process. It is one I need to begin.

And that's a wrap for this episode!

Aloha.

Episode 8: Broken Things Revisited

In this episode...well, crap. Coming up with titles are difficult for me. Unless they pop into my head from some random point in space, I struggle. I had one for my new book! And now I have to come up with a new title. I don't want to talk about it. But I will. I'll also be getting into pearls, authentic selves, and I'll even have a cameo by Michelangelo.

Now, let's get into the episode.

The struggle is real. I can write thousands of words at a time. With two fingers. But coming up with a title? Impossible. They all suck. But from some random point in space, one hit me for my new book: Broken Things: An Odyssey Through Depression.

I liked it. It perfectly described it. I dated it for a while, got comfortable with it, began writing the book, and then it moved in and took up residence in my mind.

It was evicted this weekend.

I was checking out a new group I belong to on LinkedIn, Workplace Mental Health Forum. There was a post and a meme/quote by Dr. Rani Bora:

"You are not "damaged" or broken just because you had a difficult journey so far."

Thinking about my book and this podcast, I responded, with manners--something many people forget.

"I don't know," I wrote. "I disagree? It is a semantics thing? I think of myself as damaged, broken. But I'm working on it. I reach out to others and tell my story with understanding and compassion."

Dr. Bora, a mental wealth psychiatrist based in England, responded just as nicely. --it's amazing what happens when civil communication is involved.

"Chris, thanks for sharing. No, it's not a semantic thing. You don't have to agree, and you can see it differently. I used to consider myself a Recovery oriented psychiatrist wanting the best for my patients. And I believe I was doing my best. I had a profound insight during a coaching session with my coach. The "aha" moment seemed to have come out of the blue. The insight I had was that although I considered myself a recovery psychiatrist, I saw my patients as damaged and broken and needing to be fixed. That was several years ago when I came across the three principles of understanding or Innate Health Understanding."

"Of course," she wrote, "people still need help and support, and they can work on themselves. That's something I help people with. But my foundation has shifted hugely as I began to see more and more clearly that our true essence can't be touched or broken."

And that's about when I had my "Oh crap" moment. I sat there thinking of my broken and damaged self as the movers came in and started clearing everything away. They even took the damn chair I was sitting in. They cleared the room and allowed me to see the entire field.

I started thinking.

It was good title! When a good title hits, that's all I need to begin to craft a story around it. It anchors it and allows me to explore and wander while staying on track and ignoring the shiny things. I wasn't quite ready to evict it though.

Who was this Dr. Bora anyway? How dare she challenge my perception of myself!

A long time ago, at a business conference, I learned the idea of "pearls" and knew the value of them. Ernest Cardinas had spoken about the pearls we take away from the meetings. The conference may last days, but it is the little nuggets, the pearls, that change us.

I dived deep. In an empty place, I began examining this concept, wondering if it was just one of many memes--or a pearl. I dove so deep that I came across a column I wrote a long time ago.

On February 23, 2007, I wrote the following column. It was inspired by another pearl I had picked up in the movie, The Legend of Bagger Vance, about how we can't look at things as dragons to slay.

With Soft Eyes

...and the dragon twirls around a pole and transforms into a beautiful woman. I look down at the sword and shield in my hands. Useless, they drop to the ground.

I've always had one huge problem with the 12-step programs. As much good as they do people, I just don't think that they are a solution. From what I have read, what I have seen, what I have experienced, they treat addiction like it is a dragon.

It is there in your life, breathing fire through a jaw lined with razor sharp teeth. With a beer, a snort, a shot, or a lap dance, it pounces. Always stalking you. Always there. So, you reach out to a program, and make it into a shield between you and it. As long as you keep that shield up, the dragon's fire cannot touch you; its jaws cannot rend you.

By this approach, though, you make it a fixture in your life. Ever present. Just waiting for a chance to pounce. So it is perceived, and so it becomes a reality.

…and the dragon turned lady sways up to me at the bar, places her hand on my leg, leaning oh so close that her breasts brush against my shoulder.

Are some people just hard wired that way? I've learned that addiction runs in families. Maybe dragons do exist? My perception of reality is a bit different.

I see her there, all sweet and seductive. I can feel the warmth of her hand upon my leg, and that warmth spreading through me. But she isn't a dragon. And there isn't a dragon lurking in her shadow. There isn't even a dragon within me.

There is an onion. (Don't ask. It is the way that my mind works. I can't help it; I just try to follow along.)

This is a different kind of onion, though. It is tucked away inside of my soul, my emotional growth, hidden within a fold of my subconscious. Maybe there is a little kid that traded a baseball for the onion. It is layered like an onion, but each layer is a different type of material: granite, steel, titanium…you get the picture.

Beneath all of those layers is the itch, the compulsion. I guess that I believe that if you are able to peel back those layers, get to that core, you'll find that itch. Underneath all of those layers, you will not find a dragon, curled into a ball. You'll find a wisp of smoke, that will be carried away on the breeze.

I'm not trying to knock the 12-step programs here. I wish that I could find one for Friday and Saturday nights. Help me pass the time. Ease my way through an evening, until the itch passes, until I can look upon my addiction again with soft eyes, instead of the steely eyes of a combatant. Aye, I would like a shield at times. But I also don't think that it is healthy to make that shield a permanent fixture in my life.

That there is another way. A better way for me. All that I need to do is to be able to see it.

***

Yep, Dr. Bora was right. She had given me a pearl.

[Oh. Side note. Since writing the column, I also learned more about the 12-step program. It begins as that sword and shield, but can transform, through its meditations, into something much greater. But back to the podcast...]

I replied to Dr. Bora, remembering the column written 15 years ago:

"I LOVED how you put that! I wrote a column a long time ago that talks about how dysfunction is like an onion wrapped around our "selves," that if you peel back the layers of the onion, you get back to who you are."

That's when Dr. Bora came into my mind --I imagined her with a heavy, steel handled walking stick. I guess it's a British thing? Anyway, she came in and started chivvying the movers along, "persuading" them to greater speed to evict the thought that had taken up residence in my mind for so long, that I am a broken thing that needs fixing.

"I like that analogy," she wrote.

Dr. Bora continued: "When Michelangelo was asked how he made David, he said, "I saw the angel in the marble and carved until I set it free.""

"When we work on ourselves with love and understanding, therapy, coaching, etc. we are able to let go of our limiting stories of who we are or who we are not, then we find a deeper connection to our true self."

Yeah, Michelangelo took his hammer and chisel and smacked me between the eyes.

I've never been to Italy --thanks to Covid-- but I have heard of people encountering Michelangelo's David for the first time. Men, the big, tough variety, weep.

It gave me a lot to think about. 15 years after I wrote about it. I've always been stubborn. And easily distracted.

But now I need to come up with a new title, a new anchor for my book. Ummm, any help? Inside the Granite? It will hit me eventually. Any help there, Mike?

I think it was after I wrote that column, though, that I also began reprocessing about the 12-step program. When I wrote it, something didn't jive right with me, something clanged against something else.

I have seen, and experienced, people trading one addiction for another.

Dennis Leary talks about addiction in his stand-up routine, No Cure for Cancer--another unlikely place I picked up quite a few pearls.

In his comedic way, very non-PC in 1993, he explains how a lot of people quit doing cocaine in the 70's by picking up a pound of pot and a case of beer.

The 12-Step program, working out, working, volunteering, or maybe just traveling 40,000 miles: people trade an unhealthy addiction for an addiction that might be healthier, but is still unhealthy.

I've seen it with the 12-step program, which is probably what influenced my views on it. Yes, it would help people. Save them. Save their lives. But then they became an addict to the program, making it their entire life.

To me, that is unhealthy. There should be balance in all things. Moderation in all things.

I heard, but could be wrong, that the British version of AA means just cutting back to a pint or two a night, not an all or nothing kind of thing. But I am also reminded of Leo McGarrity, a character in the TV show, The West Wing, explaining his alcoholism.

"Why can't you have just one drink," an intern asked, as Leo was about to fire her but gave her a second chance after she released private details of his life.

"Because I'm an alcoholic," Leo Replied, "I can't have just one drink. I need 12. Or 20. And then things get ugly."

I wonder what Leo McGarrity would think of Dr. Bora?

I don't know. I'm still thinking about it. My mom had bi-polar disorder. I have, among other things, Major Depressive Disorder. I know people like the fictional Leo McGarrity that are addicts. We are hard wired that way. Just like with my speech impediment.

Even when I am not stuttering, there is still something called an internal stutter that says I can stutter at any moment. I get triggered, and the external stutter comes out. Many, many experts have said that the stutter cannot be fixed, only managed.

Dr. Bora?

But...

Yes, yes: I know. There are a lot of buts and thinking going on here, devil's advocate and all that.

But I also remember a time in my life, a brief, glorious 2 1/2-week period that the experts say is impossible. I lost my internal stutter. I was 100% fluent. In between one syllable and the next, while talking to my buddy Josh on the phone, my stutter disappeared.

Nothing had really changed in my life. It just went away. I was even told by strangers, that Josh kept on throwing me at, that I was a wonderful speaker, had a beautiful speaking voice.

2 1/2 weeks later, I was pissed. I was angry. At God. I felt as if She had given me a miracle, and then taken it back. But that's another story, a tangent, a bright shiny thing to follow another time.

I think it is all a discussion for another time. Whether or not there are broken things within us, chemical imbalances that can be triggered.

But let's get back to the layers wrapped around our true selves.

I developed some very unhealthy coping mechanisms. I wrapped them around the hurt and pain, around the injury, like scar tissue. They protected me from worse, but also inhibited me from becoming my true self, my authentic self.

I remember a story from one of my favorite books, Dragonsinger by Anne McCaffery, where an injury was allowed to heal wrong, allowing the scar tissue to cut a person off from their love of playing music. She was told she would never be able to heal again and believed it. It was only when a good doctor got involved and showed her how to exercise her hand to reverse what the scar tissue had done that could finally heal and be who she was supposed to be.

A great example is my addiction to strip clubs. Yes, don't laugh. I was addicted to strip clubs. Still am as a matter of fact. It's a struggle not to go on some nights, a struggle not to go see boobies and feel that warmth of a body pressed up against me.

Besides the money involved, there was the time. Hours and hours, night after night, weekend after weekend, hiding in strip clubs. What kind of potential did I allow to pass me by while I was in there? What kind of positive things could I have been doing for myself to pursue my true self? Who did I not meet because of where I was at?

But that can all lead into the no no's of therapy. Should have, could have and would have. As I explained before, I still think they are good teaching examples, the way sports players watch their own film.

I just feel that with the strip clubs, and other things, I was adding layers of marble to the angel instead of carving to release her. But there is always today. And tomorrow. And the day after that. Days to pick up the chisel and hammer and begin carving.

Our authentic selves. We are such incredible, powerful, beautiful beings. If we allow it and get out of our own damn way.

I would love to go more into Dennis Leary's "No Cure for Cancer." There really are some incredible pearls in that routine. Instead, though, let's move into something more palatable for the post 1993 PC crowd. --though I do highly recommend watching it if you get a chance.

Even where I am going is fraught with perils in today's world. Big Willy, you made this episode difficult with that slap. That's now just added to the criticism of the "Magical Negro" stereotype that killed one of my favorite movies.

Will Smith, though, in The Legend of Bagger Vance, a movie from 2000, gave me as much to think about as Dennis Leary and Dr. Bora. It was perhaps one of the most impactful movies I have ever watched.

Dr. Bora, this one might be right up your alley.

It's based on the 1995 book by Steven Pressfield. The Legend of Bagger Vance: A Novel of Golf and the Game of Life.

If you hate golf, forget the golf part. Watch it. Every time Smith talks about "authentic swing," replace it in your mind with, "authentic self."

The film is set in 1931 Georgia. Matt Damon, once a famous golfer, was mentally damaged in WWI and now secludes himself during the Depression. For a golf tournament to save her father's country club, Damon is essentially bullied by his former fiancé, Charlize Theron, to play against the two best golfers of the time. Only, he can't play.

Bagger Vance approaches Captain Junah one night while he is trying to hit balls, coming out of the darkness.

"You lost your swing, Mr. Junah. Let's go find it."

It bombed at the box office but then, many of my favorite movies wouldn't make the top 1,000 of all-time list.

There is this one scene where Smith is talking about the field. I can't even come close to doing it justice, so I'll add a link below and on my YouTube Channel.

The field. Smith is talking about systems theory, one of my soapbox issues. How everything interacts and is connected with everything else.

A good movie for that...

Maybe tonight is movie night?

A good movie for that is Mindwalk, available free now on YouTube. I was forced to watch it in a science writing class in college. It changed my life. Mindwalk is boring as hell but a great introduction to systems theory. Break out the coffee coated popcorn for it.

It all leads back to those layers and what Dr. Bora wrote me.

Who am I? Where am I? Where does Christopher Gajewski begin and how do I get to him?

When Michelangelo was asked how he made David, he said, "I saw the angel in the marble and carved until I set it free.""

I'll leave you with that for this week.

But that's a wrap for this episode. Instead of my usual "Aloha," I'll end this one with a line from another one of my favorite movies, Bill and Ted's Excellent Adventure. Aye, it wasn't Academy Award winning material, but it wasn't meant to be. It was fun. It was authentic.

Be excellent to each other!

Episode 9: I'm Okay, Just Fine

In this episode, I'm going to be going off script, off the reservation. I had other things planned but it's Suicide Awareness Month and I recently got triggered. The suicidal thoughts are back so I thought I would talk about them.

At this point, I wish I had the money to talk to a professional. I found a good website, www.betterhelp.com, but it is tough balancing needs and dwindling savings. It's one of my triggers and I've been triggered. I triggered myself.

They say, and I agree, that money can't buy happiness. I always joke that it sure does help, and happiness can be rented for a while. People look at the rich and powerful that suffer and think, "what do they have to be depressed about," but it is not about money for some. It is about triggers.

For me, it can be about money or lack thereof. Financial stability helps me maintain a mentally healthier lifestyle. For them, it could be any number of things.

But let's get into me and see where it leads.

I'm seeing a lot of posts about suicide awareness. It's the month for it and many posts talk about reaching out to people to check on them. Call to check on me and you will find a happy, healthy, and perfectly fine guy. It is the facade I wear when the suicidal thoughts come back. You won't find the guy that was overwhelmed last night. You won't find the guy that was overwhelmed this past weekend and gave up on this podcast. The guy who laid down in bed, fully clothed with the lights on, and fell asleep--my only escape.

Then, I woke up this morning, wondering who the hell that person was last night. Hey, I screwed up. I opened the door to depression, and it came rushing through. Now, I'm clicking out of the script that I typically use so let's just talk, me and you, about suicidal thoughts.

As I've said before, they are nothing new to me. I've really had them all my life, for as long as I can remember. As I've said in previous podcasts, they are like gnats on a summer evening. I brush them aside and move on. It's only twice in my life that the swarm of gnats have become a swarm of hornets. Nobody has ever seen both the swarm of gnats or the swarm of hornets.

Only one person saw. I reached out to an old friend of mine, Rachel, first back in 2000 and then again a couple years back. The whole thing with suicide is that it starts looking like it's the only option when you back yourself into a corner--or when I back myself into a corner. It starts seeming like an appealing option. Like I said, you can talk to me all you want. You can come and visit. You can stop by, take me out for a beer, and you would never know.

Nobody ever knows. It's my secret world. It's something that I don't like to share with people for a couple of reasons. One, the type of suicidal thoughts, like gnats on a summer evening, is natural for me. It's like if you called me and asked how my back was feeling. I'm going to say fine. I mean, it hurts. I have aches and pains but hey, I'm 51. I've lived a full life. I've hiked and injured myself and worked in various trades and it hurts often. So, if you ask me how my back is doing, as long as I'm not on the floor, I'm going to say, "I'm okay."

It's the same way with the suicidal thoughts. Typically, like the thoughts that are rushing back at me now, it's just what I think of as the normal, everyday suicidal thoughts. I did find out in a therapy session that they're not normal, that most people don't have these thoughts, and that I should bring them up in therapy. I don't quite understand them myself; it's just a part of my depression, but I've learned throughout the years to just brush the gnats aside and move on and do what I have to do. I now know that things will get better.

I had hoped to never be back in that place that I was in 2000. There, I really backed myself into a corner. I graduated college in 1997. I was still pretty much of a mess, but I decided to try to save my mom from her manic depression.

I had learned a few things, got her to move in with me into my apartment when she was ill, and I tried to save her. That was my sin, my arrogance. I thought that I could do what no one else could and it got worse for her. Her illness escalated.

It is part of a larger story, but, in the end, she tried to commit suicide. She did a damn good job of it.

I was lying in bed downstairs, and I heard someone bursting through the front door. They were crashing in, so I rushed out and was immediately shoved back by cops. I saw my mom on the step with red all over the place. I'm trying to tell the cop that she's my mom, it's my apartment. They blocked me as they brought in the paramedics, who took her away.

I was left with the cleanup. It was a two-floor apartment, so I went upstairs, and it was as if someone had taken cans of red paint and splashed it all over for the place.

The doctors would later say that they don't know how my mom survived. The only thing that they can think of is that she both sliced and took pills. The pills slowed her heart rate down and that saved her. The blood coagulated.

I was left there in my arrogance, wondering what to do. How do you clean something like that up? I started reaching out to people just because I didn't know. I mean, it was a biohazard. I had a mattress that was soaked in blood. My kitchen and my bathroom were like a scene out of a horror movie because she had paced. I could hear her pacing through the night with no idea of what was going on.

That is when I began my downward spiral, what a doctor would later call a period of decompensation.

I love that word. I don't know why but I'm fascinated with it. Decompensation. I describe it as my mind was shredding. All my defenses, all my coping mechanisms, were just gone. They were being shredded by the horror that I saw.

I had finally gotten a job after college, working for a newspaper as a reporter. That job went to hell. I just couldn't think anymore. I couldn't put thoughts together. I got a job as a bouncer at a local strip club. It paid the bills.

Then, every other week, I would drive a hundred miles or so to go and work in an orthodontic lab. It was simple work, work that I could do. But I was still in the period of decompensation.

I was struggling. I didn't reach out for help. I didn't know what to do, what to think, what to say. If anyone had come up and asked me, as a few people did, "Chris, how are you doing?" The answer was always the same. "I'm fine, I'm doing okay."

Friends, who just been married, had heard about what happened with my mom and they kept on inviting me down to Florida. They wanted me to move down there with them, and I kept saying, "no" because I knew what was happening. I could feel that downward spiral and knew that a bottom was coming. I couldn't do anything about it so kept saying "no."

They were really good people, really good friends, and they kept on pushing and pushing. So, I finally said okay. I packed up all my stuff in my car and drove down there.

I got away from Philadelphia, away from the nightmare. I perked up a little bit and felt better with the traveling. I knew that I would, surrounded by friends who introduced me to their friends. We would sit around at night and during the day.

They just expected simple things out of me, like find a job and reestablish myself. They gave me a room to sleep in and fed me. I didn't bring much money with me; they were basically supporting me which is one of my triggers. So, I already had all this stuff going on and then I'm encountering another trigger, I can't care for myself, so the spiral picked up again.

If they asked me--and they did, often--"Chris, are you okay?" I answered, "I'm fine, I'm doing okay."

I got a job working as a waiter at a catering service. I was making decent money but then I started to screw up. One of my addictions is strip clubs, so the money that I would make went to the clubs. I would pay to escape. I never did drugs, was never really a big drinker outside of college, but I liked my strip clubs. I liked the fantasy. I liked the escapism that I could find there, and I found myself going there more and more--which just made me feel like a bigger and bigger piece of shit because I'm living with these people who invited me down here and I'm not doing the basic things that I need to do to better myself.

I'm spiraling down. Then, one day, I decided to end my life. I forget where my friends were. At work, I think. I was just in so much pain. I was a piece of shit. I was living off these people and I was burdening them with my troubles. I was hurting them so what other option did I really have?

So, there was a plan, and I found a lot of peace in that plan. If you had called me at that time and asked me, "Chris, how are you doing?" I would have replied, "everything is fine."

I wouldn't have wanted to burden you. I wouldn't have wanted to hurt you. I didn't want to be talked out of it. I wanted to continue with the plan, and I was ready to do what I needed to do.

Something happened. There was something in the back of my head that said this is wrong, reach out and explain it to someone, make somebody understand you. So, I reached out to a friend of mine, Rachel.

She was living in the Washington DC area, and we had been friends for a long time. I told her what I was about to do. I wanted her to realize that it made sense. I needed her to understand.

She didn't try to talk me out of it--that was interesting. She acknowledged that I was in pain and acknowledged that I was in crisis, but all that she asked for was more time. "Chris," she said, "all that I'm asking you is to give me one more year."

That made absolutely no sense to me.

Life was painful because when you're that deep in the depression, your life compresses, and my life compressed into a period where, in 2000, I was 29 and all that I could remember was the last couple months, the last month, the last week, the day. My life became that day and that day was awful. I couldn't imagine the 29 years before and all the good things in it, all the family, friends, and loved ones. I couldn't imagine any future that I was happy.

Rachel persisted. She never asked me anything. All that she kept on repeating was, "give me one more year. If you love me, you'll give me one more year. For love of me, give me one more year."

It didn't make any sense to me and then she hit me with, "if you've done it for this long, what's one more year? You can do one more year." That kind of made sense to me. It's like if I could do it for 29 years, then one more year was no big deal. I agreed.

The friends I was living with never knew this happened. I went and saw a crisis counselor who immediately put me on meds, Zoloft, and we started talking. A lot came out in those first few therapy sessions. For one thing, he was shocked that I was even able to move and wasn't hospitalized, that I could do anything, even get out of bed.

I've always considered that both a blessing and a curse because if I'm unable to get out of bed, people can point at that and say, "there's something really wrong." I was always able to keep moving, keep working, and continue to react. All that my friends that I was living with saw was me being a piece of shit, someone living off of them. So, as I'm finally starting to feel a bit better, starting to take meds, starting to think more clearly, I come home one night, and they asked me to move out.

I didn't try to explain, didn't try to reason with them. I just accepted it because I felt that it was all that I deserved so I moved out. I turned 30, alone in a house where I had rented a room.

With the crisis over, I moved back north and started working again. I was feeling better so stopped therapy and stopped doing a lot of the things that I should have been continuing to do. I found other addictions, work, and was able to throw myself into it so much that I forgot about the depression. I did continue to take my meds and would for the next 20 years.

The depression would catch back up to me. Or maybe it never really left. I was financially stable--that's one of my triggers--but there were other things that were wrong in my life, my marriage, my work, and my business partnership.

I got exhausted. I got really, really exhausted and so I gave up on everything again. By this time, 48, I had given Rachel her year and then, again, my life compressed. It somehow leaped over all those years and reconnected with the time in Florida, so it seemed like one continuous event.

I didn't think about the intervening years or the future years. All that I knew is that I was 48 and I was so damn exhausted. I didn't see any way out. So, I planned one more nice little adventure, just one last hurrah, and then find some nice, quiet place in Europe to end my life. Just find some nice quiet beach.

Again, I'm around people all the time. I was living with my wife, I was seeing friends and family and they were always asking, "how are you doing?" The answer was always the same: "I'm doing pretty damn good."

When I began giving up everything and when I sold my business, they're like, "is everything okay, Chris?" I replied, "everything is fine."

When I asked my wife for a divorce, everybody was asking if everything was okay because everybody thought that my life was perfect. From the outside looking in, it looked like I had everything that I wanted, had everything that I needed. I had the nice house, the beautiful wife, all the pretty things and everything that goes with it.

Inside, I was already dead. There was no passion in my life, no excitement about anything, and I just figured it was a good time to call it quits. I'd lived 49 years, had had a really good run and there were a lot of good things in my life. I was beyond exhausted, and the exhaustion got to be way too much for me.

Again, if anyone had asked, and they did, I'd answer, "I'm fine."

All this happened in 2019. I sold my business, helped my wife buy a new house and gave her everything that she wanted.

That really pissed off my family and friends. They were like, "why are you doing this? Why don't you get a lawyer? Why don't you keep some stuff?" The answer, that I didn't tell them, was simple enough: I was planning on killing myself. What the hell did I need it for? I mean, seriously, all that I wanted was the cash so I could go and enjoy myself in Europe for a little bit.

I had made plans. I was going to go with my family to Poland for a couple weeks. Then, for the month of May, I had an apartment rented on the Adriatic Sea on the coast of Italy. After that, for June, I had an apartment rented in Greece for a month.

Then, Murphy intervened. Murphy's Law states that anything that can go wrong will go wrong at the worst possible time. The pandemic hit.

Yes, I took the pandemic personally. It is absurd to take a pandemic personally, but I did. I had given away everything. I was planning on being away and not coming back so I'm sitting in this very large, empty house. I had a chair, a bed, a sofa and a tv. Oh. And the coffee maker of course.

When the pandemic hit, I wasn't going anywhere.

In the empty house, I started writing again. I started to reach out to people because I knew that I wasn't okay, and wasn't telling them about it, but I knew that they weren't okay. As my one friend, a psychiatrist, said, when things like pandemics or trauma happens, the best people to talk to are the people who are screwed up because we know what to do, we know how to handle this stuff.

So, I started to reach out on social media and started stopping by people's houses, picking up supplies for them. It was a very lonely time, but it was also a very peaceful time. I started reading at night.

One of the books I read was "Travels with Charley." In 1960, John Steinbeck went looking for America. I didn't have anything so grand planned, but the thought appealed to me. I couldn't go to Europe. Why not drive cross-country?

I wrote a book about the experience and the final edition is with an editor now. I sprinkle hints throughout the book of what the plan was, to go on one last adventure and then find a nice, quiet place to kill myself.

An interesting thing happened while I was traveling. I found something. I can't say it was hope, but it was a path to hope. That's the best way I can describe it. When you're on the road for 152 days and close to 40 thousand miles, just you and your car with the radio playing, you really start thinking about a lot of things. I started thinking about life. I thought a lot about my exhaustion, my marriage, the things that had gone wrong and the places where I had gone wrong.

I found something. I began to put together the pieces of what was missing in my life. I had had the conversation with Lance about a year before and had put together the mental health triangle. I started to apply it. I learned things out there about communication, about intimacy, and about being intimate with myself.

I was still depressed, still exhausted, but when I was done all 50 states, wrapped things up, I realized that I wasn't ready to kill myself yet. I needed a home, but, by that point, I was completely screwed.

There is a funny side to suicide. Sorry if you are offended by that but I find it hilarious. I didn't follow through with my plan which meant that I had given away everything I owned, didn't have anything left, and all that I had was a little bit left on my credit cards that I could not afford to make any payments on. So, I hit another crisis point.

Financial stability is one of the cornerstones of my mental well-being. I had taken dynamite to the foundation I had crafted for over four decades. Once again, that swarm of gnats turned into a swarm of hornets.

I remember one night in particular. At this point, thoughts hurt. Every thought entering my mind was like a stinging hornet. I'm on my sofa in a fetal position, shaking my head from side to side, and then I started laughing because I started thinking of Tom Cruise and Top Gun.

If you have ever seen Top Gun, or any movie with modern fighter jets in a dog fight, that's what it was like. I'm hearing the "beep, beep, beep" as the thoughts try to get missile lock. I'm physically and mentally evading them, dipping and diving, weaving through the house, as the beeping gets faster and faster.

Then, the solid beep. Missile lock. The thought would explode inside my head. Pain seared throughout my body. Crumbling into the sofa. Waiting for the wave of regrets to stop. Then, I would start hearing the "beep, beep, beep" again.

I reached out to Rachel again. "I'm there again," I told her, "and I don't want to be here." She talked me through. Talked me down.

I began doing some things right. I began working again, made it a point to meet up with friends once a week, started yoga, and started walking again. I jumped through hoops but finally was able to get back on the combination of meds that worked for me. Then, long story, but I got fired. My time in Texas was at an end.

I was soon back on the road. This time to Tijuana where I was offered a job. I found myself in a much different place mentally. I wrote my book and began on the next one. I'm writing columns every day. I would eventually start doing a podcast. The pieces had started coming together.

Then, to make too long of a story a little bit shorter, I lost my job there.

An interesting thing happened. The swarm of gnats returned, the softer suicidal thoughts. I'm here in Mexico, with some savings, and I am waiting for the hornets. I'm sitting there, waiting, waiting. Waiting some more. They were supposed to come. I'm sipping on my coffee and waiting. They never did.

Again, if you would have called me, and asked me. If you would have reached out to me, "how are you doing, Chris?" The answer would have been the same, with a tinge of truth, "I'm doing fine. I'm doing okay."

The depression still hits me. Aye, I'm not in the best situation. I'm doing the podcast, though, working on books, doing things that made me feel better and lifts the exhaustion. Most days, I don't even think of the exhaustion.

I was planning on doing a much different podcast today, but I couldn't. Last night, trying to write the script turned out to be impossible. I laid down in bed, full clothed and with the lights on and fell asleep. I decided to quit doing the podcast.

I got up this morning thinking, who the hell was that last night? Don't let that person back in. You know what you have to do, Chris. You need the counseling, you have to keep up on the meds, you must get into the self-help and at least find a yoga studio once you have money again.

I'm doing okay. I'm fine. I'm getting there. I'm getting by and that's really the best that you'll get from me. I'm 51 now and I've been through this. I've been down this road many, many, many times. I don't want to go down this road anymore. I want to start putting together a better life for myself. It's about triggers and avoiding them. I have to start adulting again, so I've been working a lot on my resume. That's what I did all weekend instead of putting together this podcast.

I guess that's really the end of the podcast for today.

I do understand if you're in crisis and if people are asking you if you're okay and you're just saying that you're fine. That's okay too but understand, like I do, that you're not fine, but there are ways to get help and there are ways to get through this. It might take a year. Hell, for me, it might take 50, but it's a hell of a ride. There's a lot waiting for you out there when you don't isolate, when you take care of yourself, when you understand what your triggers are and avoid them. If you can't avoid them, you learn better coping strategies. Things will get better.

Take the damn meds. There are side effects but what are the options? There are other treatments out there now and there's new things coming out. There's a lot of exciting things happening. Suicide is not an option; it shouldn't be an option.

There's the whole other side of suicide, of people wondering why the people that they loved took their life. I want to tell them people that it is not your fault, there is nothing that you could have done because if you had gone to them right before they committed suicide and asked, "how are you doing," they would have looked up and said, "I am doing okay. I am fine."

With that, I'm gonna wrap up this podcast. I'll post it. I don't know how it's gonna sound or how it came out.

I'm going to call it an evening, take my medication, get undressed and get underneath the blankets tonight. I'll turn off all the lights and plan on waking up tomorrow. I'm going to get back to living because that's what I really have to get back to. I have to start doing it right. There's a wrong way to do it and a right way to do it and I've been doing it the wrong way which opened up the door for the depression to come back and the suicidal thoughts to come back.

I'll end this with saying, "no, I'm not okay but I'm getting there. I'm going to keep on talking."

Aloha. Thanks for joining me

Episode 10: From Beyond the Doorstep

In this episode...I'm going even further off the reservation. In honor of Suicide Awareness Month, let's discuss the other side, the people left behind.

Since I started talking about my experiences with suicide, people have asked me about loved ones who committed or tried to commit suicide. They wanted to know, or needed to know, how I got past my suicidal period, how I am still here when their loved ones are not.

It tears them up. I can understand this as I have been there on the other side. My mom was bi-polar and tried to commit suicide multiple times. I was a witness to it twice that I can recall.

The first time I was very young. I had to be old enough to read because after trying to wake her up for hours, I opened the folded note on the bedside table and read it. Either through panic or ignorance, I did not know how to call 911 so I ran.

It was late, very late. I remember a warm rain that chilled me as I ran through the streets in my socks that quickly got soaked in SW Philly. I had no idea where to go, even with family right up the street. I was drawn to a candy store a couple blocks away where I knew the owners lived in the house next door. I banged on the door until they opened it. I don't remember much after that, but they must have called 911.

I was much older the second time. It was my greatest sin, my greatest crime. My arrogance. I was 29 and would save my mother from her manic depression. I moved her into my two-floor apartment and tried to work with her. She was too far gone in her madness, and, for the first time in my life, I met a foe, a situation, that I was powerless against.

After a couple months, I knew what was about to happen. I even called her doctor. I took my mother to see him. On the car ride over, I saw this incredible transformation. It was like watching a woman get ready to walk the red carpet for the Oscars.

My mom was completely in the grip of the madness. It shackled her and incapacitated her. All that she could do was sit on the sofa and scratch at her arms. In that car ride, though, she became the master manipulator that did not want to go into the hospital. The transformation was truly incredible to watch. Terrifying, but awesome.

We walked in and she completely conned the doctor. I tried telling him, explaining, pleading. He looked at her, asked her questions that she answered clearly and sanely, and he ignored me. I believe he accused me of trying to get my mom hospitalized so I could have a break from taking care of her.

He got a call the following afternoon. It was after the cops busted through the door, after I wandered through the apartment amazed at how much blood could come from one person, after my own madness began.

I got his answering machine. "I was right and you were wrong. Your patient is in the hospital. The doctors are amazed that she survived."

I'll give him this though: he did call me back.

So, yeah, I've been there. I guess that is one of the reasons why both my plans included not letting anybody know, not subjecting them to the horror of finding me and having to clean up the mess. Allow the waves, tide and ocean to take me into its embrace.

If you have been through this, I highly recommend getting counseling with an expert on the topic. It is most likely what caused my PTSD, but I am bad at taking my own advice.

For now, let's talk about the doorstep and beyond. You can find an essay on it I wrote on my website: In Memory of Robin Williams and others who lost the battle against depression. Some people have found it helpful.

I was so angry at my mother for the longest time, but then I began to understand it from her side. It would be about six months from her attempted suicide to when I almost exited stage left.

I made my own appearance at the Oscar's, walked down the red carpet all smiles and waves. I'm alright. I'm okay. Everything is perfectly fine.

But first, let's dive into the deep end. A person who is actively suicidal or succeeds at committing suicide. The doctor asked my mother if she had a plan to hurt herself. She lied and said no. This is an extreme case, but it illustrates the point very well. There is no room for metaphors. This is a true story.

My mother's madness had evolved to a point where she knew that she was an instrument of Satan sent to spread disease on the earth. Try to take that in for a moment. She was an instrument of

Satan sent to spread disease on the earth. It was truth to her, fact. It was her reality.

She had spread the disease to me who in turn had spread it to her grandson. She was now spreading it to everybody that she knew and loved.

In this situation, what would you do? If this was your reality?

So now let's water it down, take it back from the extreme. I know that the first time I went from passively suicidal to active, I felt like a complete piece of shit. I was not an instrument of Satan sent to spread disease on this earth, but in my reality, I was a burden, financially, emotionally, mentally and physically to all those I loved and cared about. People were taking care of me. That was my reality. My truth. Beyond any doubt and beyond any counter argument.

I got to a point where I couldn't function. It was a moment of clarity for me. My mom's "selfish" act became a selfless one. I was going to follow her lead, succeed where she failed.

It was my mom who saved herself. I don't know how. The doctors don't know how. They believe that the thing that first saved her, gave her time, was she tried to kill herself two ways. Her thoroughness bought her time. She sliced and took a massive dose of sleeping pills. The doctors feel the sleeping pills slowed her heart enough for the blood to congeal. In a moment of clarity, she dialed 911.

For me, I needed at least one person to understand. Something within me, maybe something that was still clinging to life, made me call a friend to try to explain it to her, for her to understand. Simply, because I have spoken about it other episodes, she asked for more time, and I gave it to her.

Time was the common factor. A few seconds. A week. A month.

I've read stories about people who jump from the Golden Gate Bridge wanting to commit suicide and survive. It is said that as soon as they jump, they regret jumping. I am sure you can find the stories on YouTube.

The need for survival is our most basic instinct and that of every animal. People will do amazing and miraculous things to survive. To end your own life, you need to override this most basic function.

Now, think about the stories you know that may override this. Things you may have said, especially if you are a parent.

I'm an uncle. Blood of my blood. As soon as that kid was born, I knew I would do anything for him, including giving up my life to save his. It was a love so complete, so powerful, that it placed his safety and survival above my own.

Now, apply that to the above story. Does it make it easier to understand?

...I just took a break from typing this up. Diving this deep, I need to come up for air once in a while. While taking a break, I ran across a meme a friend posted on Facebook.

"The people in your life should be a source of reducing stress, not causing more of it."

Now, I'm sane. Or as sane I get. I understand the meme. I preach it. Get rid of the toxic people in your life.

But imagine when insanity enters the equation. Imagine you become the toxic person. Toxicity becomes your identity, your reality. You are the toxic person in people's lives. The people you love and care about. Your very existence is causing them pain and harm.

What would you do?

Aye, I realize it is hard to understand, hard to wrap your imagination around it. But if you have a loved one who committed suicide, you have to try and realize that it is not your fault. There is nothing you could have done. In their reality, they did what they needed to do.

Altered reality. Imagine me trying to explain to you that the sky is really neon red and not blue, that water feels scratchy, roses smell like horses, a baby's crying sounds like Mozart, and filet mignon tastes like mustard.

I've always said that depression warps reality, it is a powerful illusion. It is so hard to pierce through it. You cannot do it alone. Please see my episode on the Mental Health Triangle.

Now, the second time I was planning on committing suicide was very different in many ways. I did not feel like a burden to anybody. I wasn't toxic. I was walking down that red carpet with waves and smiles. But the carpet was not leading to the Oscars. It was leading to the end of an existence that I could not bear anymore.

I started planning it when I was about 48. It was a hell of a plan, that Covid interrupted. The story doesn't matter, and it is one I share in other episodes. The important thing for you to know is that nobody knew and there was nothing that anybody could have done. I was waving and smiling and actually feeling great.

You see, I justified everything. It all made perfect sense, once again, in my mind. I had given my friend her year, and then another 18 after it. I was done. I had a good run, but it was time.

I said all of my goodbyes without letting on that I was saying goodbye. I wrapped things up, took care of everything that needed to be taken care of, and was about to set off on that final journey when the pandemic interrupted everything.

I was just so damn exhausted. The depression had returned after a long time and hit me with a vengeance. There was no meaning in my life anymore, just exhaustion. No purpose. No will to continue.

As I mentioned, I justified it all. It can be easy to do. Depression can alter time. As I mentioned before, as a person who suffers from Major Depressive Disorder, I think maybe 5% of my life in total is the depression. But when within that 5%, it becomes 100%.

I compared depression to cancer. In the previous few years, I had watched friends and family die of cancer. It had eaten up their bodies. To me, the depression was a cancer of my spirit. It had eaten it up and there was nothing left.

On my one friend's death bed, where I had gone every night for a month, I knew that she was entering a better existence. I did not want to lose her, but I thought that was so damn selfish of me. The pain she had been through for the last 14 years was unimaginable. I loved her, and for her sake, I wanted her to let go and finally be at peace. She did.

Peace was all that I wanted. An end to the pain, an end to the exhaustion. People loved me and I felt they were being selfish for asking me to stay. Why? For them? To make them feel better? I continue to suffer for what? To live a life of quiet desperation until something or another more natural caught up to me. It didn't make sense.

--Remember. We are talking about an altered reality here. We are talking about--metaphorically--standing on the edge of the Golden Gate Bridge. I knew I was surrounded by people who loved, and were mentally grasping and pulling at me, so I wouldn't jump. And I was pissed off at them for it.

But there were things missing in my life. Pieces that I did not know and could not find. I had never engaged the Mental Health Triangle fully. I did not have the tools to find the pieces or put them together.

Just allow me to friggin' jump and be done with it! You'll get on with your lives. You'll see me as a tragic soul who lived a troubled life, mourn for a while, and then you get to get on with your lives. Leave me the hell alone. If I love you, I'll stay? If you love me, you'll let me jump.

There was nothing left for me.

I was about to jump and then the pandemic hit me like a hurricane force wind, blowing me back away from the edge. For a while. I'd fight my way back to the edge.

I'm okay. I'm alright. Everything is fine.

That is what everybody saw. It is all they would have seen. I would have just disappeared. There is nothing anybody could have done. Nothing. It was something that I had to do for myself.

Again, I come back to time. The pandemic granted me that. Forced it upon me. In the end, I was happy for it. At the time, I was angry. I was the jumper on the Golden Gate Bridge--with a bungee cord unknowingly attached to me.

How and why? How am I still here, talking about this?

I don't know if I have a good answer for you.

The only thing I can think of is acting classes. I have lived through a lifetime of trauma. I'm good at this shit. When I am at my best, or at my worst, I know I can accomplish anything. I'm a mental monster and can be arrogant as hell. Maybe it is the SW Philly, maybe the Infantry, maybe my past, but there is something in my gut that tells me you can put me in any situation and there is a chance I'll win. A slight chance, but a chance.

This just may be altered reality, or a delusion of grandeur, or a slight touch of insanity, but I really believe that if you put me in the ring with the heavy weight champion of the world, I have a chance. Not a good one. One in ten million? I'm going to get my ass beat. But there is a chance, however slight, that I'll get lucky with a well thrown punch--or kick, bite, elbow or knee.

Aye, I'm from Philly and fight dirty.

When Covid hit, that caused a massive surge in depression and trauma, I was talking to a friend of mine who is a psychiatrist specializing in trauma and PTSD. He said people need to be talking to people like us, that we're good at this shit.

I guess that that is one of the things that saved me. Instead of turning inward and being pissed off at the universe for attaching a bungee cord to my ankle, I reached out. I wanted to help, so I started making social media posts that would eventually lead to an odyssey across America. I engaged people in the different reality that had been imposed upon them, trying to pull them from it and offering tips on way to cope and get out of it.

If someone you know tried or succeeded in committing suicide, you need to reach out to someone. You are not alone. Trauma can make us withdraw and that is the last thing you want to do.

The easiest thing to do, and it does not cost a dime, is reach out to a local Al-anon or Nar-anon meeting. They are support groups for loved ones of addicts, some of which have lost people to the addiction. An overdose, to me, is just a different type of suicide.

They have open meetings. Go, listen, find support, engage, and do not isolate.

I can't recommend counseling enough, with a trauma specialist. Your reality has been altered and you need to learn different ways of dealing with it, fixing it. You grieve. There is a process. Google the five steps to grief.

I do wish life was like a movie and there was an Oscar waiting for me at the end of the red carpet. Very apt as the movie I am thinking of is Good Will Hunting and the actor who received the Oscar was Robin Williams.

It's not your fault. It's not your fault. It's not your fault.

There is nothing you could have done.

And that is a wrap for this episode.

Aloha.

Episode 11: Why is Water Wet?

Let's get naked about mental health! --I told you I'd make it to the Robin Williams "Good Morning Vietnam" point sometime. Did it work? Too much? Not there yet?

In this episode, I'll be continuing with the "Suicide Prevention Month" theme. I've gone to the extreme where I almost committed suicide, took everybody to the other side of suicide, those left behind, and now I want to discuss the gentler side of suicide. Yes, there is a gentler side. Michelangelo will also be making another cameo appearance.

Why is water wet? It's a simple enough question, but can you answer it? Think about it. Where is Neil Degrassi or Bill Nye the Science Guy when you need them? It is a simple question that probably has a very complicated answer.

I have spent the better part of the last few years asking a similar question: what is normal? I know the complicated answers, and even the evasive ones.

"There is no such thing as normal. Normal is a range. It cannot be defined."

Yes. It can.

I see it all around me. Aye, I know everybody has issues, but I also know that not everybody thinks and reacts like I do. What's the baseline? What's the average?

The hell if I know.

It was not until a counseling session about a decade ago that I realized that having suicidal thoughts IS NOT in the normal range.

I was in the session, discussing other things with my therapist, and it popped out that the suicidal thoughts were back. Then, I moved on with the current discussion.

"Wait, wait, wait," he said, interrupting me. "Let's discuss the suicidal thoughts."

I was taken off guard. I had been on a roll with something or another, something important.

"Why," I asked.

He looked at me questioningly, "Don't you want to discuss the suicidal thoughts?"

"Not particularly," I said.

I had been through the routine. "I don't have a plan to hurt myself. I am not planning on doing it. And I definitely don't have time to be hospitalized."

I wanted to get back to the other important thing I was discussing. This session was costing me money. I had the money, but it was also costing me time that I didn't have. I was a business owner with a lot to do. An hour here and the hour and half commute were 2 1/2 extra hours I would have to spend at work.

But now I could see that he didn't understand. Him not understanding put me back on my heels. Whatever important thing I had been discussing went flittering away.

"I have suicidal thoughts," I said. "I have for as far back as I can remember. Doesn't everybody have them?"

"No," he said. "They don't."

I guess as a trained therapist --he was a PsyD-- he has been taught not to say, "This is not friggin' normal."

So, we discussed the suicidal thoughts. The softer side of suicide.

I don't know when they entered my life. My best guess would be high school. I think I struggled with them at first, but just the thought of suicide appalled me. I had been on the other side of someone attempting it. My mind could not even wrap around the idea of putting a plan in place let alone acting on the plan. A bottle of pills, a razor, a gun, jumping. My mind had catalogued and listed all of the ways to do it and discarded them as not for me.

That did not make them go away.

They would pop into my mind from time to time. Still do. "I should kill myself." Just a thought, an idea, a reaction. Then, it goes away. I refer to them as gnats on a summer evening. I wave them aside and get on with things.

Sometimes, the thought is just an individual one here and there. Sometimes, they come in clusters for days and weeks. They have even lasted months.

It is just something I got used to. It became part of my normal.

They actual swarmed a couple weeks ago and then again a week ago. I hit a couple rough patches. But I waved the gnats aside and got on with things.

When I wrote, or said, "The suicidal thoughts are back," that's what I meant. I did not have a plan in place. They really just annoy me.

Also back in high school, I injured my back. It was the summer between freshman and sophomore year. I was doing a high dive, twisted wrong, and that was the end of my football playing days.

My back has always hurt from time to time since then. I guess about 15 years ago, a new thing started. I would feel a twinge, and then I would lose all strength in my lower body. I would find myself on the floor for a few minutes. Just staring up, no pain, waiting for the strength to return. It does and then I get back up and return to whatever I was doing.

The fun times are when it happens in public, at malls or something. Everybody rushes over to me with their phones out, ready to dial 911, and I'm just like, "No problem here. Just normal. I'll be fine in a few minutes. Thank you."

That's the way I think of the suicidal thoughts. I don't talk about them. No problem here. Just normal. I'll be fine in a few minutes. Do not call the friggin' ambulance!

In the therapist's office, though, I finally realized they are not normal. Still haven't done anything about it though.

But. Why is water wet?

I did give myself a clue a long time ago. When I was in college, so 1995 or so, I wrote an article that got published. It was on dysthymia, a low-grade chronic depression. It is a mental illness that cannot even be diagnosed until you have had it for at least two years. At the time, there was debate over whether or not it was a distinct illness or just a part of Major Depressive Disorder. --I have no idea where the argument stands now.

To help people visualize it, I offered a graph. The y axis, or vertical, is a person's mental state, from 1 to 100. The lower range is depression, and the upper range is happiness. The x axis, or horizontal, is time. Days, weeks, months, years. A person's lifetime.

I used thoughts of my mother and her Bi-Polar Disorder, Manic Depression, for comparison with a normal range.

Yes, I did define a normal range.

A person's normal range will be between 40 and 60. They will live within that range with few aberrations. Major life events will push them out of that range for a time, but they will return to that baseline, that average.

The death of a loved one might push a person down to 30. The birth of a child up to 75. The low or high will go on for a while but then they return to that normal range.

A depressive episode can be devastating. It will bring a person down to 10 to 20 and they will stay there for weeks--maybe months without intervention. I would guess that 10 is nonfunctioning.

A manic episode can be just as devastating. It will push a person up to the 80 to 90 range where they will stay for days and maybe weeks. I would guess that 90 is completely out of control.

I saw my mother swing through both, the spiral downward and then the climb up to, what was for her, glorious heights.

--Just an aside here as it is suicide awareness month. I read somewhere, and know from experience, that the most dangerous time for a person is not when they are in the nonfunctioning depressive state. It is when they are still in the depressed range and climbing back out. Just something to keep in mind.

But dysthymia and that normal range. The range is from 40-60. A person with dysthymia, a low-grade chronic depression, will drop down to about 35 and then stay there. Their world is dull and gray. Happiness may strike in short, brief spurts, but 35 becomes the norm.

The article was titled, "Dysthymia: The Thief of Happiness."

Why is water wet?

I really started confusing close friends when I started talking about it with them a few years back. They didn't understand the question. All I knew was that I was not normal, and I wanted to know what that normal range was, so I had a basis for comparison.

So, suicidal thoughts are not normal. What else was I missing?

I tried to think about things for years but gave up. I went the escapism route and it worked. I allowed my profession and family to consume me.

"Consume" is a good word because that is exactly what it did. It consumed everything that I had, everything that I was. I would have the occasional suicidal thoughts, but they were very few and far between. Who has time to be depressed when they are "on" almost 24/7?

Think of a forest fire. Once all of the forest is gone, the fire burns out and there is nothing left. Eventually, though, other things will enter and begin to grow. For me, it was the depression. It was also thoughts.

Why is water wet?

I knew I had deficiencies. I would call them broken things but since episode eight, I am trying to stay away from that idea. Still reaching for new terminology. So, let's use deficiencies for now.

It is kind of ironic because the one friend who said I think too much made me do the most thinking.

I met Justine. She was this incredible woman, and we became friends. At that time in my life, I started to explore the relationships around me, especially the people I was closest to. I was most interested in the people who seemed to have healthy boundaries with their spouses, significant others, and the people they were closest to.

Justine was an enigma to me. She was a wild spirit, a beautiful soul, with a non-traditional outlook on life. Aye, she was a biker chick with tattoos and completely outside of my experiences. A tiny little thing, she was unabashedly honest and open. And she had boundaries.

I pissed her off. But, first, I freaked her out.

Forest fires and boundaries and Justine. How did I stumble into this one? But I'm going with it because it makes sense. Well, it makes sense in my mind. I hope it makes sense to you.

To fight a forest fire, they will create fire breaks. They will even create controlled fires to burn away the fuel to keep the forest fire from spreading uncontrolled. As I traveled across America, I saw breaks that had to have been intentional in case there was a fire.

I didn't have any fire breaks in me, no boundaries. I had no idea that I didn't have any boundaries. Maybe there is even something in the back of head that says boundaries are wrong, having boundaries with someone that you love is unnatural. You don't hold anything back, pour all of yourself into everything that you do.

I loved Justine. As I mentioned, I was empty, and things were starting to grow again. I got drunk one night and I told her. I saw the look in her eyes and tried to explain it. I was too drunk, and I don't think I did a very good job of it.

Special note. I am not a heavy drinker. Not many people have ever seen me like that. Justine was not expecting it because I only had two or three beers. I take a medication, though, where every once in a long while, that two or three beers can feel like 20. That's what happened.

Yeah, I think I freaked her out.

But I did love her. I loved her from the second or third day I met her. I loved her spirit. It is not like I was about to propose. We were not even dating. I loved her the same way that I love special kind of people. She was special. She became a teacher and a friend, an outlet during a dark time in my life. She awoke something in me that I thought dead.

In my condition, it didn't come out that way.

--Yes, dear one, in case you are listening, I love you.

I did manage to explain to her about the meds and she believed me. I had been with her the entire evening, arrived sober, so she knew exactly how much I had to drink.

We continued to talk--other nights--and I started to run into her boundaries. I loved her and she loved me. But she held back. That's when I got pissed off. That's when she got pissed off at me.

The anger at Justine didn't make sense to me, so I thought long and hard about the person who said I thought too much. We had stopped talking and I missed her. But I was angry. So, I thought about it more.

I realized I was not angry at her boundaries; I was angry at the lack of my own. I recognized that she had healthy boundaries. It is hard looking into a mirror and seeing something disfigured looking back at you. Justine was that mirror.

At first, I had no idea what to do with this information. Then, I think I did a healthy thing. I reached out, afraid of being rejected, and explained. We went out to dinner and had a very long conversation. We dipped and dived into deeper things but kept things light for the most part. I had my friend back and did not want to scare her away.

I'd still piss her off from time to time. I try not to anymore. She didn't understand and I don't blame her. I was probing her boundaries, trying to understand them. At times, I think she felt as if I was pushing at them, challenging them. And maybe I was. I was new at this.

I had no idea what the hell I was doing. Still don't at times.

Why is water wet?

Back to episode eight. When Michelangelo was asked how he created David, he said he saw the angel within the marble and had to release it. I have a lot of chipping to do but have to do it carefully. How do you get the nose out without chopping it off?

I wonder how long Michelangelo left his tools to the side when working on something and just considered it instead? Thinking. Evaluating. I wonder if he spent entire nights without ever picking up the hammer.

I imagine this is where a therapist would come in handy.

Instead, though, I began to examine my friendships and relationships, people watching. Friend watching. Then, learning how to step more carefully through the woods and new growth.

I want to go on here. I want to talk about Sara, another wonderful woman and relationship coach who gave me the insight I needed to talk to Justine. I want to talk about Papa Bear, Mike. Jason and Crystal are tugging at me with their wonderful children.

But I think it is time to put down the hammer and chisel for the day, step back, and consider.

Or maybe step completely away, follow Justine's advice and not think too much for a while before that nose comes off.

Perhaps the softer side of suicide is the most dangerous of places. It is filled with ambiguity and circular paths. Not dealing with it, not even knowing it was something that should be dealt with, was maybe a part of the reason that I almost did walk through that doorway.

I have some thinking to do. But not tonight.

And that's a wrap for the episode. I'll keep talking and hope that you will as well.

Aloha.

Episode 12: Something About Hope

Let's talk about hope.

I am completely and totally screwed. I am trapped in a situation that would typically have the suicidal thoughts swarming around me.

Hell of a start to an episode about hope, huh? I'm getting there.

Instead of falling into a depression, though, I am feeling better mentally and emotionally than I ever have.

It makes me wonder: how the hell did I get here?

Here is Tijuana. I know how I physically got here. I kind of got lost on my way to Greece where I was supposed to kill myself on a nice, quiet out of the way beach.

My current situation is grim.

Being in Tijuana is not that bad. It's not what you think. It is a place filled with warm and amazing people, generous of heart and spirit. The stories you hear about cartels, travel advisories, and the dangers of Mexico? To me, they are over hyped. Aye, I lived in

Philly, DC and Miami. I've been in Chicago, Las Vegas, LA and other major US cities. Downtown Tijuana is no different.

Oh. Wait. There is a difference, besides the incredible food and the whole language thing. The cartel did go on a rampage about two months ago. They burned cars and stores. Some of the violence happened just a few blocks away from me. The difference? They were polite about it.

They got the people out of the stores, busses and cars before setting them on fire and then they put out a press release. It basically said stay inside from 10pm Friday until 3am Sunday. If you are caught outside, you will be a target. We don't want to hurt innocent civilians.

They stuck with their schedule, and, by Monday, everything had returned to normal.

I wish the mass shooters in the US were as polite.

Life went on and then I think the Universe took a personal involvement in my life. For decades, She had been giving me hints to learn patience. I ignored her. For 50 years.

A couple weeks ago, it rained in Tijuana for the first time since I arrived in April, a light, misty rain that was supposed to turn into thunderstorms. I took my dog, Dani, out for her walk very early in the morning to avoid the storms. I didn't avoid the misty rain.

I take Dani up to a park. It involves a very steep hill. On the way back, I encountered a tidbit of information about sidewalks in Tijuana that I had found interesting before but had not thought of in relation to that soft, misty rain. Some of them are tiles and they can be like ice when wet.

The tidbit of information took my feet out from underneath me, my right ankle twisting inside, and I came down hard, almost passing out from the pain. It was excruciating and my vision was blurring as people rushed to help me.

Dani, who I had rescued from neglect and abuse, is very protective of me. She kept all of the would-be helpers at bay. At 35 pounds she is on the small side, but she has to be part Pit Bull and is very strong. An absolute sweetheart at home, Dani can put on a very convincing vicious beast act.

The would-be helpers finally tossed me a walking stick and got back to their day.

Dani needs a lot of training. She is only half trained, at best, on a leash. With her, and the walking stick, during the hazy part of morning right before sunrise, I made my way back to my apartment complex. It was three blocks away and almost took me an hour.

It turned into morning as I made my way back, stumbling, hopping, and resting. I almost sat down a couple times and gave up, but you have to do what you have to do.

Later, x-rays would reveal I fractured my ankle. I say broke, which is technically interchangeable with fractured, but everybody else seems to prefer fractured, so that is what I go with.

I had to wait over a week for the swelling to go down enough to get the hard cast. I am not going anywhere for six to eight weeks.

Yeah, I am pretty much screwed.

You see, I overstayed my time here. I came for a job, but it didn't work out. My friend and I had polar opposite management styles and, well, he fired me.

When I got fired, that's the first time this whole "hope" thing happened unexpectedly.

I'm on my way home from being fired, pissed off, just knowing the depression and the suicidal thoughts are going to swarm. I was happy here in Tijuana, enjoying myself, settling in, loving my apartment complex and the feeling of safety and joy I had there.

I had been talking to Leo Flowers, though, just the day before. If you don't know, Leo had me on his podcast and it inspired this podcast. He is a psychologist and personal coach. We stayed in touch following the interview.

Leo had listened to me talking about the situation here and made a point to mention that as much as I said I was feeling safe, it didn't sound to him like I thought I was. Being fired from my job, I guess he was right.

So, I am on my way home from being fired, pissed off, knowing the defense mechanism of anger will soon dissipate and the depression will settle into me.

I got home, made coffee of course, settled down outside to think about things, the anger dissipated...and this amazing thing happened. The depression and the suicidal thoughts did pop into my head, but they quickly went away.

I sat outside, sipping my coffee, and wondered what the hell had just happened. I was confused. Very confused.

I didn't feel depressed. I felt...relieved and hopeful.

Where the hell did that come from?

I mean, I knew it had been a bad situation at work, an unhealthy one, from the first day. I've been at this for a very long time so know unhealthy work environments from healthy ones. It was a job, though, a source of income, a way out of debt if I played my cards right, kept my mouth shut, and just stuck it out for the year.

I had just lost it. Relief and hope? No, no, no. That's not the way this is supposed to work. Depression, hopelessness and suicidal thoughts: that's what is supposed to happen.

Relief and hope are what I had so I went with them.

The only thing I can figure out is that I was starting to learn things and put them into action.

In my last episode, I talked about my lack of boundaries. Here, in Tijuana, I could start to explore those boundaries safely because I didn't know anybody, and nobody knew me. I could say "no" and not be overcome with guilt. I could even make course corrections, beginning to help and then having a boundary and veering away when things turned unhealthy. There were twinges of guilt, but growing pains are to be expected.

Healthy boundaries. Any boundaries. I think they are so important to mental health. I talked to Leo about it and have started to read up on them. I would be talking to someone about it but I'm kind of broke.

I did just make a connection with someone in New Zealand, a professional, that is a wellness and mindfulness coach, that I hope to have on the podcast soon. I downloaded her free workbook, and you should too. I'll include the link on my website.

I think another thing that helped me--and was my eventual downfall--was I was not broke. I had a decent amount of savings. I could pursue the activities and a job that made me happy. Without the depression weighing me down, I could. With all of the time at my disposal, I could really get to work on things.

You see, it is not just about money--though lack of money is one of my triggers. At the start of the pandemic, though, I was in fantastic shape financially, had all the time I needed to pursue anything and everything, and I didn't use it. At the time, I was still heavily in the depressive episode, there was the plan to kill myself, so why bother with self-actualization? With educating myself? I was on a countdown timer so why bother?

I squandered the time. And the money.

Here in Tijuana, everything was different. I had learned important tools during my journey across the United States. I could put them into action. Maybe I was just out of the worst of the episode, but things were working.

Friends and family wanted me to move back up to the US immediately after I broke my ankle. It didn't make sense. I had savings, but they were limited. Here, those saving could last me 3-4 months as opposed to 3-4 weeks in the US.

Without a job, I began working more than I ever have. I'd wake up at 5 am, have coffee, and then get to work on my resume, book, job hunting, website, and this podcast.

Pursuing self-actualization is therapeutic in and of itself. I was feeling better every day. Healthier every day. Very different than I had ever felt. I was acting instead of reacting.

I didn't have all of the tools, but I had a few and were putting them to use. I was not even watching tv. I had probably watched a few hours in the months I had been here.

But I lost sight of a very important fact. It is a bad habit, an unhealthy coping mechanism, that I have had all my life. I don't why I do it, but when I know things are getting tight, I start ignoring my bank account.

Things were cheap, I kept telling myself. $100 a week was more than enough for everything I needed here. Something would come through. Someone had talked about sponsorship for the podcast, I began a Patreon account for the podcast, one of the many resumes I was sending out each day would lead to an income.

I wonder what a therapist would make out of that. It's not the first time I've done it. I hope it is the last.

I ran out of money.

But it was time to head back to Philly, home. I would be sorry to leave here, but I felt that I had the tools to make things work there. I had been playing with the idea of boundaries, practicing them, and felt good about my progress. I had a job waiting for me up there and would have a source of income while I continued to pursue all of my projects. I would not have as much time, but I had created the foundation for good things.

Then, I broke my ankle. Excuse me. I fractured my ankle.

Oh yeah, I was screwed.

I lied to myself again. I had a bad sprain once before and I told myself that that was all that it was this time. A little bit of time, a boot that I ordered, some ice, and I'd be good to go to start transferring back up north. --as my ankle and then foot swelled to a pretty amazing size.

"I'm just giving it a few days," I told everyone that told me to go get x-rays. I was having to say that a lot because everybody was telling me to go. "I've been through this before," I said, "Bad sprain. I went to Urgent Care and paid a lot of money for x-rays, a boot, and aspirin. I have the aspirin and the boot is on its way."

What I wasn't telling everyone, but it had to started to eat at me, was the fact that I was terrified about how much the doctor visit would cost. I had very limited funds, just enough to get through the month and back up to Philly. Even at that, I'd be sleeping in my car most nights.

I ordered crutches.

They finally arrived and I took an Uber to the doctor's office. He examined the x-rays, and he said the good news was I would not need surgery, that it was a clean break, but it was close. The bad news was I'd be in a cast for a minimum of six to eight weeks.

Alright, I thought, c'mon. Let it hit and sweep me away: the suicidal thoughts and depression.

I got home, spending another 100 pesos or so on an Uber, and waited for the wave to hit. I waited. And waited. Waited some more. The wave that would sweep me away into an inability to do anything, act on anything, never came.

Hmm. Interesting. I made some coffee and waited some more. Nope. Nothing.

I was paralyzed for a little while. But not with depression. I was confused as hell. I think the word is poleaxed.

Yep, that's the word: poleaxed. I just looked it up. Verb. An old word meaning hit, kill, or knock down with or as with a poleaxe; cause great shock to someone. --a poleaxe is a medieval weapon.

I got over it, with some help of some coffee, and then got to work.

Is this what is supposed to happen? Is this normal?

Yeah, I'm pretty much screwed. Did I mention that? I was even forced to start a fundraiser, asking for medical and living expenses. I had a couple bouts of depression about the entire situation, but they went away quickly instead of what I consider my normal: spiraling down into a deeper depression.

In a previous episode, I discuss it. I'm Alright, I'm Fine. It is what I say when I am not alright, and not fine. I think it is ironic because YouTube, where you can now find this podcast, reached out to me asking if I was okay.

Now? I am alright. I am fine. With no idea why.

I'm getting good medical care, have friends helping me out as I adjust to life without the ability to do everything --or really anything-- for myself, and I have redoubled my efforts on the job hunt, expanding to any and all positions.

My book editor told me to back off on my book, that she would take care of it, so I had more time to pursue the job hunt.

And I'm feeling pretty damn good. I continue to wake up each morning excited about the day. I think I spoke about it before, but I am like a kid on Christmas morning, every morning. I wake up and there is no struggle to get out of bed. I make it to my coffee maker and then get to work.

I have hope again.

There were so many times in my life that that is how I made it through the rough times. I could tell myself there was hope. Fake it till you make it. It would come.

This time, there was no faking it. It was just there.

No, I am not doing everything that I know I should be doing. Check out my episode on the Mental Health Triangle. I am still not in therapy. But I am doing everything else that I can.

I am still taking my meds along with the other things the doctor prescribed--no pain killers, only Motrin. I am searching for that self-actualization each day. I write, the warmth and support of the connections I made continue to lift me up as I have not retreated into isolation. I'm looking forward to the day when I get out of my chair and start exercising, working a little bit with the crutches and some recommended exercises.

I do watch more tv here than I ever have, but I am supposed to. Bed rest and ankle elevated.

In short, I am living my life, looking forward to each new day. I am so far away from that garage in Texas, both in miles and thought processes, where I spent so many nights contemplating suicide. Where a situation like this would have pushed me further down.

Is there a succinct way of summing up the change? I'll try.

1) I gave myself what I tell other people contemplating suicide: time. I know the depression is just a distortion of reality and that the healthier reality will reassert itself eventually.

2) I reentered the world and stopped isolating. I am remembering and using that web of connections I have built over a lifetime. Many people, I just reach out to and say hello. I know, and remember, that they are there.

3) I'm having fun with this. I make videos. Maybe not the best use of my time, but I have fun and share them so others might get a smile out of it.

4) While I work on my job hunt, I am also expanding the reach, or trying to, of my website and podcast. I am taking steps towards self-actualization and am embracing the future.

5) I am engaging on social media, talking with professionals, both to expand my network and to share my experiences.

6) I am looking at my situation with a different perspective.

Something I have always said is, "Perspective: use it or lose it." Instead of looking at my situation as "I am totally screwed and there is nothing I can do," I am looking at it as, "There is a lot of opportunity here for growth. I need to learn patience. I need to learn to accept help when it is offered. I need to learn to ask for help. I need to keep in mind that I am not alone, of which I am being remined of every day."

So, I am embracing the opportunity for growth.

After coffee each morning.

Yes, there really is hope.

You are not alone.

I am not alone.

And that is a wrap for this episode.

Aloha.

Episode 13: Make a Right at Philly

In this episode, I had something different planned. Much different. Then, a post I read on LinkedIn, well, pissed me off. I know Big Willy, via The Legend of Bagger Vance, you have to look on it with soft eyes. I tried, and did eventually, but the SW Philly boy came out as well. As a Philly boy yourself, you should understand.

So, I get into my response, teletherapy, health care professionals, and just talking.

Now, let's get into the episode.

Let them eat cake?

I was triggered by a post I saw by a mental health professional. They posted the following and a picture of an advertisement they saw on Facebook for teletherapy:

"I find this advertising to be misleading," she wrote, "traditional therapy can provide most of this and with better quality. I might add in [the traditional therapy] column: "Choose your own therapist. Use your insurance benefits. Get a diagnosis and treatment plan. Have a motivated therapist who is making more than $30." Now if I only had millions of dollars to run competing Facebook ads...."

I looked on it with soft eyes. There was a part of me that agreed with her. Then, there was the Philly boy, the Philly attitude, and 50 years experience dealing with the mental health care system in the United States. That part of me interpreted the post, by a woman who calls herself Maryland's Mental Health Maven and practices psychotherapy with about 5,000 followers, as "Let them eat cake."

"Let them eat cake," wrongly attributed to Marie Antoinette, "...is taken to reflect a princess's frivolous disregard for the starving peasants or her poor understanding of their plight."

Yes, there is the Philly in me. There is also a seasoned journalist and critical thinker that would like to invite constructive dialogue on the matter.

But I found myself back in SW Philly, in a working-class neighborhood. Though I have seen some improvements in recent years, I am a child of the 70's that witnessed the devolution of the mental care system, particularly for the poor and underserved.

My mother was diagnosed as manic depressive with schizophrenic tendencies. When she was hospitalized in the 70's and 80's, it was mandatory 30 days. Over the decades, that would drop to 15, then 10 and then finally three, where she would be sent home so medicated that she could not function. I don't even want to get into the hospitals that I have heard have gotten worse.

I replied to the post that I both agreed and disagreed. More SW Philly came out than seasoned journalist I'm afraid.

"I've been doing the therapist dance now for decades," I wrote. "I need it now. When I had insurance, I didn't have the time. When I didn't (don't) have insurance, I can't afford it..."

There is the issue of finding the right therapist. I jump through hoops, make the appointment, do the intake, make the commute, and then find the therapist is not a good fit. I give it a few more sessions hoping for...something. I am typically already in a depression because therapy has become more like triage than anything else.

You need patience. I think I read that each medication has a 40% chance of being effective and you need to take it for 30-60 days to see if it works for you. I see therapists as the same.

You need to find a therapist that is a good fit for you, that you can establish a sound therapeutic relationship with. As with meds, you might get lucky on the first try. More often than not, you make do with what you have or start the dance again.

I did finally find one who was truly making a huge impact on my life. I was working with a combination of weekly therapy sessions and monthly psychiatry sessions. I felt that after 45 years, I was finally on the right track and making a lot of progress. Dr. Ralph of Spectrum Behavior Services was amazing.

Just as with medications, though, you can become resistant. Dr. Ralph had guided me through the process of switching from the Zoloft I had been on for 15-20 years to a new med, Viibryd. My very good insurance did not cover it, so she supplied me with samples as she fought with the insurance company to force them to cover it.

I did not become resistant to Dr. Ralph. I had, and continue to have, the highest and utmost respect for her and her abilities. She was the best doctor, psychiatrist, I had ever dealt with. But she sold her private practice to a company.

I couldn't get through anymore to refill my meds. Then, Covid hit, and a difficult situation turned ugly. I ran out of meds.

Every doctor on the planet will tell you to not stop taking these kinds of meds. Hell, even if you are suffering from bad side effects, you are still cautioned to wean yourself off of them. I finally went to the emergency room.

The ER doctor said she was not supposed to give me a prescription, but, given the special circumstances, she would, but urged me to find another provider.

The SW Philly did come out in the letter I mailed to that company. Or maybe it was just the withdrawal symptoms?

No, it was definitely the Philly. After singing the praise of Dr. Ralph like the Vienna Boys' Choir, the terms "shit show" and "cluster...[edited]" came up a lot. I remember in the closing of the letter, I mentioned how Dr. Ralph was part of the solution to the mental health care crisis, but the company was part of the cancer in the mental health care system.

After the medications were back in my system and I was feeling better, I was finally able to make an appointment with a telehealth provider, a psychiatric nurse practitioner who was very good at her job.

Telehealth as opposed to traditional therapy?

I wrote in my reply to Maryland's Mental Health Maven, "On a battlefield, you take whatever is offered."

At that point, during the pandemic, with everything going on, with my depression and anxiety really kicking into high gear, the last thing I needed was to worry about running low on meds.

She replied, "I'm sorry to hear that was your experience. Do you think a platform like [teletherapy] would have given you the quality care you needed?"

The SW Philly boy heard the echo of, "Let them eat cake."

I replied, still trying to look with soft eyes, but then memories surfaced that had the SW Philly boy punching me between the eyes. "What is quality care," I wrote. "Where do you get it and who do you get it from? Would, say, the head of a psychiatric hospital, with multiple degrees, provide better care than a therapist from a teletherapy provider?"

One of the potential triggers of my PTSD occurred the day after I sat with mother and her psychiatrist, the head of a psychiatric clinic. This amazing transformation had taken place in the ride to the emergency visit. My mother was deep into a psychotic state, considered herself an instrument of Satan sent to spread disease on the earth, and was about to kill herself.

You are taught in writing classes to never talk about a person's eyes, that the eyes are merely parts of the body, and you can't see anything in them. The only thing you can see in them is the lens and the pupil. You have to describe it, show it, not write some corny line like, "I saw insanity in her eyes."

But I did, and the insanity was the smallest part of what I saw. She had sat there on the sofa, scratching at the disease on her arms, and there was something beyond madness in her eyes. Looking into her eyes was like looking through a window into hell. Madness radiated off of her like heat waves as she rocked back and forth and scratched at her arms.

In the doctor's office, she was a woman with an IQ well beyond genius level, a master manipulator, who did not want to be hospitalized--it was in the hospital during her last three-day hospitalization that she "caught" the disease she now spread.

I was told my mother was fine. There was an unspoken disapproval, a glance at the multiple degrees and awards hanging on the wall, as if I just wanted a break from caring for my mother.

The following morning, police burst through the front door of my two-floor apartment. In a moment of lucidity, my mother had called 911. The doctors said it was a miracle she survived. They could only guess that it was fortunate for her that she attempted suicide by two routes, slicing and pills. The pills had slowed her heart enough that the blood congealed and gave her time to make the call.

I was not so fortunate. I still remember walking through my apartment in October of 1999, wondering how much blood there was in a person. My mom had paced after she sliced and it looked as though someone had taken multiple cans of red paint and splashed them throughout my kitchen, bathroom, hallway and then poured a can or two on her bed for good measure.

My own period of decompensation began, my time of madness. Without insurance, and without access to therapy --not to mention teletherapy, I wonder if it would have made a difference? It would be six months before I came the closest to following my mother.

Would a platform like teletherapy offer me the quality therapy I needed?

"I would have to research it more," I replied. Had she even researched it before posting? "But I know that just having someone to talk to is a huge help. I know that BetterHelp.com is another one where you can switch therapists as often you like until you find a good fit."

I did not know of the company the Maven had posted about, Talkspace, but I do know BetterHelp. Following an interview on a podcast with a licensed psychologist, who spoke highly of them, I reached out to them online.

I had not been thrilled with the intake interview questions that "matched" me with a therapist, but I did get an appointment right away. I also knew that I could switch therapists as often as I needed until I found a good fit.

The cost was something I could afford. Well, I could afford it but lost my job before I began therapy so was forced to cancel. They refunded me the money I had paid upfront.

Perhaps beating the saying, "Let them eat cake" to death, I put myself on bread and water rations until I could find a new job and possibly get insurance.

"Quality care is expensive, beyond the means of most Americans," I replied to her. "The health care system has been circling the drain now for decades."

"...I welcome any and all alternatives. I would like it to be quality care, but I wish everybody just had access to care—and took it. I hope to help end the stigma of getting care and will promote any way a person can reach out to talk to someone."

I reached out to the mental health professional in a private message. I told her I understood her position and apologized if I had come across too harsh in their post. I wrote that a lot needs to be done and I would welcome a conversation about it.

She wrote back, "...I know care navigation is a huge problem. Good luck."

Let them eat cake?

I need to do more research. I need to talk with professionals and teletherapy care providers. I am trying to arrange an interview with Leo Flowers, host of the podcast, "Before You Kill Yourself!" who interviewed me about my new book.

Are you there, Leo? As one of my few subscribers on Podbean. Leo? Leo? Buehler?

That's just my sense of humor. Nothing Philly or passive aggressive about it.

One thing I worry about on my podcast is bad information. As I stated at the beginning of my show, and every show, I am not a psychologist, psychiatrist, therapist or any kind of profession with an --ist at the end of their title. I am just a guy who has been there.

I just try to be an authentic voice to get people talking. To anybody.

We definitely need a better answer than my podcast. We also need a better answer than, "Let them eat cake."

But let's make a right at Philly. Coming from the south, we'll cross over the Walt Whitman Bridge and soon be on the Atlantic City Expressway, one of the most absolute boring rides I have ever taken in my life. In an hour or so, we'll be in Atlantic City. We drive through the casinos, maybe park in one.

Forget about it! We're not here for the that. The women we pass? Forget about them too. No, let's just stroll down to the boardwalk, cross over the wide wooden walkway, and make our way down to the beach, and then the quarter of a mile or so to the ocean.

We can sit in the sand and look out over the waves. It is much easier to look at a sunrise with soft eyes.

Or, in my case, wait for the sunrise and even the pre-dawn. Something happened to me a while back. I started waking up early, very early. 4 AM today. I look at my clock, know that I could go back to sleep, but something pulls me to the coffee maker instead, makes me start it and then begin my day.

I'm tired, know that I will crash for a nap about 10, but I just want to start my day and begin doing something.

This morning, Saturday, I feel guilty. My dog, Dani, woke up with me. Before I broke my ankle, I had her trained. I'd take her out when I woke up to do her business. She begs to go out. I can't do anything about it. I have a tiny back patio where I leave puppy pads. All I can do now is hope she uses them.

But what can you do?

Bagger Vance would say to look at the upcoming day with soft eyes, look at the entire field. It is not a dragon to slay.

If you are struggling, if you are jumping through those hoops to begin therapy, or to get meds, there are things you can do right now.

First, don't do what I do. Don't start the coffee maker. Go back to sleep and get your rest. Leo made it a point to talk about it in our interview and I found it odd at first. He wanted to talk about sleep, good sleep. I looked into it after the fact and remember something that I learned.

There is a direct correlation between sleep and depression. I figured it out while I drove across the United States on my odyssey. When I was exhausted, started out the day exhausted, my mood was directly affected.

But you don't have to take my word for it.

There are a ton of articles online about the bidirectional relationship between sleep and depression. It is the chicken and the egg question, which came first? Bad sleep leading to depression or depression leading to bad sleep. Doesn't matter to me when looking at the pre-dawn with soft eyes.

7-9 hours of sleep each night is essential. Do what you have to do to get there. Therapy and meds can help, but if you don't have access to either, or are waiting, there are steps you can take to get there anyway.

First, establish a routine. Make it a point to go to bed at the same time each night. For me, that is about 10 these days. Before I broke my ankle, I'd go to bed about 10 and then wake up at about 5 or 6. My 7-8 hours. It makes a difference.

One thing about being stranded in Mexico is access to meds is much easier. I can buy most over the counter or with a prescription I get from the doctor who is in the pharmacy. I get a 3–5-month supply of my clozapam for $25 or so. 1.5 mg enables me to turn my mind off at night and fall asleep.

All of my life, I was a coffee addict. I could drink coffee right before bed and still fall asleep. That changed. Now, I know that I have to stop in the afternoon. I still crave coffee but have switched to decaf. With the help of my friend, Sara, I found an excellent one that I enjoy. I have a funny video about it on Instagram that I will link to on my website for this episode.

Cafe Bustello. It is a Cuban coffee I make in an Italian Expresso Maker and then add hot water to make a full cup.

Avoid booze. I was never a big drinker, but I did enjoy my beers. And I know the struggle. That booze should help me fall asleep. Enough of it and I pass out. But I also know what happens.

Booze is a depressant. Yes, it does relax me. Yes, it can help me fall asleep. But I also know it metabolizes in my body and starts working as a stimulant mid-way through the night and it wakes me up, whether to go to the bathroom, stomach issues, or a sugar rush.

I also know how it affects me the next day. It brings me down, makes me feel like shit. Even just a few. The older I have gotten, the more it affects me the following day. It can make me unproductive the following day, which then makes me feel like shit, which then makes it harder to fall asleep because my mind is racing with all of the things I should have and could have gotten done that day.

Yes, I take a break from my routine once in a while. I go out and have a few beers, but I try to limit it to only once in a while and stick with two, maybe three, beers. I know that that is my limit. I can still function the next day. Four beers? Nope.

If you do have access to healthcare, I highly recommend talking to your doctor about a sleep study. And there is an app for that as well. Many people suffer from poor sleep because of snoring or sleep apnea and never know.

I never knew that I snored until my wife pointed it out to me. She never knew that she snored until I pointed it out to her. She didn't believe me of course so I recorded it one night. On video. I got a great shot of one of the dogs being startled awake.

There are dental appliances that can help with the snoring as well as light to moderate sleep apnea. I swear by mine, the D-SAD by Panthera. One of the best things about it is that it is covered by health insurance, not dental insurance, which is typically better.

As I told Leo, though, as a professional in that field, don't get one of those over-the-counter things unless you absolutely must. I think they are all crap and the ones you get nowadays from the direct-to-consumer companies where you make your own mold and send them in even worse. They need to be fitted by a qualified specialist or else you run a risk of damaging your teeth and jaw.

Something else you can do, that I make it a point to do each day even with the broken ankle, is get the hell outside. All the studies are clear on that. Getting outside and spending time in the sunshine helps.

Hell, my doctor here, Dr. Sibeja, wrote me a prescription for it. No shit. At least one hour, but I should be doing three, in the sunshine. So, I gimp my way up to the roof with my iPhone and listen to music while soaking in the sunshine.

Let's face it. If you are suffering from anxiety or depression the last thing you want to do is go outside, you want to isolate. Don't.

Aye, I know what I am asking here. I am asking you, like I told myself, to change lifelong habits. I am also telling you to work against the depression and anxiety. It is hard, difficult, but there isn't a magic bullet here to solve all my problems. It takes work.

I think just by doing the work, just by taking action, helps me with the depression and anxiety. Popping that pill I don't want to take, doing the small things and the bigger things, makes me feel better, makes me feel like I am more in control of my life, wresting the power back from the depression and anxiety.

It empowers me.

But let's back to the list. There are still a few more things that you can do, that I do, to empower myself.

Exercise. There is a direct correlation there as well. Exercise releases endorphins, something missing in the right quantity in those with depression.

Be realistic like I am, though. I stare at the gym right across from my front door. These days, laid up with my ankle, I stare at it even more. I see the people using weights and jumping on the treadmill or the elliptical. I stared at them even before I broke my ankle and there is a really good chance that I'll be staring at them after I heal, though I know I need to get in there.

I went for walks each day instead. Just strolls, with my iPhone and headphones, at least two miles a day. These days, after sitting on my butt for two weeks and having bruised my ribs that made using the crutches impossible, I couldn't do anything until I healed. Now, I crutch my way up and down my apartment complex. And make my way up to the roof.

Yoga was a huge help for me and in many places, they offer free classes. I don't like the apps and videos to use at home, but you might. It was part of my "getting out" thing.

Besides being exercise, yoga also teaches an important lesson that is especially helpful for those suffering from anxiety, depression and PTSD: mindfulness.

I personally noticed huge improvement in my mood and energy level when I was practicing a couple times a week.

Mediation is something I can and do practice at home now. There are many free apps for it. It is part of the mindfulness thing. Just 10 to 30 minutes a day. Just like yoga, it is difficult at first. Practice. It really does make a difference.

Aye, I know. I'm from Philly as I mentioned. I didn't believe in any of that crap. Yoga, chakras, meditation? Exercise? Quit drinking? Sleep? I always said I'd sleep when I'm dead. Well, I almost was, so started looking into things.

I did an episode a while back where I discuss the Mental Health Triangle. Self-care, to me, is the base of the triangle, that supports the other two sides, psychiatry (or meds) and psychology (therapy). It's the part I ignored the most throughout my life.

Don't be like me. Start putting in the time and effort on all of these free things and see what a difference it makes.

And that is a wrap for this week's episode.

I'm now going to gimp my way up to the roof and enjoy my hour of doctor prescribed sunbathing.

Aloha.

Episode 14: Boundaries and Blind Squirrels

In this episode, I go deeper and into the background of a topic I've spoken about, boundaries. Healthy boundaries. It was a few years back that I realized that I had none. Learning about them and starting to build them is perhaps the healthiest thing I have done for myself. I've learned how to say, "No." I'm not very good at it, but I'm working on it.

Now, let's get into the episode.

I just had one of those revelations that occur from time to time. Eh, even a blind squirrel finds a nut once in a while.

I have spoken about it a few times. When I am in a depression, everybody offers me advice which can boil down to, "Just get over it." And then they wonder why I can't just get over it and get stuff done.

I talked about how one time in particular, I was in tears because I could not put on a sock. There were no physical impediments to me doing it, but the depression made it impossible at that moment.

But what is it like? What is that kind of depression like?

Well, it is like now: I can't put a sock on my right foot. I have a broken ankle and there is a cast preventing me from doing it.

The broken ankle is preventing me from doing many things. I wrote that this is probably one of the worst situations I have ever been in.

The sock thing, with the cast, is laughable. When it gets cold, I cover it up with a towel or a blanket, but I am unable to do anything. I have to depend on other people for everything, mostly strangers, because it happened in Tijuana. I'm stranded.

I even complicated it by bruising my ribs in a fall, so even short trips to the store were out as the use of the crutches aggravated the bruised ribs. One day, I got tired of not doing anything and went around to the grocery store on my crutches. I got to ride the electric cart, filled up my backpack, and then crutched my way home.

About an hour after I got home, every breath was painful. I had to stay completely immobile for a week while my ribs healed, just rolling around in my office chair to make it from the bed to the sofa, to outside my front door to smoke.

I was helpless. Still am, although after a week of immobility I resumed my use of the crutches to make it to some stores and get upstairs to the roof. I'm under doctor's orders to not do anything else.

People are being extremely helpful and kind. Neighbors pass me and offer to do anything I need done. Staff are cleaning my apartment and doing my laundry--and refusing to accept tips. Friends are buying me the big things I can't carry in my backpack like the jugs of water.

I have been looking for somebody to help me take a shower, but I am still on my own with that. Every lady I have asked thinks I have an angle. You try taking a shower in a stand-up shower stall while trying not to get the cast wet. --my doctor mentioned to this blind squirrel to put a dining room chair in there and that helps.

With my background, there is a certain irony to it. When I do make my way around to the store or wheel my way down through the apartment complex to do my laundry, people get angry with me for doing anything. They see me with my laundry basket in my lap and snatch it off of me, shooing me back home. My laundry appears at my door later on, folded. My trash bags I leave outside disappear before I can crutch them down to the cans.

My doctor told me he wants me doing nothing. I am not even allowed to do the exercises I read about online. He said I can start exercising once the cast comes off in four more weeks. The only thing he wants me doing is taking my supplements and sunbathing for at least an hour a day. So, I am doing as little as possible.

The ironic thing is that the cast and a broken ankle is considered an acceptable reason.

Nobody is telling me to just shake it off and get things done.

I did have to shake it off once and do what may have been one of the most physically excruciating things I have ever done in my life. When it first happened, I was a few blocks away from my apartment complex walking my dog before the heavy rains came. I tried calling a few people, but it was too early, and nobody answered their phone.

My dog, Dani, kept would be helpers away from me so they finally just tossed me a walking stick. It took me over an hour to get home. I almost passed out a few times from the pain. Almost gave up a few times. A broken ankle and a half-trained dog were almost too much for me, but I made it.

I did what I had to do, but at least I could do it.

When I am in a depression, I can't.

I've been through a lot in my life. I would just get stubborn, put on my Philly attitude, and make it through physically difficult situations. The walk three blocks was the worst, but it was just the top of a long list. There was bootcamp, working seven days a week for years while visiting friends and family in the hospital--making it happen on little or no sleep. I wrenched my knee deep in Arches National Park and made my way back to my car.

You get the picture.

There was that one time, deep in the depression, when I was unable to put on a sock. There is an equally long list there as well.

I can't just "shake it off." I try to put on the Philly and do what needs to be done and I can't. I slump back into the bed or a chair and just wait it out.

With the cast, I am hobbled, disabled. Without the cast, I am being lazy and a piece of shit. With the cast, I am not expected to "shake it off." Without the cast, I am.

They are really the same thing...

Instead of being depressed about the entire situation, I find myself...happy? Maybe happy is not the best word. I'm excited in the morning to wake up and get to work. Well, I am excited to get to the coffee maker. After the coffee is done, I am excited to roll outside...and sip my coffee in peace. Then, after a little while, a cup or two, I am excited about getting to work.

What's the difference? As I mentioned, this is one of the worst situations I have been in: almost completely helpless, stranded in Tijuana, and depending on the kindness of others. Everything from my experience screams that I should be falling into a deep depression. But I'm not.

Hell, I'm even having fun with it. I graduated from Instagram stories to TikTok videos. I think I'm funny. If you need a laugh, or maybe just to laugh at me, check out my other YouTube channel, The Chris Chronicles.

So, what is different? One thing is connection, something I finally picked up as I traveled. I write about disconnecting in my book. It's called "Disconnected: An Odyssey Through Covid America."

While I was disconnected, I was reconnecting again. Then, I disconnected again to fall deeper into the depression in Texas. I even removed all of my social media accounts for a long time. People noticed and reached out to me.

At the time, I was still struggling with the suicide thing. A titanic struggle that would occur every night as I sat in my garage, fighting the urge to turn on the car and allow to carbon monoxide to carry me away.

I never fully disconnected though. I was living about a mile away from close friends and made it a point to see them every week and spend time with their family. I talked to them a few times about the struggle. Mostly though, I just spent time with them. We would go out to a restaurant on Thursdays, Margaritas, where I would sip my coke, and then every other Friday was pizza night at their house where I would buy pizza for everybody.

Then, I began further reconnecting again. But differently.

At some point in time, I ran across this on Facebook, that I just ran across again. It is about addiction, but I apply it to mental health. I do not know who the original people are, but the latest post I read is credited to Johann Hari:

Rat Park

"Put a rat in a cage and give it 2 water bottles. One is just water, and one is water laced with heroin or cocaine. The rat will almost always prefer the drugged water and almost always kill itself in a couple of weeks. That is our theory of addiction.

Bruce comes along in the '70s and said, "Well, hang on. We're putting the rat in an empty cage. It has nothing to do. Let's try this a bit differently."

So, he built Rat Park, and Rat Park is like heaven for rats. Everything a rat could want is in Rat Park. Lovely food. Lots of sex.

Other rats to befriend. Colored balls. Plus, both water bottles, one with water and one with drugged water.

But here's what's fascinating: In Rat Park, they don't like the drugged water. They hardly use it. None of them overdose. None of them use in a way that looks like compulsion or addiction.

What Bruce did shows that both the right-wing and left-wing theories of addiction are wrong. The right-wing theory is that it's a moral failing, you're a hedonist, you party too hard. The left-wing theory is that it takes you over, your brain is hijacked.

Bruce says it's not your morality, it's not your brain; it's your cage. Addiction is largely an adaptation to your environment.

Now, we created a society where significant numbers of us can't bear to be present in our lives without being on something, drink, drugs, sex, shopping... We've created a hyper consumerist, hyper individualist, isolated world that is, for many of us, more like the first cage than the bonded, connected cages we need.

The opposite of addiction is not sobriety. The opposite of addiction is connection.

And our whole society, the engine of it, is geared toward making us connect with things not people. You are not a good consumer citizen if you spend your time bonding with the people around you and not stuff. In fact, we are trained from a young age to focus our hopes, dreams, and ambitions on things to buy and consume. Drug addiction is a subset of that."

***

I don't know who this Bruce character is. I'll look it up.

Okay: Bruce K. Alexander, a psychologist and professor emeritus from Vancouver, British Colombia in Canada. He retired from active teaching in 2005 from Simon Fraser University. I included the link to his "Rat Park" study below.

As I said, I apply connection to mental health. I've also mentioned in the past that I think we can become addicted to our depression. But I add another level to Bruce's experiment. It is not only about connections, but about healthy connections.

In the experiment, and for the sake of this book, let's put a "Rat House" into the setting. The rat is alone in the house. They have to leave it to get to the "Rat Park." There are two paths to take.

The first path, the easiest route, is passing through the original box, where there is nothing but the two bottles and bunch of addicted rats. The other route, harder, is a roundabout way that bypasses the addiction box to bring them to the Rat Park.

The depression makes us go the easiest route. Eh, it is hard putting on socks. For decades, I took any kind of connection I could find. My dating history shows that. I took the path of least resistance and ended up in places and relationships that fed the depression or the co-dependency. It was only recently that I began to connect the dots and stumbled into Rat Park. Then, I began leaving my front door to take the long route to Rat Park, bypassing the empty place.

I am vastly oversimplifying this. I did have very healthy connections and relationships my entire life. For the most part, they never knew about my secret world, the depression. They never knew that when I did connect with them it is because I was stumbling through the empty box to get to them. When they did not see me for a long time, they had no idea I was spending time in that empty box.

It was really when I began examining (and overthinking) the healthy connections, comparing them to the questionable ones, that I discovered the alternate route to Rat Park.

It was hard taking that alternate route at first. So damn hard. The more I took it, though, the easier the way became. After a while, I started waking up eager for the day to begin. And the coffee is pretty damn good too.

Yes, I do trip coming out of my door at times and fall into the empty box.

That brings us to the next part of the episode: the Universe being tired of me ignoring Her and taking direct action.

There is an untold part of the story about breaking my ankle. It isn't really important, except as a part of this episode.

Everything I have related in my videos and posts about fracturing my ankle is absolutely true. There is not even a lie of omission.

I was NOT drunk. I was taking my dog out for a very early morning walk in a misty rain. The heavy rains were supposed to hit, and I wanted to get her walk in, so I left about 5 AM. It was a Friday.

I talk about it in the latest video I posted on the SOMA Chronicles (The Sitting on my Ass Chronicles). You might think I am nuts, but I do believe the Universe broke my ankle on purpose. She got tired of my shit.

For decades, She had been giving me subtle hints to learn some patience and humility. I ignored her. She made it so I couldn't ignore Her anymore, so now I am learning patience and humility. Struggling with both.

I also think She placed Dani, my rescue dog, in my path. All that Dani is teaching me is to puppy proof my house. I now have all my shoes in drawers and everything that she can gnaw on hidden away. She comes up with something new from time to time, and I have to figure out ways to keep her from that. The latest was toilet paper rolls. She ate half of my last roll!

But Dani cramped my style.

Maybe as a rescue, or maybe just as a puppy (she is 18 months old), she does not like being left alone. Since adopting her, I had been staying very close to home, not even heading to the bar on occasion.

She had gotten better, though, not going completely nuts when I left. I felt I could start venturing out for short periods of time.

That Friday? When I broke my ankle? I had every intention of going out. I wasn't going to stumble and trip out my door into the emptiness; I was going to walk boldly into it. I was heading to the strip club that night. Eh, it's an addiction.

Then, I broke my ankle. I wasn't going anywhere. Instead, I had to start reexploring the longer route to the Rat Park, the healthier route. The Universe didn't give me much of a choice.

Fracturing my ankle, being stranded in my apartment complex, and running out of money all turned out to be good things. It's funny how things work out.

It has even brought me more revelations. Aye, I'm bored. I can't work all the time. I page through social media. I'm stumbling across things left and right, shiny things, things that tickle my brain and lead me down paths I might not have discovered otherwise.

I ended a few unhealthy relationships and started to explore new, healthier ones. I really started exploring the word "no" and how others were applying it to me.

Things catch my eye that leads to thoughts and then columns and then podcasts.

At first, to be honest, I did think about taking the easy way. Eh, I just broke my ankle. I was in pain. I have been against drugs and pain killers all of my life. When I have gotten a script for them for something or another, I always stopped taking them before I ran out.

My thoughts strayed to a very unhealthy path. There was the case of beer I have in my fridge and offers of more. I knew, or at least thought I knew, I could get a script for pain killers from my doctor.

Dr. Sibeja, my specialist, disabused me of that notion. "Have some beers," he said. "I'll even take you out for one or two. But no pain killers."

Healthcare is very different here in Mexico. They don't have an opioid epidemic. They are against prescribing pain killers.

Pain is good for the healing, he explained. He prescribed me a heavy dose of Motrin, that I am now off of. He also prescribed me this medication that made no sense to me and some of the doctors I spoke to in the US.

Prikul, or Pregabalin in English, has nothing to do with broken ankles. It is prescribed for nerve damage, which I didn't have. According to Medline Plus, "[It is] used to relieve neuropathic pain (pain from damaged nerves) that can occur in arms, hands, fingers, legs, feet or toes if you have diabetes and postherpetic neuralgia..." It didn't make sense to me, or my docs in the US, so I didn't fill the prescription. I was counting my pesos.

Dr. Sibeja gave me samples to take. My doctor friends in the US said they wouldn't harm me so take them.

A neighbor I have seen a few times in the complex passed me and asked about my ankle. He turned out to be a semi-retired ankle and foot specialist from the US. He explained the Pregabalin is ideal for my situation. It would relieve pain without the narcotic effects.

But that's not the only reason I wanted the drugs. I wanted to escape. Eh, I'm in Tijuana. It's not like I need a doctor's prescription. My friend took me out to a restaurant, dropped me off across the street while he went to park, and I crutched my way over to the place. On the short hop there, a minute, three different people approached me and offered me the best Percocet cheap.

I went and had my two beers.

Aside from a beer here and there, I'm sticking with my caffeine and nicotine.

So how did I create healthy connections? Well, first, I ran away from home. I was too embedded in unhealthy ones. You can't run from your problems, they always stay with you, but sometimes I think you need to get some distance from them. --though I did find you don't really need to.

Out on the road, I started to find out about boundaries and how I didn't have any. That creates very unhealthy relationships with the wrong people, either people who are users or people who have no boundaries themselves. I found myself pouring everything that I had into everything, which left me with nothing.

The basic idea of a boundary is the ability to say, "No." I suck at it. A few thousand miles between me and the people I could not say "no" to helped me establish the once nonexistent boundaries.

I'm getting there. I found some incredible teachers along the way. I think by learning about boundaries is what has helped me maintain a healthier mental state. I'm not pouring myself out into everything. I'm saving something for myself while exploring balance and other tools.

Not that I have much of myself left, but I am finally rebuilding the reserves as well.

I am a natural giver. It even says so in all of the personality tests I've taken. When I was interviewed by Leo Flowers, he asked me an interesting question. I had spoken about both the unhealthy giving of myself and dedicating my life to helping others. He asked if they were a contradiction.

It made me think. No, I replied. It's not a contradiction because of boundaries.

Let's go back to the rat box and Rat Park. Co-dependency, and unhealthy giving, is exactly like sipping on that heroin infused bottle. It's an addiction. Healthy boundaries are the walls you form to create the tunnel to take you to that Rat Park.

You are avoiding the takers, and the other addicts, while making your way to mutually beneficial relationships. Giving, in a healthy way, like doing this podcast, doesn't deplete me. It revives me, gives me something back, connects my spirit with an inexhaustible supply of...pardon the pop psychology or new age-ishness...energy and good vibes.

I did take things a bit too far. An addiction to being healthy? It made me forget things like being financially healthy. I started working on the whole balance thing, made plans to return to Philly to start working...and then the Universe broke my ankle.

I was hesitant about returning to Philly. Okay, okay: I was scared shitless. It was taking me far too close to that empty box. I had done well with things here, but could I continue it with the empty box so close and integrating work into the work life balance?

With some more time, and some more lessons, I know now that I can.

And that is a wrap for this episode.

Aloha.

https://www.brucekalexander.com/articles-speeches/rat-park/148-addiction-the-view-from-rat-park

Episode 15: The Anatomy of a Slide

In this episode...a friend gave me a much-needed kick in the butt. I was sinking into the depression again without even realizing it. I caught it in time. It is much like those big slides at amusement parks. They start with the slight decline and then you hit the steep part. Instead of a "weeeeeee!" though, it is...well, not so fun. I was still in that slight decline.

Now, let's get into the episode.

How the hell did that happen?

I did not even realize it, but the depression had gotten me. I was even thinking the opposite. Shit. It took a friend reaching out to me to make me realize it.

An old friend is helping me out with my book, editing it. She sent me pages on Wednesday. "I'm all over this," I thought to myself, as I opened the email and downloaded the attachment.

Then, nothing.

On Friday, she reached out to me again. "What's going on?"

"...I sent you those pages on Wednesday," she wrote, "and you should have been finished reading. Just read them and if anything jumps out, we will discuss. Again, the priority is those pages.

I think you have some sort of block with the book because we keep going back and forth on the same things and I don't think your energy is in it. You seem scattered. What's going on?"

She was right, I realized: I was scattered. I am grateful for all that she is doing for me and always reply instantly to her texts and emails. I drop everything and get right to work. I've been waiting for this next edit as it marks the halfway point of the book. I had opened the file, quickly scanned through for comments and highlighting, and then...nothing.

I am not even sure if I closed the document or not.

I explained to her what is going on.

"You're right," I wrote back. "I'm actually getting it done right now. I'm seeing a few things and adding notes. Not many.

The anxiety is kicking into high gear. My fundraiser helped but I'll be out of money soon. I'll have to get on the road before I'm healed and I'm worried about it...I'm not sure what to do about me, my dog or my stuff.

My mind tends to start shutting down. Sorry. I needed the kick in the pants. I'm focused now and getting it done. And getting it done right..."

She replied back that if I needed some time, that was okay, that she would just continue on the next section.

"Seems like you have your hands full," she wrote. "Why don't you solve what you need to solve and pick the review up when you are calmer. I know, money issues are the worse.

No sense in concentrating on the book when your heart is not in it. I will continue editing from where I left off when I have more free time. And you'll just check two edits at once. All will be well.

Don't worry about going into what has not been edited. I'll handle it."

That's when it hit me. I was sliding into the depression again. She even offered me a way to gracefully slide deeper in.

"Oh no," I wrote back. "I'm all over this. I'm having fun! It's what fulfills me and keeps the depression at bay. I just needed to refocus. I'm about a third through the edit now. But I do need to nap because I'm exhausted from waking up at 3.

I'm calm. My heart is 100% into it. I needed to get my head to follow my heart and it jumped on the bandwagon finally.

I'm LOVING this. I'd continue but want to sleep for a little while so I'm clear. I ran into an issue with the Ft. Benning info and started to stumble with the edit.

This is my norm now. Sleep from 11-3, get to work, sleep from 9-12, make breakfast for me and Dani and then get back to work. Maybe nap another hour in afternoon.

I can guarantee 100% of my best effort. After a nap..."

I was still a bit scattered, ran into some issues with exhaustion because I am not sleeping well, but I did get it done and back to her.

That scattered feeling is one of my first signs that the depression is coming on. It is tough to recognize though. I am at work on a half dozen different projects, working on things to promote myself, my resume, my podcast and...

...I found myself on dating apps and wasting time having conversations with fake accounts on Facebook Messenger.

I didn't even get to work on this, the podcast script.

The book and the podcast are what everything else is about, it is what fulfills me and keeps me going. They really do make me happy. They fulfill me. They are what have added purpose to my life again.

But let's back up.

I broke my ankle. I wish I had a good story for it, but I was just walking my dog in the morning rain. That bothered me. After all of the shit I have been through, including train wrecks and natural disasters, I break my ankle walking in the rain.

I talked about how I've been having fun with it. I'm under doctor's orders to not do anything except sit on my ass (which inspired The SOMA Chronicles--Sitting on my Ass Chronicles) and had me graduating from Instagram and Facebook to TikTok.

It really could not have happened at a worse time. Money issues, or lack thereof, have always been a trigger for my depression. Asking for help is another one of my triggers. The ankle had me facing both.

I had overstayed my time in Tijuana. It's a long story that I cover in a previous podcast. I had already had to reach out for help to get me through September. But I had a plan to start adulting again which included a move back up to Philadelphia for a while where I could start working again.

A few days before I was about to leave, I broke my ankle. I can't go anywhere until the end of November.

I have never been in this situation before. I am completely dependent upon others. For everything. Some bruised ribs even made it more difficult at first as it made using the crutches impossible.

And, I had to start begging for money.

It killed me inside, but I posted a fundraiser. I needed rent, medical and living expenses until I could start working again.

I think that is when the depression started trickling back in, when I started that slow decline on the slide. People reached out, contributed. I was embarrassed, but grateful. The embarrassment put me on the rug to the slide. The people not responding were the push to get me started.

Bitterness and a touch of anger, that should not be there, started intruding into my thoughts. And a song. I made a video--that was pulled off of TikTok for copyright violation. I told myself I was just having fun with it. That I can't be bitter or angry for people not helping me.

"Nobody Knows You When You're Down and Out" by Eric Clapton became a bit too popular for me.

Aye, I'm human. I'm not perfect. I work at it every day but what can you do?

Once I lived the life of a millionaire
Spent all my money, I just did not care
Took all my friends out for a good time
Bought bootleg liquor, champagne and wine

Then I began to fall so low
Lost all my good friends, I did not have nowhere to go
I get my hands on a dollar again
I'm gonna hang on to it till that eagle grins

Cause no, no, nobody knows you
When you're down and out
In your pocket, not one penny
And as for friends, you don't have any...

I know that's not true. I have a huge net of friends and family and people who love me. But the depression begins to warp reality. I guess I began to wonder: where the hell were they?

And the bitterness began to intrude as well. It's not healthy, it's not me, but I'm human. I've always said to give without thinking of getting anything in return. I never loan money. I give it if I have it and don't if I don't. I always gave until it hurt, and then beyond...but I'll get into that one when I finally get around to discussing unhealthy boundaries.

I gave freely of my time and money to anything and everything. It is only recently I began pulling back. But I did have to start wondering where everybody was.

The fundraiser got off to a quick start, but then slowed to a trickle and then stopped. I got October covered, but November is creeping up on me.

The rational side of me knows that everybody has lives, they haven't gone anywhere. I've spoken to some friends who never even saw my posts about my fundraiser.

I know that that is a part of the depression. I start overthinking things, takings things personally that are not personal. Not having anything else to do besides sit on my ass gives me far too much time to overthink things. It is almost like a paranoia begins to set in. Why are people against me?

Things begin jumping at me out of the shadows.

The right way to think about things, as I have mentioned, is people have lives. Hell, I've gone years without talking to friends. It's a comfortable kind of friendship where we slide right back into where we left off, catch up, and move forward.

Facebook posts? How many do I miss? How many do I pass on? Because of my feelings about asking for help, I have not been very good about advertising the need for help.

Nobody is against me. Nobody has abandoned me. Just like I never was against or abandoned anybody else.

But the depression makes the specter start to loom.

Bitterness really started to kick in when I tried to post about my situation with the national association that I founded to help small labs. They would not even post about it. It went against their new rules.

That just pissed me off. And made me feel rotten all at the same time. I chose to do things and I own everything I did, all of the consequences of my actions. Yes, it was the unhealthy boundaries that made me pour myself into that association, all the time and money, but I did it to help, not to get anything in return. But I had personally allowed posts from small labs in trouble that needed help.

Looking back now, I can see how all of the things combined to push me into the depression. The feelings of abandonment, the bitterness, the anger, and the guilt of asking for help and the guilt over the anger. I was on the rug on the slide and then the feelings pushed me, so I started that slow decline.

The depression started whispering to me. No, "wheee" as I began the slide, but a "you are alone and need to do what you have always done. Figure it out. Isolate. Retreat. Escape."

Lack of sleep was not helping either. That had nothing to do with the depression. I am able to fall asleep easily. Staying asleep is the issue. It's the cast. But I have learned that not getting enough solid sleep drastically effects my mood. And there are a few hundred studies that support me.

I'm going about my day, doing everything that I can be doing, telling myself I'm doing well, but the depression was sinking its claws into me again without me even knowing it. I started missing beats, my thoughts scattering. My 100% productive days started being filled with diversions and trouble concentrating on particular projects.

Resumes were going out every day. Wasn't that enough?

No, it's not.

I know this. This is truth. This is the truth I discovered not too long ago. I need to be pursuing a purpose. I need to be working on self-actualization. I need to be working on the projects and videos that get me beyond the day to day.

What's there to binge watch on television? How about that stupid ass dating app again that I hate? Where the hell was everybody? Without realizing it, I started slipping into escapism.

But I'm fine. That's what I told myself. We can rationalize anything. Even as the resumes began to trickle off, I'm still fine. Aye, the hundred or so I put out there will produce something--ignoring the fact that even if they did it was too late to help with my current situation.

Scattered, I froze. Time froze. It became about my ankle, recovering, healing, and making it through the day until I could go to bed again. But time doesn't freeze. The days of the month are ticking down. My bank account is trickling down. I ignored it.

Until my friend kicked me in the ass.

Getting kicked in the ass is a good thing when you have depression. But I had to jump on it. She gave me options. She even gave me ways out, would have allowed me to sink into the depression, maybe hit the steep part.

When dealing with any kind of mental health issue, from depression to addiction, there is a fine line between helping and enabling. It is not my friend's job to be my personal coach. That's my job.

That's why I stress about that base of my mental health pyramid: the self-help (episode 5). The small things we need to be doing each and every day to help ourselves out. I can't do much with a broken ankle, like my walks, but I can still do some things like mediating and staying away from the useless conversations. I can continue the resume barrage as I put more pieces of my projects into place.

And I have to keep begging because that is my reality.

I want work. I want to start adulting again. I'll accept charity because I must. But I know there is a point if I hit it, where I'll say, "stop, enough." I know the line between helping and enabling. I know it well because I crossed it from the other side many times.

I did stop adulting. Long story. I went looking for oblivion and found that I needed work/life balance. I forgot about the work part. Yeah, home runs are nice. The long ball. But it's the singles that win the game, get you through the day.

So, with my butt hurting--it really is hurting from sitting so much--I slowed the descent. Stopped. And am now making my way back up the slide.

Have you ever tried making your way up a slippery slide? It's a pain in the pass--I'm not asking for pardon for that pun.

I do need to regroup a little bit. Tuesdays, when I upload these podcasts, I give myself off. That is kind of necessary. As much as I enjoy doing these podcasts, they drain me, so I leave my mind to wander and recharge.

So, what the hell do I do? What would you do?

First, don't do that. --I really have no idea what that line means from Good Will Hunting but I've always wanted to use it.

Second, I have to take some steps backwards. Whether I wake up at 3 AM or 4 AM or 7 AM, I need to go back to an old routine: making my way to the mirror while the coffee brews and giving myself a choice: be happy or be miserable.

It's a tougher choice than you think. Being miserable is easier, far easier. Being bitter and angry, being paranoid and abandoned, being guilty is far easier than starting to think right. It's a comfortable feeling, an easy one, like following ruts in the road. The easiest thing to do is allow myself to slip down that slide, hit the steep decline, and stop thinking about anything and everything.

I need to start choosing each morning what I have been faking each day, to be happy and productive, strive towards my goals and purpose.

I don't think there is much I can do about the sleeping, but I am hoping that resolves itself when the cast comes off in a little over two weeks. I don't have to sleep with the boot, do I?

I have to get back into my meditating. Mindfulness. It is especially important now that I can't do yoga which allows a natural meditation and reach towards mindfulness.

I've already ended the useless conversations on social media.

Maybe Sara will talk to me? She was a personal coach I met in Seattle during my travels. She's the one who taught me about the net, gave an idea substance, an architecture for my mind. She doesn't give herself enough credit. She's given quite a few ideas the architecture so people can have a symbol to hold onto in their minds, but she says they are simple ideas. I reply if it is so simple, how come nobody has done it before? But an affirmation, a reinforcement, would be nice. --I actually just stopped typing this up and texted her.

We are all connected, and the connections are like the strands in the net. The people the knots. The net is the safety net over that chasm--or, for the purpose of this episode, the barrier between the slight decline and the fall to the bottom.

My life has gotten quiet again. Another sign of the depression. It is time to recharge the speakers and get the tunes going.

It is time to continue that flood of resumes. In between, I need to work on marketing and SEO research to build my projects better.

I'm going to keep at the funny videos. It's fulfilling for some reason. I have a whole other website, the original one, and a few YouTube channels I am trying to organize.

Next week, for the podcast, I want to do something that I have not done in a long time but have been promising myself I would do, be a journalist. I want to research and write an article. Most of the jobs I am applying for require writing samples. Some are specifically asking for translations of difficult subject matter into an easy-to-understand article. I know how to do it, but all of my clips are 25 years old. I'm getting it done.

What I am not going to do is isolate. I will not dwell in the negative thoughts. I'll tell them to go away--it really does work.

Finally, I am going to keep talking.

And that is a wrap for this week's episode.

Keep talking everybody.

Aloha.

PS. Sara texted me back. It was a simple text. She's busy as hell. I asked for something simple, a minute or two of her time, a hello, to hear her voice. Knowing we are connected is different than having an affirmation. It's not weakness to have need. She feels the same way. She called.

Be kind to yourself, everybody.

Once again, until next week, Aloha.

Episode 16: The Non-Comedy Routine

The missing episode.

The episode is not missing but it did not make it into the book. It is available on YouTube as a movie.

I tried transcribing it a dozen times without success. It just did not fit to me, had no place in the book. I went live, without a script, and just found myself saying a lot of things I had already said or would say later in other podcasts. I rambled.

This is why I stick with a script. Much of it came out much better in the following episode.

I started it as my story: where I am, where I was and where I am going. Recent conversations with family members, though, and being laid up with a broken ankle, along with memories of things that are no more, brought me to a place removed from aloha.

That is what struck me the most as I was relistening to it and reading the transcription. It lacked the love, compassion, peace, affection and mercy I try to bring with me into every episode.

I'll leave it on YouTube for anybody interested. I think, however, it is best if it stay on YouTube and not be a part of this book.

Aloha.

Episode 17: The Tangled Path to Listening

In this episode, it got complicated. I started writing the transcript and then fell down a rabbit hole. If you have ever seen someone finish a bottle of tequila and then try walking home, that's kind of what it was like. Aye, I made it home, sobered up, and then retraced my steps to find a more direct route.

When I post, I always use the hashtag #keeptalking. A couple episodes back, I started posting with a new hashtag, #startlistening. I first discussed it in the interview I did with Leo Flowers on his podcast that inspired me to do this one. I do talk, but then I stop because people aren't listening. They hear what I say but aren't communicating with me.

Last week, a few things came together, like conversations, realizations, my sense of humor, being in a cast for eight weeks and a couple songs. Jake and Elwood Blues and Pink Floyd will be joining us for this episode.

Now, let's get into the episode.

I now understand Robin William's quote better, about how he always felt being alone was the worst possible thing and then realized that being made to feel alone while being surrounded by people was worse.

I've spoken about it before in podcasts, that an issue that I have is people not listening, not comprehending what I am saying. Aye, I get it. I understand. Clinical depression can be very difficult to wrap your head around unless you have been there.

As humans, we try to understand things by comparing it with our own experiences, the known. Most understand depression as a bad day, the feelings associated with bad moments. Clinical depression is not that. Talking about the desire to commit suicide can be like talking about an alternate universe where our laws of physics don't work.

Especially during Suicidal Awareness Month, I saw a ton of posts about reaching out to people to check on them. It is a good start. But there was something off about the message for me and I didn't understand why.

I spoke about it in previous episodes, about how when I was suicidal, or even just in a depression, everybody and anybody could have reached out to me, and they all would have gotten the same answer: "I'm fine." Hell, people could have stopped by for pizza and beer, and they would have found somebody that was fine, a-okay, laughing and joining in the conversation. They would never have known I was not okay, not fine, and planning to kill myself.

Why?

Both times I stood on that doorstep to suicide with my hand on the knob, about to pass through, there was a long, long list of people I could have called. I come from a huge family, and they care about me and love me. I have an even larger group of friends. Both times, 20 years apart, I called one person, Rachel.

I can remember going through the list of people in my mind the first time. In 2000, I called Rachel, though we had really only known each other for a handful of years. In the second instance, in 2021, I remember going through my contact list on my phone. I called Rachel again.

Why her? Out of the hundreds of contacts? The simple fact is that I know that I am truly blessed. Those hundreds of contacts are not merely acquaintances. A large, close-knit family makes up a large portion of them and even larger group of close friends ring them.

Other conversations, about other situations, began to intrude on my thoughts regarding communicating about depression and suicide. A web of understanding began to form. Large pieces were missing, but the framework began to appear in my mind. I started following the paths open to me.

There was a conversation I had with a friend of mine on another topic. He was upset with me. I would talk to everybody at work except him. I would also stutter more when I spoke to him. He took it personally and finally told me so.

I told him he should take it personally.

I explained that we had had a few conversations about it. Half a dozen? He's one of those fast talkers that cut people off. He explained that he does that to everybody. I countered that I wasn't everybody; I was a person who stuttered. Him cutting me off and talking over me made me stutter more and just not want to talk to him.

He finally understood, stopped cutting me off, I stopped stuttering, and we had good conversations. We still do.

It was a lesson I learned a long time ago as a PWS, a person who stutters. I consider my stutter a superpower. For 50 years now, I have called it my asshole meter. It saves me a lot of time.

It works like this. I begin or enter a conversation. Immediately, how they respond to the stutter tells me if it is worth investing anymore time in the conversation and the person. If they don't listen to me, cut me off, or talk over me, I move on.

Yeah, it might sound harsh, but after 50 years you pick up on things. I do give people the benefit of the doubt, try again, but that is about it. It is just something that I know. I don't take it personally.

Aye, it is a lot like dating. I am not everybody's cup of tea, and they are not mine. I don't take rejection personally. I see rejection as an opportunity to meet someone else that is more compatible, for the both of us. The sooner we break up the better.

But what happens when I am left as the only person in the room not talking? When I don't have a date for the prom? I take a break. I step back. Leave to collect myself.

Mix in the depression and I isolate.

Leo Flowers and I spoke about it when he interviewed me on his podcast, "Before You Kill Yourself."

I forget exactly what we were talking about, but it comes in at about 18 minutes into the interview that can be found on my website.

"Your friends," Leo said, "don't really know how to be supportive when you share your suicidal idealizations, and they believe they and their friendship should be enough to keep you around...and I think people miss out on the opportunity to be curious as to why [you] might have these suicidal idealizations. And try to understand where it is coming from as opposed to saying, "don't kill yourself because I'll miss you."

"To me," Leo continued, "that response is selfish because [they] haven't taken the time to hear [you] and listen to [you] articulate where these emotions are coming from."

Then, this framework in my mind, this web of thoughts and ideas, began to have a soundtrack. Or at least my favorite line to a Blues Brothers song.

In the song, "I Don't Know," Jake says, "Baby! What did I do to piss you off this time?"

--sorry, it's the way my mind works and, when I'm following ideas, I've learned to just allow it to wander down any path that presents itself. This particular path led me to Jake and Elwood Blues and then a book I read a long time ago.

Aye, just go with me on this one.

Deborah Tannin taught me what possibly could have pissed off Jake's "Baby."

In her book, "You Just Don't Understand; Women and Men in Conversation," first published in 1990, Tannin talks about how men and women hear differently, approach conversations differently, have different conversation styles. If you have ever had a relationship, I am sure you have encountered this.

The book, a NY Times Best Seller, was published before sexual roles got complicated, so generalizations are made. For the sake of the podcast, I'm going to use the generalizations, but keep in mind that I have realized that my approach is much more "feminine" in nature though I can also be very masculine in my approach.

A woman comes home from work and tells her husband that she had a bad day. The conversation quickly makes the day even worse for the wife and for the husband.

The man approaches the conversation from the masculine, "how can I fix this?"

The woman approaches the conversation from the feminine, "I don't need anything fixed, I just want to be heard."

The man gets frustrated because his attempts at fixing things are being rebuffed and he feels ignored. The woman gets pissed off because her attempts at being heard are being ignored.

The wife stalks away and the husband starts hearing the line of from the song: "Baby! What did I do to piss you off this time?"

As I said, I am very much in touch with my feminine side. When I talk to people about my depression, and particularly about my suicidal thoughts, I don't need things fixed. I know how to fix them. I want to be understood. I want to be heard. I want to connect.

Rachel heard me, both times.

If I don't think I am being heard, I walk away.

"Baby! What did I do to piss you off this time?"

Jake, I now have an answer for you: "You pissed me off by not hearing me and I just wasted a lot of time and emotional effort for nothing."

Maybe that is why I withdraw and isolate when I'm in a depression? Why I hide it. It is the path of least resistance, and the path of least resistance is the best I can do at times. If I am in a depression, it means my emotional reserves are gone. When the depression becomes severe, I barely have the energy to function let alone explain myself again, try to talk over the noise and the people talking over me. Talk over the rejection.

It is much like when I broke my ankle. I had to walk home three blocks. The best I could absolutely do was the most direct route, and I almost didn't make it. Talking to people when I am in a deep depression would have been like if someone had asked me to go out of way and pick them something up at the store. It ain't happening.

...and that does not ring true to me. Parts of it. Where the hell has the path led me now?

It's led me to SW Philly and my Coci Carol?

My Coci Carol is popping into my head, so I am going with it. Bear with me here. There is a whole other twist that is coming into play. Rejection and abandonment. Follow along as best as you can. I think it's important.

Coci means "aunt" in Polish. I grew up calling her Aunt Coci. I finally learned better, but she was still Aunt Coci to me. Some of my earliest memories of childhood revolve around her and her home, a block up the street from my house.

My own home was, well, not safe. Not stable. My mother was bipolar, so things were always interesting and a surprise. Coci's house was my safe place, my comfort place. Her and her own children, all older than me, were my home. When my mother would have an episode and go into the hospital, my father would eventually drop me and my brother off at Coci's house.

This is where there is a dichotomy, a story of polar opposites-- no pun intended. One of my earliest detailed memories is being at the shore with Coci in North Cape May, NJ. I was laughing and playing in the bay. I was probably about four or five? I stepped on something slimy, and it came up to stare at me with one eye. I went screaming to my Coci on the beach. She laughed and said I should have grabbed it, that it was a flounder and was dinner.

Another of my earliest childhood memories is bolting out of my Coci's house in SW Philly. I was six or so and running away from home. My safe place was being ripped from me. I forget why, but my father had stopped by to bring me home to my mom, even though she was still sick. I ran.

I got about a block before my very huge cousin caught up to me. He was crying and apologizing but scooped me up anyway. I fought. It was like, well, a scrawny six-year-old against a giant. He carried me back to my Coci's house where my father brought me back to my mother. I was taken from safety to a place where I was not safe.

So, I run from the unsafe place, where people are not listening, to the safe place, the depression? Where the battle is not with other people, only with myself. Alone, I have been taught, is where I feel safest. Me against everybody. Me against the world. Me against the universe. I might fail, but at least I do not have to count on anybody.

--there is really something important there you can find in the movie, Good Will Hunting. Robin Williams talking to the math guy about Will's friends.

There is still that inner child, that scrawny kid with the skinned knees and bad haircut, that felt rejected and abandoned often, most often by the family that loved him. I was abandoned by the people who were supposed to take care of me. I started taking care of myself. Maybe not well, but somebody had to do it.

It was another part of the interview with Leo: adultification. I was forced into the role of an adult, independent, when I should not have been, when I was too young to handle it. Without ever having really come to grips with it, I brought those survival coping mechanisms into adulthood where they became unhealthy behaviors.

When things get bad, I count on me because I am the only one who I can count on. There is no safe and stable place for me unless I create it.

And now another song is starting to play, the opening of Pink Floyd's "Keep Talking."

"For millions of years, mankind lived just like the animals. And something happened that unleashed the power of imagination. We learned to talk."

After those millions of years of not talking, partners were finally able to communicate, and I'd guess it was about three days after that Jake and Elwood Blues appeared on the scene singing, "Baby! What did I do to piss you off this time?"

So, I stalk into the other room to be alone, where I might not be okay, might not be fine, but it is where I feel safest. The other room might be a path to self-destruction, but at least I walk it alone where I am not reaching for someone's hand for help, and it is not there or torn away when I need it most.

Why Rachel? I imagine there was a gut feeling that she would not pull her hand away.

As with many things, I don't really know.

This has been a tough transcript to write. Imagine what it would have been like without the script.

But let's get away from Leo, Jake & Elwood, Coci, and Pink Floyd. Let's find our way back to the main path, communication. What can you do to start listening to a person who is struggling? If you are struggling, what can you do to keep talking?

On International Stuttering Awareness Day, I repost a piece I did on how to talk to a person who stutters that has simple rules. 1) Don't finish their sentences, 2) Don't tell them to relax and 3) Don't talk over them. You have to keep in mind that you are having a conversation with someone that is different and different rules apply. I write that all that we want is to be heard.

Their reality, my reality, is different than yours. Fluency is natural for you whereas it is a battleground for people who stutter.

The same goes for someone suffering from depression or other mental health issues. For some reason or another, we are pushed into isolation, and we should not do that and should not be there; it is the unhealthiest place for us. How do we end up there?

The first thing you need to think about is should you reach out? Seriously. The best of intentions can go wrong. What's the saying? "The path to hell is paved with good intentions."

I understand. I really do. I have a family member who has told me they have the emotional intelligence of a shrub. They are just going to try and fix things. If they reached out to me? And I was desperate enough to respond with something beyond, "I'm fine, a-okay"? That would end up being a step along the path deeper into my personal hell.

Another thing to think about before you reach out is do you have the time and the emotional strength to hear what the person has to say? Again, I do understand if you don't, and I do not hold it against you if you don't.

I've been on both sides. I've been in a place where I knew a close friend, a loved one, was going through a bad time but I just couldn't do anymore. It really took me about 40 years to stop being pissed off at my mom's family and to start understanding that they have lives and issues as well.

You have to put yourself first.

If you are ready to make the investment to reach out, be prepared. You will not be having a conversation with someone who's reality is the same as yours. It may be completely beyond anything you might know or have experienced.

The absolute worst thing you can do is point out to them that their reality is wrong. You can't just tell them to suck it up. You need to be prepared to approach them from different angles as opposed to head on.

That's what Rachel did with me the first time. I remember the conversation from 2000 vividly. Not once did she say, "don't do this because I love you." She came at me from a different angle.

Remember: suicide made perfect sense to me. It does not make sense now, it did not make sense to her, but that was my reality at the time. So, Rachel approached it from, "just give me more time. Hold my hand and just give it more time. You've been through so much. You can give me another week, another month, another year."

That made absolutely no sense to me. I was in so much pain and my reality was so altered that I could not see beyond that moment. But Rachel was right. I had been through a lot. I knew I could make it through anything. I could give her the year that she requested. In that year, I got help. Rachel helped give me perspective. She allowed me to have more time to regain a better reality.

Another thing you can do if you do reach out is don't be a guy. Don't try to fix things.

When I get calls like that, it just pisses me off.

"You should get counseling. You should get meds. You should do yoga. You should walk two miles every day. You should..."

Yeah, no shit Sherlock. I'm not stupid! Is that what you are trying to tell me, that I'm stupid? That I am just being lazy and a piece of shit? --That's how I interpret it in the depression. Which doesn't help. It makes me more depressed, reinforces the depression and makes me isolate even more.

I'm actually a very intelligent person. A hell of a researcher as well. Mental illness smothers that intelligence. You need to figure out a way to reveal it. How?

I don't know.

I've been there too, on the other side--with no answers. My mother had an IQ that well surpassed genius level. Her mental illness had her focused on a fact that was not true. Every expert in the world would agree. There was no shaking her from that reality.

I wrote a long time ago about an experience where my intelligence was smothered. Long story short, I was hammered by a depressive attack while at work.

"Do you know what it is like," I texted my wife, "to be a failure in every aspect of your life?"

In that moment that I texted her, that was my reality, my truth. I started getting a flurry of texts from her. This was just a depressive attack, much like an anxiety attack that comes and goes, not a long drawn-out episode. Reality reasserted itself much faster.

"What the hell did I just text" I thought to myself. I'm a failed business owner, husband, father, uncle, son, nephew, etc.? Am I nuts? I'm not perfect, I've made mistakes, but a total failure? No. And then I began to resurface from the depths, the attack passing, and I made it to the surface where my real truth existed.

But apply that to an episode that is lasting weeks or months.

The second time I reached out to Rachel was much different than the first and her response was different. It was a long conversation we had, with me in tears for most of it. The pain was more awful than what I encountered walking three blocks on a broken ankle. The agony was real, physical.

I think it was a depressive attack while in the depressive episode.

From a couple thousand miles away, Rachel hugged me. That's it. That's what I needed. She knew. She just had to be there to understand and to hug me. She didn't try to fix anything, didn't try to approach it from another angle like the first time, she just instinctively knew that all I needed to hear was "I understand" and to hug me.

Maybe it has to do with the inner child thing? I just had the same thing happen under different circumstances a few months back. It was not about depression or suicide. I had been triggered by something.

The friend I texted understood immediately and called. As a child of trauma herself, she talked to me from experience. "I'm right there with you, we're standing there with your inner child and hugging him and telling him that he is safe. We won't let go."

She didn't let go until the attack had passed. Rachel didn't either. And that is really all that it took.

Within me, a part of me, is a very accomplished adult, 51 years old with a hell of a resume. Also within me is a scrawny kid with skinned knees and a bad haircut. I think a lot of this is coming down to that. If and when you reach out to me, you are reaching out to that child, not to the adult. The approach is very different. The adult needs to be coaxed out while keeping the child safe.

How do you keep talking? I think the same rules apply but just reversed. You have to be aware of who you are talking to and what their limitations are, understand where they are coming from talking to you. It's about communication styles. Different people are going to give you different things, approach you different ways.

I say often that when I am in bad shape, before I completely withdraw, I throw out lifelines. I just start tossing them out. I've been amazed at who has picked one up and surprised by who has not.

The people who have not picked one up, or let go before I was safely ashore, I am not angry at or disappointed in. I now understand.

But I am going to keep talking. And I am going to start listening better.

And that is a wrap for this episode.

Aloha.

Episode 18: Finding a Way Home

In this episode, I decided to go way, way back in time. Last week, I spoke about that scrawny six-year-old with skinned knees and a bad haircut. Let's go back and meet him. He stutters a lot but is a friendly kid who talks too much in school and is probably too intelligent for his own good. He is a child of trauma.

Now, let's get into the episode.

I did go back and meet him once. It didn't go well.

It was during one of my brief stints in therapy. I forget when and where but it was a long time ago, maybe 30 years. The therapist and I were doing role playing. They wanted me to meet him, talk to him. I was game.

I forget exactly what the therapist did, but I really got into the moment. I saw him sitting across from me. He was always a scrawny, small kid, not hitting his real growth spurt until high school. He always had skinned knees but what little boys don't? His jeans had holes in the knees until he was in double digits.

He was in shorts that day, in a tank top, maybe a tank top half-shirt. Aye, it was the late 70's we are talking about here and that was the style. He sat across from me with his feet swinging. His sneakers were tied in double knots, tied with rabbit ears, the same way I still do it today.

I don't know what my therapist did but that kid, Chrissy, was there, existed. He was staring at me, the slight scar on the chin far more visible from where he had run into a moving car. Long story. He was waiting for me to speak.

This was my moment. I could say anything I wanted to him, and it would be real. He would hear me back through the decades.

I wanted to tell him so much. I wanted to explain to him that he was doing well, the stutter would improve, he would be going to Miami to a new life. I wanted to explain that his dream of being a writer was more than just a fantasy, that in just a couple of years, when he was around eight, he would be published in the Philadelphia newspaper. That would be the first article of many.

He edged closer to the edge of the chair, closer to me.

I opened my mouth to say all those things and more.

"Suck it up kid. You have to be tough. Tougher. The tougher you are the easier it will be."

He sank back into his chair and nodded his head, his feet motionless. I sank back into my chair and covered my closed eyes with my hand.

I opened my eyes, and he was gone.

Yep, that did not go well at all.

I have always thought about that moment, wondering where the hell it came from. The years would pass, the decades, and I would realize that I really needed a much better relationship with him. I needed to go back and undo some of the things he learned.

He was scrawny, but he was a scrapper. Tough little kid. That was forced into being tough far too early. He even had to be an adult sporadically.

I remember this one time I think I almost set the house on fire. It was my first try at cooking. Mom wasn't doing well. Maybe she was up in bed in a depressive state--which was far better than the manic state. I was hungry.

I remember that I tried cooking rice and peas in a frying pan. I put them all in the pan, turned the flame on, and then I forgot about it. It was a blackened mess when I came back and was starting to smolder. The paper towels got knocked into everything, caught fire...and I forget what happened next. I think someone showed up to toss everything into the sink with the fire alarm going off. Or maybe I did?

My attention span never got too much better. My cooking only mildly better. I now know to boil rice.

Adultification. It's a term that Leo Flowers threw at me during our interview. I had never heard it before. Obviously, my computer has never heard the word either because it keeps underlining it in red every time I type it.

I did a little bit of research and came up with scholarly articles going back to 2007. It is what I thought it was, what it sounds like: a child having to step up into a parental role.

Adultification? I don't know. I would need to talk to an expert more about it. I don't think it applies to me. From what I read, it is when children must step into parental roles for extended periods of time, maybe even becoming adults at a very young age.

Me? I was surrounded by adults. I had to step up once in a while, but it was very sporadic. Mom would get sick and eventually something would happen that would put me back into the care of an adult.

Is there adultification or trauma in the waiting?

I remember this one time I was about five or six. My uncle met me at the corner store. I'm not sure how I had gotten in touch with him, but we were out of food.

I was crying, pleading, for him to come home with me. He was crying. Said something about his own children and handed me $20. I wiped away the tears, went into J&N's, and bought lunch meat, rolls and cheese.

I did what I had to do. It became a common theme in my life.

Any adultification I encountered ended when I was about 10. Something had happened, mom was in a manic phase, my stepfather had entered her life, and I guess a call had gone out. An aunt, who had I had spent some summers with, came and picked me up and brought me to her home down in Maryland during the middle of 5th grade. I would stay there until the end of 7th. I was safe.

She and my uncle did what they had to do, I guess. During the summer between 7th and 8th grade, I went to my mom's and stepfather's apartment for a visit. I remember the friends I left in Maryland, expecting to see them again at the start of school.

Towards the end of the summer, all of my stuff began to arrive in boxes. I was told that I would be staying and starting 8th grade there.

I remember tearful phone calls. The payphone. They did not accept the collect calls, so I got change somehow or another and started making calls.

"Why? Why, why, why? Come and get me. Please!"

I forget what the answer was, but I started grade school in Springfield, PA at Our Lady of Fatima. I began a new life again with new friends. The following year, I would start High School at Cardinal O'Hara.

It would not be until I was in 11th grade that I ran away from home, from the mania. Had a room in an apartment and everything. Had a job to pay for it all at Macy's Department Store. But when the high school would not switch my classes to allow me to work full time, I quit school.

I was being an adult. But I was closer to adulthood anyway. 16? I thought I was doing a pretty good damn job of it. But, with the threat of cops from my mom and something about truancy, and not knowing about emancipation yet, it was back down to Maryland for me.

I would move back down to finish 11th grade, go to bootcamp, get thrown out--again--and finish high-school at Cardinal O'Hara where I would live with my mom and stepfather until I properly moved out after I finished school.

That led to a shared apartment with my best friend. It didn't work out. He got addicted to drugs and I would come home one day to find all of our stuff missing. We had been "robbed."

I moved back home, then back to Maryland, then on to Miami for college. It was my "bouncy" days, bouncing from one location to the next, looking for a home. The idea of "home," a place I was safe and couldn't be thrown out of or chased from became embedded in who I was, became all that I was, my Golden Grail.

I don't know if any of that counts as adultification. While researching it, though, I ran across memes for unhealed trauma.

The internet search algorithms got involved in my research for self-help. How thoughtful of it. Information and quizzes about untreated childhood trauma began popping up throughout my social media accounts.

I finally looked at one, read it. Read the checklist of signs of unresolved childhood trauma. Now, checking off those requirements was like shooting fish in a barrel.

"Unhealed trauma can look like.."

Low sense of worth -- check, something I struggle with

Codependency in relationships -- check, oh yeah

Fear of being abandoned -- check and double check and triple check, something that is constantly being reinforced.

Putting your needs aside for other people -- check

Craving for external validation -- check, but a small one, though others might disagree?

Always fearing what might happen next -- check

Resisting positive change -- Big red check mark

Tolerating abusive behaviors from others -- check, but getting better

An innate feeling of shame -- check. How many of these do I need to test positive?

Being overly agreeable -- had to think about this one, but check. Nobody would ever accuse me of being overly agreeable. They would say the opposite. It was much more of a subtle thing, being agreeable by not disagreeing when I should have or giving in when I should not have.

Not being able to tolerate conflict -- Nobody will believe me, but check. I enjoyed the hell out of conflict. When it didn't matter. When it mattered, it was difficult, or see above and apply it to avoiding conflict when I should not have.

The kid is sitting across from me now. I can see him. He's not swinging his feet anymore. He's not waiting for me to talk to him. He wants to talk to me.

"Check," he asks. "That's it? You should have been tougher. You should have done what really needed to be done so that we would be safe now."

The scar on his chin...

"They don't need to know about the scar," he screams as he balls up is fists. "Tell them! Admit it!"

It is tough staring at him because he is right. I did what I needed to do to survive, but I never did what I really needed to do to heal. It is why I can check off the list in the present tense instead of in the past tense.

Finding a home became my Holy Grail and I gave up everything for it without ever finding it. It became one of those quests that does not have an ending.

He nods. "Go on," he says.

"I was getting there," I say. "I might have been there if it had not been for that damn piece of slippery tile. That's why we're stranded in Tijuana, unsafe."

He shakes his head.

I've tried having arguments with him before. It usually goes like this.

But he's right. I should have been gone from Tijuana long before that first rain, long before I broke my ankle. Staring at him, I am looking at a truth that is being uncovered as I write this. It has to do with that big, red check mark? On resisting positive change?

He nods his head.

I was looking for positive change. No, I say to him as he begins shaking his head violently. Let me finish.

He calms down.

I came to Tijuana because it was the best I could come up with. Personally, I think the little brat is being a bit too harsh. Correct, but harsh. I was surviving. I had a plan. I was feeling good. And then I lost my job.

I was working on positive change, but I needed to be doing it in a far healthier way. I was forced into making a correct decision instead of making it myself. Right after making it, I broke my ankle. I tumbled even further down into unsafety, into instability. The kid and I were screwed again and vulnerable because of choices I did not make.

It's an argument I've given passionately, but with him as a mirror, the argument seems hollow.

I did the best I could with the tools that I had. But it is like the story of the three little pigs. I should have had better building materials, worked on getting better tools. I know what the answers are but didn't pursue them. I pursued self-destruction instead. I was doing a pretty damn good job of it until the end. Then, I failed miserably at it.

I forget how old I was, but my parents were still together, so maybe the third grade? I have no idea. But I remember they took me for a psychiatric evaluation. I still think the story is funny. I just laughed out loud about it as I am writing this and am now giggling about it. They wasted their money.

--yes, I am going down a tangent to avoid the main path for a little bit, but I think it ties in, so I'm going with it.

I would just start laughing and then follow up with giggles. My parents kept asking me why. I would start laughing when nothing was going on around me. When they asked, I started laughing. Then, when I saw that they were concerned, I made it a point to do it more often. --I can really be an asshole at times.

I tried explaining to them that I found the stories in my head funny. That's what I was laughing about. That's it. I had a very vivid imagination. I would create entire worlds populated with characters inside of my head. They would do funny things and I would laugh and giggle. Aye, I still do it. I just don't do it out loud as often. Of course, in today's world, I probably could with everybody seemingly talking to themselves on ear buds.

Fantasy books became my escape. I don't know about Adultification, but I was reading at an adult level when I was very young.

I found this secret bookshelf in my house. I grabbed a book off of the shelf. My mom caught me and snatched the book from my hands.

"You're too young for this," she said.

I had no idea why. The book smelled good, old and musty. It had an awful cover but an interesting name: The Fellowship of the Ring. Of course, as soon as I could, I stole it, hid it in my room, and then spent hours and days diving into Tolkien's fantasy world when Mom wasn't looking. Then, I grabbed the other ones. The Two Towers. The Return of the King. Finally, The Hobbit. What was wrong with that?

The kid is nodding now so I must be doing something right.

The enormous box of Playboys my father had in the basement made me a very popular kid on the block, but those old, musty books held far more interest to me and far more entertainment.

Funny how things work out. I was eight? At 51, it's still those old, musty books that grab my attention more than anything else. I can still smell them when I open them on my iPad to read them again. Times have changed, technology has changed, but I have not.

I look up at the kid and he just stares back. I must be on to something here.

Those old, musty books and that fantasy world is where I screwed up. Where I continue to screw up. The kid knows it.

I don't know what the hell to do about it.

In the top five rules of "how to be a professional writer," if not in the top three, is "read. Read, read, read, read. Voraciously and across fields and genres. Read what you want to write." It is a very basic part of education as well as the business of writing. Read your competition so you know how they are writing and how to position yourself against them for editors and publishers.

I don't. I never have.

I did start writing a fantasy series once. Aye, I created the entire world in my head and even started on the mythology. It's not my style though. I love to read it. Write it? No.

My genre has always been creative non-fiction or literary fiction. I've dabbled in reading it. Hemmingway, Faulkner, Steinbeck. Recent stuff? Nope. Magazines and periodicals? Nope. Hell, right now I should be listening to other podcasts and researching what mine is up against. Nope.

I know. The kid knows. I have had a solid two months now with a broken ankle where I am doing nothing but sitting on my ass. I am unemployed to boot. I have tons of time. I don't watch television. Even applying to every job I find consumes 5 to 8 hours of my day.

I think that that is one of the reasons that brought me to the brink of suicide. I had gotten so exhausted and so disgusted with myself. Then, there was no escape. I couldn't read anymore. I tried rereading the old books. I tried finding new books to read. I tried listening to music. Nothing. Nothing interested me anymore.

I wanted to feel something, anything, just to feel again. Nothing. There was only an emptiness.

It was time. I was used up, empty. There was nothing left. There was nothing left in me to even try to push forward anymore. Not even having a home mattered anymore.

I had a home. It was joyless and loveless, but it was stable. I had found my Holy Grail, completed my QUEST...and found it empty. For some reason, the house actually felt better to me when it was empty, after my wife had moved out, and I was alone.

At the last second, way past when it was feasible, I did try to hold onto it. I loved that place. But Covid had hit, and I had already put a most excellent plan in motion, and I couldn't back out of it. So, I set out across America and towards self-destruction.

I tell people I ended up in Tijuana because I got lost on the way to Greece. It's kind of true. I just had a few pit-stops on the way. Austin, Texas. Justine, Kate and Sara. An alohaless beach. A self-published book. Pieces of something that could lead to hope. The new books by Robin Hobb. The coldest winter in Texas in 35 years. Dances with Murphy and then finally breaking up with him--you won't be reading or hearing about Murphy's Law anymore.

And then the realization that I am not doing this adulting thing very well. Then, I adopted a dog. Finally, I broke my ankle.

I look up at the kid and he's nodding his head.

Everybody was right. I dove into a fantasy world here in Tijuana. It was so damn easy, too easy. I had savings and a hell of a resume, and the savings would last until I found a remote job.

Maybe it was a good plan, or at least a plan, but, realistically, it was a plan that should have had a two-month time limit to happen. It didn't, and instead of being an adult and finding a home, a base, I entered fully into the fantasy world.

I look up at the kid from my ruminating and self-reflection. He's waiting now.

"And that's why," I tell him, "we are screwed and not in a safe place. Why we don't have a home. I failed you. But I'll do better."

He climbs down from the seat across from me and gets up into my lap to lay his head on my chest. He is a scrawny, little thing.

He looks up at me, flashing the scar on his chin. He nods.

This has been some heavy stuff. I need to think about a lot of it more. I really need to start talking to someone about it. For now, though, I'll leave you with the story of the scar. It's still visible, a tiny bit, on the left of my chin, an effect of a few stitches a long time ago.

At a very, very young age, I was a pervert. In my defense, I was supposed to be. That was the game we made up in SW Philly. It was tag with a twist. It was summertime, we had come out of someone's pool, and we all wrapped the towels around us like we saw our moms and sisters do.

One kid, me that time, was the pervert who ripped all the towels off and then ran. The chase was on. I ran out in between two parked cars right into a moving car. That's how small I was: my chin hit above the wheel well. I bounced.

The man slammed on his breaks and jumped out of the car. More of a kid now that I'm thinking about it. He rushed over to me where I was lying on the ground and helped me up. I wasn't even shaken up. I was laughing. I had been caught but everybody had a shocked look on their faces.

I felt something on my chin and reached my hand up. "What," I asked, "am I bleeding?"

"Yes," the man/kid said.

I screamed. And went running to the safety of home and my mommy.

And that is a wrap for this episode.

Be kind to yourself. Be kind to that little child inside of you. Keep them safe. Do right by them.

Aloha.

Episode 19: At the Wall

This episode is the natural progression of the previous episodes. I am at the wall, clinical depression, slumped against it. Maybe setting up camp with a sleeping bag and my coffee maker. Not depression, clinical depression. There's a difference. And I can't figure out a way to get beyond it. Never have.

I've been able to ignore the wall for years at a time. Maybe even a decade? But get beyond it? Nope. I know there is no cure for clinical depression, no magical pill. I could spend years in therapy, read all the books, do all of the treatments, and the wall will still be there. Or will it? Now, let's get into the episode.

...but before getting into the episode, I wanted to talk a little bit about the here and now, what my life is like.

If you go by the podcast, as some of my friends and family are doing, you might think that I am on the edge. Maybe even leaning over the edge. Hell, some podcasts have sparked phone calls and one even caused an intervention by YouTube. No, it is not like that.

One friend says I think too much. Another friend warned me about doing the podcast, that the constant negativity is harming me.

It's really not like that. As I mentioned in a previous episode, depression causes time to compress. Yes, I do struggle with Major Depression, PTSD and Anxiety Disorder. There is also the childhood trauma and few other things and acronyms. It has been this way all my life. But it is episodic.

I would hazard a guess that 5% of my life is the bad times. The other 95% is the normal, or whatever normal I have been able to squeeze out of it. Depression can make that 5%, though, seem like a 100%. This podcast is about that 5%.

It is much like last night. I was having a good day. Not a damn good day, but a good day. I got work done, went to the store, and came home to find out that my dog had gotten out. I was living close to the 95% and the 5% caught up to me.

I was terrified and almost in tears, thinking my friend would never be back. The wall of depression compressed around me, and I started thinking about all of the worst possible things. I was shaking and angry, unable to go out looking for her because of my broken ankle and feeling helpless and hopeless.

Then, I reached out. Friends and people I barely knew got involved and the search was on while I sat outside waiting.

Dani returned about an hour later. She had had a nice run. All was right in the world again. I even made a funny video about it. After thinking about it a lot, and experimenting, I figured out that the little bitch figured out how to open the door from the inside to let herself out. Really. No shit.

I was exhausted from worry so went to bed soon after, about 8:00. But it was not an "escape to bed." It was just your normal, "I'm friggin' exhausted and need sleep" going to bed.

The podcast is about living in depression. I dive deep. I need to move forward. And to maybe help others move forward. I want to push against that wall, examine it, and study it. I want to figure out if it is a wall, chains, or just a cage I built around myself.

I do think the effects of the depression, PTSD and everything else affects me every day and that is what I am attempting to figure out how to break free from. But I do go to bed feeling hopeful and happy and then wake up happy that I can turn on the coffee maker, and that the day, today, is filled with hope.

I think that that is the main reason why I have allowed myself to ignore the wall, or whatever it is, for so long. For a year, and for decades. My true self is beyond it but also a tidal wave of regrets. I am terrified.

Afraid that my salvation may also lead to my destruction?

It's a scary proposition. 51 years of having something control me in ways that I do not understand. If I unlock the potential for the next however many years, I also release knowledge of all of the things I could have, should have, would done differently.

In any case, I am going to continue to dive back into that 5%, dive deep, and ask the question that I have asked myself hundreds, perhaps thousands, of times.

"What the hell is wrong with me?!?"

I think of the old expression, the grass is always greener on the other side because it is fertilized with bullshit. That's not the case this time. I know that beyond that wall is my true self, a life to be lived without the weight of depression and PTSD. Without the suicidal thoughts. A life of self-actualization. No, there is no cure for depression but there are much better coping mechanisms.

I think that that is what caused the last depressive episode which lasted years. So maybe that 5% ticked up a few percentage points. I can only ignore the wall for so long, allow life to make it seem dim and almost not there. But I also know that throwing myself against that wall has become a common thing in my life.

A long time ago, I wrote a short story about another wall, writer's block. I wrote about how I don't believe in it, that there are ways beyond the wall if I but choose to take them. Sex, music, and letters to friends allow me to seep through it or get beyond it. Simply battering myself against it allows me to eventually break through and write.

This wall is different. In 51 years, I have not been able to get beyond it. Three years ago, I began ferociously throwing myself against it, trying to batter my way through. I screamed at it, "what the fuck is wrong with me?!?"

There was no reply, not even an echo. No sound came back but a feeling did. An utter exhaustion, so deep and so terrible it filled me until there was nothing else to me.

Tired, exhausted beyond anything I have ever felt, I slummed against the wall and decided to give up. The 5% had compressed into the 100%. The depression engulfed me, became my world. It sucked everything out of me, and I decided to end the battle, end the fight, and check out. I decided to end my life.

At 49, I decided I had had enough. I had had a good run, but the exhaustion overpowered everything. I was tired and just wanted to sleep. It was far beyond, "an escape to bed."

In my journey towards self-destruction, though, I found pieces of things that could lead to hope. It was like walking along a beach and finding pieces of shells and sea glass that could eventually lead to art. I stuffed them in my pocket for no reason whatsoever. The end of the journey along the wall, on the beach, would lead to a nice, quiet place to end my life and end the exhaustion.

I was still exhausted when I got to the end of my journey. I slumped against the wall. Instead of ending my life, I started sifting through the pieces I had found. Maybe, I thought to myself, I should do something with these pieces before I ended my life. It would be a waste not to. Maybe help others that were wandering along the wall. I couldn't get through it, but maybe they could with the help of the pieces that I found.

I put some of the pieces together into a book, that is still being edited. "Disconnected: An Odyssey Through Covid America."

Other pieces led to other things. The transcripts of this podcast will become a first edition of another book that I want to write: "An Odyssey into Depression." Then there is the biography I want to write about my mother and then...

So now I am setting up camp against the wall. Instead of trying to throw myself against it, I am exploring it and examining it from time to time as I live my life. Throughout my life, I learned a major truth: there are always ways beyond walls. I have pieces and am finding more in the oddest places.

When you start looking, stop ignoring, is when you find things. That's another lesson I learned as a writer. I hate when young writers ask me how I find ideas. I'm not even nice about the answer anymore. "Open your damn senses," I tell them. Just spin in the place where you are at, with your senses open, sight, smell, taste, touch and hearing, and there are 20 story ideas right there.

I spun through America and am spinning now, through the internet.

It is much like a jigsaw puzzle with missing pieces scattered throughout the world. I opened myself to finding them, waiting for the clicks.

I just saw a post by a friend on Facebook. Well, a Facebook friend who I never met. But her post "clicked" in somewhere or another.

Anna Fotiou reposted a quote by Irish author Brendan Behan. "At the innermost core of loneliness is a deep and powerful yearning for one's lost self."

Click.

It is the piece that joined the quote from Michelangelo with the rest of the puzzle. When asked how he carved David, he responded that he saw the angel inside and had to release it.

Click.

It joined with the piece about how I was so lonely because I was in relationships with a business partner and life partner who took but didn't give, draining me.

Click.

Robin Williams quote, about how he always felt that being alone was the worst thing until he realized that being made to feel alone while surrounded by people was worse.

Click.

That deep chasm inside of myself is depression, a blackhole that sucks everything into it, all that I am. The funnel towards it is loneliness. Especially at night, it is like doing a highwire walk across the chasm. Sara's lesson about the safety net below me, the connection of people and relationships that will catch me if I fall.

Click.

Hell, I know now that if the stress of walking that highwire is too much, I can jump off it, fall on purpose, to land in that net and bounce instead of falling into depression. Papa Bear and Mama Bear, Dawnie Dear, Sara, Rachel, Justine and all of the other people in my life.

Click.

Just moving the puzzle pieces around, the new segments I formed. Knowing it is not so much as battering against the wall until it crumbles, but if I put the pieces together into the right pattern, it will make a spell that will make the wall simply disappear.

No, there is no cure for depression. I don't know about PTSD and Anxiety Disorder. But I do know that if I click enough pieces together, get enough segments together, I can learn things so the depression will not determine my course in life, my reactions and my inability to act.

I really want to go back and focus on that quote from Michelangelo and compare it to the idea of the wall. It doesn't fit and needs new channels and pathways. It's not a wall. It's more like a mountain of marble that I created. I need to start chipping away. I have started chipping away.

I am floundering a bit here, trying to be coherent. Many times, as I start writing the script for the podcast, I'll uncover things that make me go back. That happened this time. From the wall to the mountain. This time, though, it is not going to happen.

On top of everything else, I got sick, the flu or something, that just left me escaping to bed. Or falling into it because I could not do anything else.

And I am really going off on a tangent here because 1) it is the best I can do and 2) it kind of makes sense.

Having a broken ankle is bad enough. It's getting better but it is still hard having to depend on everybody for everything. Then, add the flu on top of it and you have a recipe for probably what would be just a normal kind of depression.

Aye, I'm a man. I am sick. Hear me whine.

Nobody was there to listen to my whining, so I just thought about things. Okay, there was some wallowing in self-pity as well. All of the things to be depressed about rode the waves of my fever. I have a bit of a list going on here, and I am a very typical male when it comes to getting the flu.

The fever finally broke last night. The exhaustion is still crushing me. But I also know it will pass. So, I slept through it all and will continue to do so. Physical therapy is going well, though I had to skip it today, and my foot is healing, and I have some movement back.

It all makes me think of a meme that I saw that I want to make into a video once I learn how to combine them.

The Universe: Are you listening?

Me: I know, I know. I should be doing things, but I had a shitty day.

The Universe: I know you had a shitty day.

Me: I'll get started right now. Before you break my other friggin' ankle.

The Universe: I'll ignore that, but no. I'm here to tell you to cut yourself some slack, give yourself a break. You've been doing well. Not great, but well. Find a movie to watch or break out one of those books you reread constantly.

Me: Seriously?

The Universe: Yes. You are allowed to just say "fuck it" once in a while and become a vegetable here and there. I even take time off. Just don't make a habit of it.

And with the that, this episode is a wrap. I'm going to bed.

Be good to yourself. Be kind yourself. And give yourself a friggin' break.

Aloha.

Episode 20: Stumbling Through the Darkness

In this episode, I'm, well, depressed. I'm stumbling through the darkness. It was really difficult to start writing the transcript. Nothing is popping, nothing coming to me. I have tons of material and was thinking I was just in a slump but then it hit me: I'm depressed. It's not so bad.

My life right now is like Rocky III. Depression is usually like the first fight with Mr. T, Clubber Lang. Pretty much just taking a beating. Vicious, brutal, until you lay there on the floor hoping for the ring of the bell so the beating stops. This depression, I guess, is more like the normal depression? I feel like Rocky getting ready for the second fight, pushing at Clubber's face with my glove.

"You ain't so bad. You ain't so tough."

Ding.

Now, let's get into the episode.

Aye, I got a lot to be depressed about. The Friday before uploading this episode marked exactly 70 days since I broke my ankle. You try sitting around and depending on everybody for 70 days with the doctor and physical therapist telling you that you are doing exactly what you are supposed to be doing.

It's been about six months now since I've been employed, and the job search continues to not go well. It's been a struggle here and I've been lonely. I did learn I could get by on next to nothing but discovering that knowledge depresses me.

I reached out to all of my friends and family with a plea, a fundraiser. Begging for money. I reached out to the national association I founded to help others. The association rebuffed me, even punished me. The response from family was a few "best of luck's" and some friends responded to the fundraiser but not enough, though I appreciate everybody who did. Where is everybody?

Like I said, the depression wants to push at me, push at my thoughts. Push my thoughts down darker paths. It fills me with questions that I do not like the potential answers to. It even alters the answers.

I read something from The Depression Project, something everybody listening to this should check out, that people don't talk about depression because they don't want to burden people that they care about. That's a part of it.

Who really wants to listen to all of this crap?

But it is also about expectations. The depression tells me the old saying, "Have no expectations and you will never be disappointed." Disappointment leads to that deeper depression. Reaching out, burdening people, and then not getting the response I need, is disappointing.

When cries for help go unheard, you learn to just keep them inside. As I have said, both the depression and life have taught me some harsh lessons that I need to unlearn.

Even this podcast is dragging me down--through the lens of depression. Are people listening? Am I being heard? Is it worth it? Is it a pushing outward to find something that is inside?

Posting the podcast is frightening. Is that why my job search is not going well? Are potential employers comparing my resume to my podcast and moving on to the next candidate that doesn't talk about depression and mental health? A candidate who isn't, well, nuts?

There is just a twisting of the paths here, a convoluted thought process that I must be wary of, to dance along the depression without falling into the deeper depression. I'm not ready for that battle yet.

That battle is the Russian in Rocky IV. I need training first. But I do know now what I need to do. I have a trainer and people in my corner. I need to go into winter to find the strength and abilities to chip away and find my true self.

The self that people will not be afraid of or dismiss? The person that I showed everybody most of my life, including those closest to me? The person that thought themselves so alone when surrounded by people that...

This lighter depression can make things start to swirl. I just have to be careful of that funnel downward. Very careful. The questions piling up inside of my head push me down. Paralyze me. So instead of doing the things I need to be doing, the things I should be doing, I do nothing, which depresses me even more.

I can feel time compressing in on me, where the "now" becomes the past and the future. My world gets very, very small.

It even makes me forget the most important lesson I learned in life, as reflected in the opening to this podcast. This is not a battle.

I'm not Rocky and depression is not Clubber Lang. Major Depression is not the Russian.

I need to look on it with soft eyes and remember.

No, it's not a dragon to slay. I need to look upon it with the softest eyes. I need to take a few steps backwards to gain some perspective. Or, in my case with the ankle, hop a few steps backwards. See the forest through the trees. The field.

In the field, I am doing pretty damn good and there is a lot of potential. I have good friends and people who do understand. I'm expanding my professional network to people who understand with organizations that I can be a part of and pursue self-actualization. I'm learning and growing.

I need to push away the self-doubt and the questions and focus on the confidence and answers. I need to get my Philly back.

But it is hard.

I need to focus on the fact that though it has been 70 days since I have been sitting here, I only have two more weeks until I can start walking again. The field, if I but start walking through it--or hopping through it--is filled with potential.

Yeah, I'm all over the damn place here. Stumbling. I've started rewriting this a few times. It hasn't gotten any better. This is my depression, so I am going with it. It's my party so I'll cry if I want to?

A bomb went off inside my head. As you might be able to tell, it has to do with my ankle.

It was three weeks ago when I went to get the cast off. I was doing well, staying in good spirits, making videos, writing often, being productive. I was even being funny about it. I had enough to get by because I KNEW as soon as the cast came off, I would be fine. A couple weeks and I would be able to drive and start working again, fend of eviction.

I got the x-ray, praying the doctor would read it and say the cast could come off. A lot was depending on this. He read the x-ray, said everything was healing great, and cut the cast off. It had been seven weeks since I had broken my ankle. It was more swollen than when he put the cast on, and I couldn't move my foot. I couldn't feel my foot. The muscle had atrophied. I expected it, But I KNEW once I got moving again, everything would be fine and...

He then informed me I was halfway through, that I couldn't put any pressure on the foot for another six weeks. He wanted me to do ten sessions of physical therapy in the next two weeks. Ten sessions I couldn't afford, two weeks of Uber rides, six weeks of continuing to depend on others, two more months of rent...

If this was a video, there would be a cut scene to a nuclear bomb going off.

That was my brain. The depression. The moment that started the cascade of thoughts and questions. Everything shattered. I wanted to cry in the doctor's office. Everything started swirling around me and I couldn't think anymore.

I put on a good face, the front I would show everybody, thanked the doctor and said I'd be back for my next appointment. I made my way down and outside and ordered my Uber home.

I arrived home. It was about 2 in the afternoon. I went to bed and stayed there. Except for coffee and a little bit of food, it is where I stayed for a few days, trying to figure out what to do. I made a feeble attempt at begging for money again, reposted my fundraiser, reached out to a few people personally. Made a deal to get November's rent paid.

Then, I started to move again. Not well, and my concentration was total shit, but I did start moving again and made it a point to eat. Then, I got the flu and stayed in bed a couple more days.

I did another podcast.

My concentration is still shit and my thoughts are swirling. I wonder if this is normal depression. It's not the deeper kind, I think. No suicidal thoughts. No crushing weight. I can shrug it off for the most part and go about my day. I'm eating, and only sleeping a little bit more than normal. There is no swarm of hornets stinging me.

I think I get exhausted by the swirling thoughts, the inability to concentrate, so I lay down and fantasize about when this is over, when I am walking and driving again. I fall asleep to wake up a couple hours later to start the process over again.

Two more weeks, now, until the physical therapist said I can start walking on the foot again. I look at that. December 1st. I know I can hold off until then. I know I can keep busy and keep hacking away at things.

Let's compartmentalize things and clear a path through the depression. It's what I do when I can't write. I organize my desk and my desktop on my computer. Clearing everything and putting everything away makes it easier to start making my way towards my goal.

Let's get into the nuts and bolts.

--the depression is telling me not to, or at least not to write about it. That it is silly, stupid. Nobody wants to listen or read about this mundane crap. Nobody wants to hear about your boring struggles.

But isn't this why I do the podcast? Isn't this why I write? Just exploring things for the podcast, joining other groups and reading other posts have given me insights. The truth is I couldn't care less if only a single person is listening. This is something I want to do, something I need to do, so I'll keep talking.

A podcast is supposed to be about metrics and numbers. I'll eventually learn how to figure it out or buy the software to do it for me. But this is something that is helping me.

The ankle has me bummed out, but I can move it a little more each day. It looks a little better each day. I'm not in pain and know I'll be back to mobility in two more weeks, two more podcasts, and full mobility not too long after that.

In two more weeks, I won't have to depend on everybody for everything anymore. I'll be able to take my dog for a walk, make it to Cosco on my own and not have to depend on Uber anymore.

No, the job search is not going well, but a friend mentioned I may have to take a few steps back sometimes to move forward.

Orthodontics? Possibly. I know what I need to do now. I have to learn SEO, search engine optimization, maybe get certified as a life coach, organize my portfolio better, write some articles that are true journalistic endeavors to have in my writing samples.

A home. I have one waiting for me. I know that with November's rent paid, I can hold out on getting evicted until I am ready to drive. A friend has an apartment waiting for me in Minnesota with a yard for Dani. It is a job rich environment. She even has some furniture waiting for me.

No, the fund raiser has not gone well but I know I also sucked at promoting it. People have their reasons for not donating. Everybody has their lives going on. It's easy to miss.

The association I formed was a real disappointment, but it finally allowed me to sever an unhealthy relationship. I created some incredible friendships and will just take the positive with me moving forward. Knowing when to walk away continues to be a lesson I need to work on.

When the depression hits, I know I need to remember. When time and the world compresses in on me is when I need to push back. It makes me want to exist in a tiny moment and in a tiny place.

I know how big the world is. I know many people who populate it. I know how time works. When I get home, when I get stabilized, I know exactly what I need to do to continue my journey. I know what I need to start doing and continue doing today. It's just hard getting to the starting point some days.

I don't know why I don't. Even when the major or minor depression is not hitting, I just can't seem to function the way I want to or need to. This is exactly where the question posed in the last episode comes from, "What the hell is wrong with me?"

I wanted to get into The Mental Health Triangle I spoke about, the path to self-actualization, and Maslow's Pyramid of Needs. Today, though, I don't know how. Today, I just want to beat the living hell out of myself so, instead, I turn away from everything. Instead of a photo album of my life and glimpses into my future, it becomes a snapshot of a life.

I know the snapshot is not a true picture. In no way can it encapsulate what I am or what I have done, but the snapshot is of me sitting in my chair, sipping coffee, and doing nothing.

I've spoken about it before, how I am very good at reacting. Reacting is what has gotten me through life. It is what made me an excellent business owner. As an orthodontic lab owner, a pile of work would come in and I would react to it. It would all get done and get done well. It would go out the following day. I would end the day invoicing everything, seeing a result.

I find myself reacting to the here and now, not future potentials. I'm sitting in my chair and have to wait. Have to wait for my ankle to start working again. Have to wait for a job offer and then the right job offer. Have to wait for the right thing or person to come along. I wait for the things that I need, instead of going after what I want.

This is where, if I allow myself, I can break out the cat of nine tails and really start beating the hell out of myself. I can hear the sound of the leather unrolling, the iron tips scritching against each other.

What the hell is wrong with me?

I've had 70 days in a chair and far too much time on my hands. Yes, I take my meds each day religiously but that is as far along the Mental Health Triangle I've gotten.

There are three books to be written, articles to write, websites to work on. Hell, I could have been an SEO expert by now. I could have packed my portfolio with work that would have wowed any potential employer.

There are things I know I could have done about the self-care part of the pyramid that I have ignored. Meditation and simple exercises.

Psychology, or therapy, the third side of the pyramid, is beyond me right now because I'm counting my pennies, but it is something that I have ignored most of my life anyway.

I sit and I wait. What the hell am I waiting for?

Reaction vs action.

Maslow's pyramid of needs. I think that is one of the things that has gotten me into trouble all my life. Pyramid of Needs or Hierarchy of Needs. If you don't know it, it was a paper that was published in 1943 and outlines what motivates us.

It is, well, a pyramid. Go figure. At the base is things like food and shelter. You move up the pyramid towards love and self-esteem and then further up towards self-actualization and transcendence.

I feel as if I have been stunted all my life trying to build the perfect foundation, meeting my basic needs. I build it and an earthquake comes along and shatters it, so I rebuild it better. Another earthquake. I've ignored the upper levels to concentrate on the lower levels. Knowing the upper levels existed, and that I could and should be reaching for them, make me depressed and ignore them.

My motivation has always been solely concentrated on that bottom level. Why?

That's what made me a good business owner. As a good business owner, with money coming in, I could build the best, earthquake proof foundation ever made. But why can't I apply that to other things that I want as opposed to the things that I need?

Yeah, I'm whining a lot. Bitching. Having a pity party. But this is the current snapshot of my life, of the depression. I know it will pass and I will get back to work on the books and the other things I need to be doing.

But this is also why I had such a great time on my path to self-destruction, when I knew I was going to commit suicide at the end. I could say the hell with the pyramid, couldn't care less about the future, and gave absolutely no thought to self-actualization. All thoughts and feelings of depression faded into the background of the here and now. I was alive like I had never been before. 152 days on the road, only existing in the cities, towns and parks I was passing through, all of my senses alive.

The perfect foundation I had worked on building all of my life? I blew it up. Set explosive charges and allowed the pieces to rain down on me and into my bank account. I mean, screw it. It's not like I needed it anymore. All I needed was my Subaru Outback, my credit cards and my life insurance policy.

It was only when I got back from Hawai'i, state number 50, with the journey over, and the knowledge that I wasn't going to commit suicide, that I could feel the tidal wave of depression starting to build again. I'm kicking at the pieces of the foundation I had been building for 50 years and thinking, "ahhh, hell."

It was time to start over. I knew, though, as I made my way to Texas to rent a house with the last of my money, that I first had to face down the Russian and take a beating.

The beating came. If there is a freedom in planning on committing suicide, the opposite is true when you don't follow through. I was screwed, in the corner, and could do nothing except allow the punches to come. There was no "ding" to end the round. The only ending would be the depressive tidal wave to pass or for it to sweep me into oblivion. I had decided against oblivion, so just had to wait.

A snapshot with a broader focus.

I just hung onto the pieces I had picked up along my travels that might lead to hope and health.

I took what I learned to Tijuana. I didn't want some grand, impervious foundation anymore, just a place to start looking at the pyramid and motivations. A bed, a place to set up my computer, an income. That's it. And I did start stumbling in the right direction. Well, kind of sort of in the right direction. I still have a lot to learn.

Then, I broke my ankle.

What can you do?

It is so, so, easy for the depression to tell me to do the wrong things. So easy to stumble along in the darkness. I can take a positive from this though. There was no tidal wave. No swarm of hornets. There was a bout or two with the gnats. There was the question, "what the hell is wrong with me."

But there is direction. And hope. There is hope every morning I wake up and am excited for the day to begin. Excited about sipping that cup of coffee. The darkness swirls with the thoughts but I know it is a passing thing.

And that is a wrap for the episode.

Be kind to yourself. Be patient. Learn and follow the better paths.

Aloha.

Episode 21: The Holiday Special

Everybody has a holiday special. Even the most ridiculous shows on television have a holiday special. I decided to have one as well.

I think I came up with a pretty awesome title. Let's get naked about mental health! The Depressive's Holiday Special. Brought to you, in part, I think, by Sir Isaac Newton.

Beginning at Thanksgiving is an especially rough time for me. And for many. The holidays create a unique kind of conflict. I think it has to do with the nature of the holidays combined with Newton's Third Law: for every action, there is an equal and opposite reaction.

Tis the season of joy! Of family and friends, of giving. It amplifies the depression to an equal extent. I don't understand why and the hell if I know what to do about it.

Now, let's get into the episode.

Aye, I'm okay. I'm fine. I'm dealing with stuff but, this time, I am sincere about it. I really am okay. I really am fine. I have my dog, Dani, and everything that I need. I have my books, my movies, and my coffee. I even have a home waiting for me.

I both love and hate the posts on Facebook. Hate is too strong of a word. It is not the right word. What is the word? It has something to do with seeing the pictures of family and friends gathered and they trigger me, so I try to avoid them. Kind of. It's complicated.

I am truly happy to see your joy. I want to see your joy, especially the joy of the little ones. It is the little ones that make the holidays for me. I feel blessed that you share them on Facebook.

There are no little ones in my life anymore. There is no immediate family, and the holidays became an ugly thing for me, filled with stress, anxiety and became a time of the year that I just wanted to make it through. I'd breathe a sigh of relief on January 2nd, when life would return to normal. I couldn't wait to tear down the decorations and put them away.

The holidays become a tightwire act for me, teetering between joy and depression. I try. It is a very unique conflict for me, one that I do not know how to deal with or what to do about it. The best I have been able to come up with so far is to withdraw, isolate. Like I said, I really am fine. I have my dog now, my books, my movies. And I wait for January 2nd.

All I really ask of you is not to take it personally and give me my space while I figure it out. It may take a couple decades.

How do I describe it? It started much simpler. Thanksgiving. Where do I go? With divorced parents, I was torn. I loved both sets of my parents and stepparents. A fracture began to form a long time ago. It grew over time and did not improve when I had my own family.

Thanksgiving began a time of extra stress. I enjoyed being with family, but I had to push away the stress and conflict to do so. That got even worse after my separation. Everybody invited me over. I had offers everywhere. Every place that I went, though, I felt as if I was bringing that internal conflict in with me. I felt as if I was a boiling pot on the inside with the lid on while enjoying time with people, but the pressure would build and build. The last thing I wanted was for it to burst out and be inflicted on the people who had invited me.

Finances have not helped either. "Just bring yourself," I'm told. I know that is all they want and expect. But I expect more of me and I just can't, which adds a layer of guilt to everything.

Then, we get into Christmas.

I'm sorry, but I truly abhor Christmas. I hate it. I have for many years now. I started liking it again when I got married but quickly began hating it even more. It is for many of the same reasons as Thanksgiving, but there is more to it.

Just 34 more days until January 2!

Bah humbug? Maybe if there was a little Suzie Whosit in my life, and little ones, it would be different. A little bit at least.

Christmas was always a stressful time. Working in the orthodontic laboratory industry, that stress was compounded. December is always a big month, and four busy weeks' worth of work is done in three. That means long hours while you are preparing everything for Christmas day.

A very long time ago, I stopped being upset about it. Aye, it was money coming in and I knew there was a week off coming up. I told myself it was worth it.

During all of this, there is an entire day spent putting up decorations, hours spent trying to figure out why the lights aren't working, and then there is the shopping.

I hate shopping to begin with. I don't like crowds. During the holidays, there is a something like a dark vortex pulling me into the pit of hell: the mall.

I did figure out a way around the shopping thing. A trick I learned. A secret. Nobody believes me though. I'd go to the King of Prussia Mall, one of the largest in America. I'd go the Sunday before Christmas, an hour before they opened. Seriously.

I would get a front row parking spot that would allow me easy egress. The mall was closed, but the restaurants were open. I'd order myself some breakfast and a Bloody Mary, or two, for fortitude. I'd be finishing the second Bloody Mary when the mall would open, and I'd be in the doors.

It was always empty. I'd finish my shopping as the crowds began to make their way in. I'd see the long lines of cars waiting to get into the mall as I was leaving. With my credit card whimpering in my wallet.

I joke and say that we go from waiting for Santa Clause to being Santa Clause.

It is more than the stress, time and finances. Like I said, I'm still figuring things out.

I remember when my nephew was young, Christmas was the best time of the year, the best day. I am pretty sure I would spend the night and be there for when he woke up. But there were all those years before and all those years after.

I particularly remember one Christmas when I was in the fifth grade. I was living with my aunt and uncle with my mom in the hospital and they asked me what I wanted. I didn't know how to ask for anything. They were well off and I could have asked for anything. I told them, "nothing."

I got my first stereo that year, and two cassette tapes. Men at Work and Styx, Paradise Theatre. I loved my uncle and aunt, but there was a cloud over Christmas. Mom was in the hospital.

Fractures forming? Conflicts that a young boy was not prepared to work through? I don't know, but I do know that things never really got much better until my nephew was born. Christmas was just a day to get through.

My nephew was born in 1999. There were issues, but for a few years, those issues were completely obliterated by my nephew's smile. To me, there is nothing as powerful as little ones' smiles on Christmas morning. --which is why I so much enjoy the posts on social media.

There were more conflicts. I have to dive back into the Mom story. Here is a piece that I wrote when I found out my Mom was dying of cancer. There was nothing the doctors could do. It was only a matter of time.

An Angry Little Boy

Protect your queen.

It is from a television show, The West Wing. The master against the amateur. A flurry of moves with pieces being taken from the chess board. Protect your queen, with fewer and fewer pieces, fewer and fewer tools. Once the queen is gone, the game is over.

That is what I remember from my childhood, my oldest memories, how I was taught to be a son. Forget childhood: protect your queen.

I'm not sure if it was from the micro culture of SW Philly or the old country culture of my family, but a mother was the queen, the matriarch. I remember my grandmother being something more than human and my uncles and older cousins being more than men. They were soldiers, warriors, the queen's guard.

And there I was, with my tiny sword and shield, with my own queen, unsuited to the task at hand. Sometimes part of the queen's guard. Sometimes the only queen's guard.

Protect your queen.

I learned anger. It is a powerful tool, both sword and shield. You really haven't lived until you have felt that primal rage coursing through your body. It was all that I had. The only coping strategy, the only recourse, the only defense. And so, I used it, made it a part of me.

Protect her. Against any and all. Protect her from herself, from the manic depression, from the insults and slights, from people and neighbors and friends and family. And from myself. --I was never allowed to turn that anger on her and so I never figured out a way to release it.

I was only a little boy.

There is this cute little meme going around Facebook, something about the approaching storm, and the warrior responding, "I am the storm." Yeah, buddy, you have no friggin' idea.

The storm came upon me in my earliest childhood, and I sometimes feel as if I have spent my entire life on that battlefield. Warrior and soldier, field medic, hero, craven and deserter trying to find a way off that damn field. But the storm would continue to rage, and I would always make my way back to the middle of the field, the highest ground, to see what else could be thrown at me, to see what else I could stand against, to see what else could beat me and rip at me.

Without anger, where would I have been? How do you survive something like that, how do you maintain a grip on sanity, without anger?

Protect your queen.

So, yeah, I lived my life pissed off at a lot of people. First and foremost: myself, and the conflict to live my life versus doing my duty. Second on the list is my mother, and the fundamental conflict that particular relationship brought to the storm. But nobody and nothing escaped it. Dad, brother and sister, cousins, aunts and uncles. Doctors, illnesses, episodes, surgeries and pretty much everybody and everything.

I know. I shouldn't have been angry at anybody, especially myself. But tell that to the little boy that doesn't want to see his mommy hurt.

I once set my anger against the manic depression. Not a flanking maneuver, not a rear-guard action or surgical strike, but a full-frontal assault. I was no little boy anymore. I was a man grown, with intelligence and abilities, and with a will and determination probably unmatched by anything you have ever seen or experienced. The anger coursed through me, and I embraced a powerful arrogance, a terrible strength that would allow me to set my will against the illness that had ravaged my mother's life, my life.

In that apartment, with the turn of the century approaching, with almost 30 years of dancing in the storm, I called the lighting. I shoved that lighting rod in the ground at my feet as a banner and challenged it.

The lightning came. It kicked my ass. It was brutal. Defeat does not even come close to explain what happened to me there. A total shredding of everything that I was, had been, would be. There were so few pieces of me left, that I did not think I could ever put myself back together. There was not even a shred of anger left to help me repair myself, defend myself. The aftershocks of that defeat battered a defenseless mind.

Protect your queen.

The hell with the queen. I turned from that battlefield and quit. I had nothing left. I retreated to Florida. It was a turning point for me. A climatic ending or a climatic beginning. The battle became against myself, as I tried to figure out what to do with this anger.

I'm thinking now that all of the progress that I thought I had made was only an illusion. I never left the storm, the battle. I could ignore it from time to time, push it aside and live myself. Become a man. Become a husband and father, a business owner and homeowner, a friend and acquaintance and maybe even a writer. But there is still that angry little boy.

Protect your queen.

I cannot.

It's cancer. Like manic depression but totally unlike it. An illness with an inevitable conclusion. I have no tools to deal with this. But the anger returns, with the should haves and could have beens. And I dread the passing of the storm. The event that will herald the passing of the queen will also herald the passing of the storm and I will finally be able to drop this sword and shield? What do I do next?

Protect the little boy.

***

157

It would be over 15 years between the birth of my nephew and the day my mom died. For his own reasons, my brother had cut off all contact with my mom, and that meant my nephew as well.

I thought I summed it up pretty succinctly during my mom's final days. My brother had flown down with me to Florida, seen my mom, and then he and I got drunk. It seemed like the thing to do.

I turned to him at one point. "Brother, I love you." He nodded. I went on, "There is a part of me, though, that hates your fucking guts." His eyes opened wide and then he nodded to that as well.

Protect your queen. I could not protect her from my brother. I was reminded of it every Christmas. I knew the pure and utter joy of holding my nephew in my arms would be forever denied my mother.

Protect the queen? In her later years, all that I tried to do, wanted to do, was give her a better quality of life. Give her some joy and happiness. Every time I held my nephew, particularly on Christmas, the joy was tinged with a deep sorrow, a blush of anger and a brushstroke of guilt. I had hoped my brother might relent but he never did and, as the years passed and my nephew grew into a little man, the joy could not quite be pushed out and away.

Christmas meant 8 days to January 2nd.

Then, I got married. That added a whole other level of conflicts and stress. I always promised myself if I ever got married, I would never fight about money. It is something I remember my mother and father doing and then my mother and stepfather.

My wife loved Christmas. It was her favorite time of the year. As a business owner herself, doing craft shows, it would really pick up all the way to, and past, her cut off day for mail outs. I was a business owner at that point, and I was crushed even more while helping her with her craft shows. And decorating even more. And shopping even more. And my credit cards whimpering louder.

My brother is the finance guy in the family. He always said, rightly so, I sucked at budgeting and finances. He was right. My wife made me look like the budgeting king. My wife and I were both doing well, well enough that there didn't need to be any fights about money. There never were. But there should have been. That promise I made to myself always hung over my head.

There was a lot of joy with having the family, but the Christmas onslaught grew to be too much quickly. My wife had come from a poor family. To say she overcompensated with our daughter was an understatement. It would be like comparing your kid's clay sculpture with Mt. Rushmore.

No, I am not being overly harsh or critical because she is now my ex-wife. It is just the simple truth. 6-8 hours of opening presents? The kid would get tired and have to take breaks. I thought it would let up as my daughter got older, became an adult. Nope. I think our record-breaking year, nine hours, was when she was 26.

January 2nd? Hell, I just wanted the damn day to be over.

Year after year, we had the talk. Stop it. Ease up. A couple things is enough. We should save our money, put it towards a vacation--that she would take anyway. Yes, yes, yes. And then the onslaught would begin again.

It had nothing to do with jealousy, and it includes issues I may get into another time, but it all just made me hate the holidays even more.

It was a dysfunctional family, but it was a family. I still grieve the loss. It was my choice to divorce, but that does not make the grief any less. There is the extra added piercing of sorrow at the loss of my daughter, who decided to stop talking to me after the separation.

Every day became just another day after that. The last holiday I enjoyed was Father's Day. It was the only holiday I looked forward to. There were no mother's involved, no conflicts. Married and with a daughter, my dad and stepfather would get a card and a phone call.

Then, it was gone.

It all just gets heaped upon the pile. Layer after layer of, "what do I do about this?"

My family has a Christmas Eve party every year and I always enjoyed going. I don't anymore for much the same reason as Thanksgiving. There is that boiling pressure pot and I am so damn afraid of it spilling over and infecting the people enjoying themselves.

The Christmas before my divorce, I said the hell with it. I could counter all of my family members' entreaties with, "I'm just not up for it. I'm fine." I was still sharing a house with my wife so spent the night at work on a very comfortable sofa. The following day, I escaped to a friend's house who was spending the day with his in-laws and their family.

It was nice.

The following year, I couldn't fend off my family and went to the party. One point found me outside, crushing tears away. I went back in, made my goodbyes, and ran like hell.

There is so much that is influenced by the depression. I'm not sure what this is. A very common thing that you will hear from people suffering with depression on why they isolate is because they don't want to bring people down. I really don't think this is that. There is that element to it, but it has more to do with the fact that I just want to be alone until January 2nd. I really am fine.

Maybe it does have something to do with Newton's Third Law. For every action (force) in nature there is an equal and opposite reaction. The joy that I see, hear and feel from others reverberates in my soul. Those vibrations are like harmonics on glass. Hit the right frequency and it shatters. I will shatter. So, I just like to muffle the sounds. It is much like being at a concert where I like the music, but it is too loud, so I put ear plugs in. They don't deafen me, but they allow me to enjoy the music without it hurting.

I scroll through Facebook until the sound gets too loud. I stop, only to return. I do enjoy seeing your posts.

I really am okay.

I really do rejoice in your joy and happiness.

There is no conflict in that.

The conflict is in me, and I need to figure it out. I wish I could recapture those few years when my nephew was a tiny one and the pure joy could obliterate all of the dissonance. Or maybe if I figure it out, there will be no dissonance.

And that is a wrap for my holiday special. The holidays are a tough time for people who are struggling, whether financially, emotionally, or otherwise. Just like you cannot tell a person with depression to "snap out of it," or a person with a broken ankle to "just walk it off," your joy cannot erase all the things that are going on.

I really do wish all of you all of the joy and happiness this season should bring. I wish you all the peace and miracles and movies and songs, all of the family and presents and giving and receiving. I look forward to seeing your photos.

I just hope you understand and respect my feelings, and do not take offense.

Aloha.

I have a late breaking PS to add to this one. As I was reviewing the script one last time before recording, I checked out Instagram. There is a group I follow, Real Depression Project.

During Christmas, with everything closed, I'll be diving into one of my old fantasy fiction books. I always wondered why I kept rereading the same books and watching the same old shows.

Real Depression Project's latest post had to do with "Things Those with Depression Secretly Do Alone."

First on the list was, "Rewatching reruns of old tv shows you used to enjoy to feel a sense of comfort and safety."

Hmmm.

Episode 22: Are We Okay?

I forget what famous author said it, but they said, "an amateur writer borrows; a professional one steals."

In this week's episode, I'm stealing. A friend sent me a link on Instagram to a group about a month ago, Real Depression Project. I am in awe by what they are doing on Instagram. I highly recommend checking them out. There is also a website.

Everything they post hits me in some way, makes me feel better. I know that I am not alone, and not being alone is a message I preach. Real Depression Project are the choir, singing the hymns.

I thought I would share some of the things that have struck me the most. As I said, if you are struggling, or trying to understand someone who is struggling, I highly recommend following them.

Now, let's get into the episode.

I follow the Real Depression Project on Instagram. It is sometimes hard reading their posts. They are educating me on things I needed to know decades ago. They are also educating loved ones of people struggling and even helping to validate many of the feelings I have.

As I have mentioned, depression, anxiety and PTSD are not what many people think, the caricatures we come across in everyday life. They can be, but most often are not. It is like how I explained PTSD once.

I took all of the online tests for ADHD and passed with flying colors. Finally, I thought, something I can grab onto and address. I went to see a specialist. After a battery of tests, I was told I did not have ADHD. When telling a friend of mine about it, a psychiatrist and expert on PTSD, he asked me if anybody had ever told me that PTSD can present itself as ADHD.

Mental health struggles can be insidious. From the Real Depression Project and other resources, I am learning that depression and childhood trauma really did have complete control of my life and I just did not know it. I was looking for the caricature, not the reality; I was looking for the dragon to slay instead of looking upon it with soft eyes.

After five decades, it is hard coming to that realization.

I can't imagine how difficult it must be for an addict to walk into that meeting for the first time, admit they were powerless over their addiction and that their lives had become unmanageable. But what if they really had no idea their lives were unmanageable and could have been managed? I don't know enough about addiction but what if they really, truly believe that not only were they in control but they did not even know they were using? As if someone close to them was slipping something to them when they did not know about it? (That's an episode of NCIS.)

When my last major depressive episode hit, I was pissed. I was angry at the depression, God, the Universe and everything else. I was doing well! I was taken my meds religiously! My depression was managed!

Only, it wasn't.

Memes, conversations, and posts by the Real Depression Project are teaching me that according to my Mental Health Triangle, I had flatlined a long time ago. Signs of it are scattered throughout my life. It was never a question of if the episode would hit again, but when.

It is so damn hard to come to that realization, and then look back and see the evolution of a life controlled by the depression.

The caricatures can be easy to spot. I learned that a long time ago. The onset of my mother's manic episodes were marked by music, candles and religion. It was episodic, hence the word episodes. The gentler insanities, as I call them, the less pronounced versions, are much different.

Hints and allegations. I've always said I am a man. We don't do well with hints. We need to be hit with something heavy. Those light brushes, though, have been touching me all my life and I didn't realize it. I just thought of many things as character flaws. I never put together the pieces that they were all a part of something larger, something looming over my life.

One post by the Real Depression Project hit me right between the eyes, with something heavy last week. Think 5 lb. masonry hammer.

Right before I was about to record the episode, I read their post on "Things Those with Depression Secretly Do Alone." The first slide after the title post got me.

"Rewatching reruns of old TV shows you used to enjoy to feel a sense of comfort and safety."

Though not old TV shows, I've written about this and spoke about it often. I've been writing about it since I first launched my website in 2001. I wanted to be a writer. I know what it takes. I am a voracious reader. I could have read all of the classics by now, the top 1,000 books of all time. Hell, I could have read an entire library by now. A smaller library, but a library.

I didn't.

Throughout my podcast, I write about my addiction to fantasy books. It was not new fantasy books, though. It was the old ones. The ones I have been reading for decades. I first read Tolkien when I was about 8. I have now read the series 20-30 times.

I remember when I went to Scotland for a semester abroad. I was broke. I was beyond broke, counting every penny. Due to various issues, I had to get by for a month and a half with very little money. I went on January 4th and my student loans would hit in mid-February.

Meals were one piece of meat on two pieces of toasted bread. Sometimes, I would splurge and add a second piece of meat. I had an entire country though! Things that cost nothing! Just explore. Meet people. Be a part of things. Hell, I could have been going to class.

Instead, I found my way to a bookstore. I bought books I owned at home in the States, spending money that I did not have, and sat in my flat and read them.

I never put 2 and 2 together until I read that post, though I switched it around a little bit inside of my head, [Rereading old books you used to enjoy to feel a sense of comfort and safety.]

All of the other slides in the post hit just as hard.

2) Neglecting chores/habits because you have no energy--all of it is used up fighting depression/faking a smile when you're with others.
3) Spending long periods of times distracting yourself/finding an escape from your inner turmoil.
4) Planning out how you'd explain your struggle to others (and even typing it out via text) but then not following through with it because you fear being a burden (or that you won't be accepted).
5) Getting lost in / fantasizing about a memory you cherish.

I can hit all of these. Or all of these can hit me. That is just one of many posts by the Real Depression Project. Each one educates me a little more. When I can stand being educated.

Like I said, when my last episode hit, I was pissed. It seemed to come out of left field. It didn't. It was a pitch right down the middle of the plate and my psyche hit it out of the ballpark. I was primed and ready for my depressive episode, with the exhaustion from two nonexistent partnerships triggering it all.

I have a lot of work to do. A lot of homework. A lot of healing.

This is what this journey is all about though: the work, the homework and, most especially, the healing.

...and this is the part where I get stuck. This is the part where I want to swim out deeper into the posts by the Real Depression Project, but I can feel the demon circling underneath me. It reaches out a claw to my foot and I kick it away. It reaches again.

And I am drug down to the depths, through 51 years. Many things carry me down, helping the demon along. What my friend said about how PTSD can present itself as ADHD. Episode 18, where I talk about what childhood trauma looks like in adults. This episode where I am learning these hints and signs of a life controlled by depression. The question I have always asked myself, "What the hell is wrong with me?"

It goes back to a rooftop in Chicago in 2019, when my friend Regina asked me why I refer to myself as a person who stutters and yet as a depressive.

The demon drags me down through decades of me writing, pushing at the boundaries of who and what I am, of what was wrong with me. Though I began publishing my Coffee Chronicles online in 2001, I was journaling since I was about 14 in 1985.

In the silence of the depths, the roar is overpowering. I wasn't writing journal entries. I was writing self-prophecy. I was answering the question of, "what the hell is wrong with me," but never putting the pieces together.

It brings me to a flat in Scotland where I was rereading The Belgariad by David Eddings. It brings me to Miami in a dorm room where I read and reread Tolkien, Eddings, McCaffrey, and Jordan. It brings me to so many places where I stand with my back revealed and hear the rustling of whips being unrolled, the steel tips scritchity schritching against each other, the could have beens, should have beens and would have beens.

It brings me to the present, where I ask myself a simpler question. "At this point in my life, do I really want to know any more?"

The answer, of course, is, "yes." But there is the strong undertow, and the demon is carrying me along. Perhaps it is the current depression whispering to me. Aye, you would be depressed as well after 90 days in a chair. There's a lot going on. The flu is not helping.

It can be overwhelming. So, I'm just going to do what I do and keep talking and see if I can't make it past that overwhelming feeling. But it is hard. So damn hard. I can't help but feel as if I have been going through life with one arm tied behind my back. I did not even know it was tied behind my back. But now to see the entire field, see the great expanse of a life lived, a full life...

Even the tiny glimpses in the slide have the ability to both make me feel more comfortable and repel me at the same time.

"Hide, Chris," my mind screams. "Stop! Halt! Cease! Desist!"

It just all wants to make me find a nice orthodontic lab to get back to the day-to-day work, the satisfaction of seeing a mountain of casts become appliances. Collect a check at the end of each week. Watch my movies, read my books, play with my dog, and really say the hell with this self-actualization bullshit.

The overwhelming feeling is so strong, so terribly powerful.

I also know, through the experience of that long lived and full life, that I can only hide for so long. Weeks. Maybe even months. But then one of two things will happen.

First, the depression will catch up to me again. Or two, the desire, the need, to learn more and push out more will return.

I've said it in previous episodes. All my life, I just wanted to be like others, my friends and people that I love. People that I respect. To come home from a day's work and put on the ball game and open a beer. To be satisfied and comfortable in a smaller world. I've tried it. It does not work.

I've also said I wish I was like my mother, with explosive and devastating depressive and manic episodes, with huge billboards in my life that scream, "There is something very, very wrong here! I need help!"

But I am me. That means continuing to write, continuing to talk, continuing to learn and explore. It means standing in the face of that overwhelming feeling and waiting for it to pass so I can continue my journey outward and beyond what I am into what I can be. Even at 51.

But as I have been taught, let's try things from a different angle. I'm stuck here. So, let's look at another portion of the Real Depression Project that I love.

Affirmation.

Self-doubt can be such a powerful tool we use against ourselves. It can be especially hard when we see or perceive it reflected in those we love. Again, there is the caricature we can recognize for what it is but then there are the subtilities that we may miss.

The caricature is when I wrote about when I texted my wife one night at work. I was slammed by a depressive attack, not even knowing depressive attacks existed at the time.

"Do you know what it is like to be a failure in every facet of your life?"

It's become easier for me to shrug them off, laugh at them even. No matter how bad the attack, the lightning strike of self-doubt, even when my shoes get blown off, it is easy for me to pick myself up, dust myself off, and get my swagger back. Aye, ya know, I'm from Philly. Infantry. And I've done a lot with my life. Even helped out an entire profession. The swagger can even push itself into arrogance and all is okay again.

With the depression pushing and nudging me, I begin to doubt the small victories, the everyday ones. I even begin to question if the major victories were victories at all.

And then I come across a post by the Real Depression Project.

"Mental Health Achievements that Deserve More Recognition."

The first one is the biggie for me: "Not acting on suicidal thoughts." I think of it as an achievement, a huge achievement, but I get the feeling that not everybody does. I mean, they are happy I did not, but many of the reactions I have received from the people closest to me fall far from the recognition I think it deserves.

It was a battle not to do it. Then, the war began. It was like the D-Day Invasion. I got past that day, but there were so many nights afterwards that were just nasty, ugly, street fights. I knew I wasn't going to do it but sat night after night in my garage wondering if I should start up the car and drift off in the carbon monoxide fumes, where the pain was so intense I could only rock back and forth and wait for it to pass.

It is so hard to explain to other people, hard to get them to comprehend the scope of what I accomplished. Many never will. I understand that. Some days, though, the understanding is harder than others.

I talked about it previous episodes, about how I felt like I just climbed Mt. Everest of hiked Death Valley in the middle of the summer. Or maybe did both. And family members responded, "yeah, but you were wearing the wrong shoes."

And then I run across the Real Depression Project. They understand it. They get it.

I question this podcast at times. Am I really doing anything? Am I helping? Or am I just talking to hear myself speak? The depression whispers to me that I am harming myself, wasting time, that nothing really matters. I particularly worry that I post these episodes and advertise on them on LinkedIn, the same place where my unsuccessful job search has been. Then, I come across the second slide in the post:

"Opening up about a mental health issue that you may be judged/stigmatized for."

I also receive messages and notes here and there. No, I am not looking for daily outside affirmation, but I do like to hear it once in a while, need to hear it once in a while.

It is the difference between knowing someone loves you and hearing them say it.

Maybe I'll get to the point where I will just know. Where the results of what I am doing do not matter. Just doing it should be enough. I am a huge proponent of "the means must justify the ends" as opposed to the "the ends justify the means," but it is nice to hear and read the affirmation once in a while, the support, the held arm to steady my steps.

The other slides were just as meaningful to me:

3) Putting in boundaries because you no longer tolerate toxic behavior.

4) Allowing yourself to be vulnerable after you've been hurt (e.g betrayal, abuse, heartbreak).

5) Moving away from what is familiar and towards what you are worthy and deserving of.

They wrap up the post with the slide, "Be proud of yourself-- All of these achievements take so much strength, courage, and hard work."

But I'm still struggling with one. I'm struggling in general. The flu pushed back more than this episode. It pushed back my departure. I'll be leaving soon to start a new chapter someplace else. Minnesota this time.

My friend is worried about how I will handle winter. I haven't been in one in a long time, and I have never been in a winter like they have in Minnesota. I am not worried about winter at all. The cold and heat don't bother me. I have a home waiting for me and my dog. That's all that matters. It looks...perfect, white stuff on the ground and everything.

I can feel that certain tingling all throughout my body, the pause between two breaths. I've been caught here for too long.

I did go for a walk today, though. It my first walk in a long time. A long walk to the pharmacy to stock up on meds it is tough to get in the United States. Today, as I write this, marks exactly three months since I broke my ankle. Today was my first long walk. It felt good.

Yeah, I still have a lot of work to do. A lot of homework. It all reminds me of a song by the Grateful Dead, Just a Little Light. It is a song that acknowledges the darkness within while looking for a little light.

It is just a little light that illuminates my path somedays. That's all I need to know that I am moving forward. The light can come from the oddest of places. The darkness can as well. The interesting blending of the two creates shadows that must be explored to discern their reality.

But that is going to be a wrap for this episode. I need to start packing. Or maybe just lay down for a little bit and acknowledge that I could use a little bit of extra rest today.

Be kind to yourself. Educate yourself. If something feels "off," look into it. Our mind plays tricks on us--something else that the Real Depression Project reinforces. Our senses can be lying to us. It is the nature of depression. We need to trust our gut and go with it.

I highly recommend the Real Depression Project if you are struggling or someone you know is struggling.

Aloha.

Episode 23: The Space Between Breaths

I wasn't planning on doing another episode this year as I was supposed to be on my way to or settling in Rochester, Minnesota, but I am still stranded in Tijuana. As I was sitting here, waiting, a title popped into my mind. Things typically start with that. Things are a bit scattered with everything packed, but I'm going to try and plow my way through and maybe make some sense.

The space between breaths brought a memory of a stupid little kid. Everybody told me I couldn't breathe under water, but how do you know if you don't try?

It didn't work out well to say the least, but, in retrospect, it wasn't nearly as bad as when I stuck my finger into the empty lightbulb socket to see how that worked.

We really don't know anything until we try. Until we start talking. Until we start listening. Until we understand. A lot of the time, and the most difficult thing I think, is knowing what we don't know.

In business, I say it is important to know what we do know but more important to know what we don't. I think life is the same. Mental wellness especially so.

I'm stuck in the space between breaths, still stranded, with everything packed. My lungs burn at times. And that is what it was like when I wanted to commit suicide. The first time, I didn't know to come up for air. The second time, I didn't want to come up for air.

Now, let's get into the episode.

Yeah, that was stupid. I sucked in as much water as I possibly could. Aye, I was young and Aquaman was my favorite cartoon character. If he could do it, maybe I could? I sputtered to the surface coughing and choking where I was scooped out by an adult who knew better.

I was stuck in the space between breaths the first time I wanted to commit suicide. A timeless moment that I discuss in previous episodes, with my lungs burning, my skin on fire, my brain ablaze with pain, and I did not know to come up for air and just breathe.

The second time, I knew to come out for air, but I didn't want to. The effort was too much. I was too exhausted and just wanted to drift into nothingness.

Both times share similarities. A major one is loss of perspective. My world compressed into a timeless moment of pain and agony. Another similarity was loneliness, a deep, dark loneliness that could not be touched by the huge circle of friends and family who surrounded me.

One of my favorite personal quotes is: "Perspective: use it or lose it."

It connects directly with another quote I ran across recently by Irish author Brendan Behan. "At the innermost core of loneliness is a deep and powerful yearning for one's lost self."

They both connect with a post I recently saw on LinkedIn by Mark Carolan. He posted about a book he recommends, Man's Search for Reason by Viktor Frankl. Frankl relates his experience of his time in Auschwitz. It is about finding meaning.

Meaning is what I lost. It is what I found again. It is what makes this experience in Tijuana so different than all of my other experiences.

My situation still sucks. It sucks a little bit more each day I am stranded here. It is probably the worst one I have been in. I thought I had been in bad situations before, but then I broke my ankle in a foreign country with no money. The experience really forces perspective on you, whether you want it or not. Instead of being pushed deeper and sucking in water, I was pushed to the surface of a different kind of reality. I sucked in air and knew that I had to learn patience to get through this. It became about that space between breaths.

I have been pulled back under constantly the last few months. I guess that the stories of "why" are unimportant. The direct "whys" lead to bitterness and anger, and the last thing I want to do is start sounding like Yoda.

Depression, anger leads to.

I am trying to get at the "whys" behind the "whys" and that is a tougher proposition.

Imagine you are struggling, drowning, breaking the surface to gasp in a lungful of air. Standing just beyond reach is a yoga instructor saying, "now remember to breathe with the belly, in through the nose..."

Yeah, screw you.

But that's what it can be like. In that space between breaths, you need to remember how to breathe, the mechanics of breathing.

"Like a leaf on the wind," keeps popping into my mind for some reason so I am writing it down. That's an awesome scene in the movie, "Firefly."

That's something else that just struck me today from Facebook. Dori Holt, author and group moderator of Voices Unearthed, for parents of children who stutter, wrote something about how talking for a person who stutters can be like driving an icy road. The more you try to force it, the harder it becomes.

It is what I was taught and taught my daughter. If you start going into a slide, you never fight the slide, as counterintuitive as it may be. You go with the slide, thereby regaining control.

I really have no idea what any of this has to do with anything. It almost makes sense in my head. Aye, like I said, I'm just waiting. It is the space between breaths.

I do know that I felt at my absolute best when I was on the road to suicide. I had a plan in place, a great plan, and was having one last hurrah before finding a nice, quiet place to end my life. Check out the movie "Scent of a Woman" if you haven't seen it already.

I felt great. Wonderful! I was free. It was not the space between breaths. I was breathing. I felt utterly calm and relaxed. The anxiety that I had felt? Gone. I've always been afraid of flying and the dentist. Phobias. Gone. In the Great Sand Dunes National Monument in Colorado, I think I felt silence for the first time in my life.

There is something so damn important in there, something beyond and deeper than not having to worry about anything because I am about to die. The 500lb weight I had carried on my shoulders all of my life was gone. I was lighter and could breathe.

I was no longer living in between breaths.

I had purpose. I had direction. A destination. I was also living a life of service. Without telling anybody my final destination, I took everybody along with me on my journey through social media. All 50 states, close to 40,000 miles, and 152 days, I posted to help others to shake free of the hibernation and trauma caused by Covid.

When the journey was over, and I decided to live, that's when things got really ugly. I knew it was about to happen though. I was expecting it. I knew that I was not going to kill myself. Wave after wave of depression slammed into me. I just continued to breathe through it, knowing it would pass.

Knowing I had purpose again?

There was no happiness or joy in the decision. I was not expecting either. There was no hope. I wrote that I did not find hope in my journey, but I found pieces to start putting my life back together. An authentic life? A direction to find my lost self?

Just breathe.

There is a lesson to be learned in breaking my ankle. --I really have no idea where that came from.

I was told I did not actually break my ankle in the initial fall. I really did not need to be told that, but I was told anyway. I just sprained it very badly. I broke it doing what I did next.

I had adopted a dog who had been abused, neglected and never been on a leash. I slipped and fell while walking her in an early morning rain. People rushed to help me, but the dog kept all my would-be helpers at bay. They finally tossed me a walking stick.

The pain was excruciating, unlike anything I had ever felt. Add in a terrified puppy who was savagely attacking anything that came close to me, and my thoughts left me. I couldn't think. I couldn't process anything resembling logical options. I had one thought in my head. Get home.

I had a walking stick. I had three blocks to go. I had a puppy I needed to get home safely. I got home. It took me over an hour. I was living in between breaths because each breath brought pain.

That's where I broke my ankle. Somewhere along that three-block walk, hop, crawl, my ankle went from bad sprain to fractured.

Various things in life have taught me to breathe through the pain, endure by keep breathing. By concentrating on the mechanisms of breathing, we can endure and keep going. There is a disconnect with that in the space between breaths. There was a disconnect with that during that walk, hop, crawl. I endured, but I stopped thinking.

I think of tWitch, another seemingly happy person, who had everything, who took their life. We will never know his story, and I would never want to intrude on the family to better understand it. Like with Robin Williams. I can only understand my story, and try to understand it better, try to figure out the things I need to know, and pass on that knowledge to others.

It all makes me think of the space between breaths. Of what it takes to bypass the most basic instinct of any organism to survive. Of either a loneliness that goes so deep that it cannot be touched by all those around us or a greater need to end the burden that we think we are placing on those around us.

I am trying to breathe right now, breathe through this podcast, breathe through the space between breaths.

I am scarred shitless of what comes next. When I can stop breathing in Tijuana and begin breathing on a long road trip that will bring me to Minnesota. I am afraid of those frigid breaths in Rochester where the high next week is 11 degrees. As much as I need to continue my journey, as much as I am desperate to start breathing again at a job and with an ankle that works, I am afraid of that next breath.

Yes, in the space between breaths, I have considered suicide again. There is a painfulness in the space between breaths, but there is also a comfort in it. Opening the door to opportunity also opens the door to stress and anxiety.

They are just passing thoughts, the gnats on a summer evening that I write about. The ones that have no purchase on my reality. They are the thoughts of the path of least resistance.

The last few months, the last couple years, have taught me I need the resistance in my life. There is something about coming up for that lungful of air and the surface of the water has a tension to it. I would use the metaphor of a layer of ice, but I am trying to avoid thoughts of cold. There is purpose breaking through it. There is a step towards an authentic self. That my lost self lies beyond the tension, along the path of more resistance.

It is so easy to get caught up in the comfortable and known, too easy. I watched years and decades pass. Was that the feeling that I got over time, that I moved further and further away from my true self? The path of least resistance led to the most resistance until every day was a struggle.

In the space between breaths, what I did not know makes me ache.

In the space between breaths, I grow more and more tired.

In the space between breaths, I have choices to make.

In the space between breaths, I know that I need to learn more to make better choices.

In the space between breaths, I struggle, my thoughts scattered, but I choose to move forward with another podcast. Whether I'm walking, hopping, limping or crawling, I'm still moving forward.

Maybe I should have called a cab or an ambulance. Maybe I shouldn't have tried to breathe water. Maybe I shouldn't have tried to figure out what makes the lightbulb go on. Maybe I shouldn't have given away everything. Maybe I shouldn't have done a lot of things.

But I am figuring things out. And you have to admit that some of the more stupid stories are entertaining.

And that is the best I have for this episode. I hate writing or saying that. I always hated the John Cougar Mellencamp greatest hits album name, "The Best That I Can Do." Maybe there is a lesson in that? Let me think about it and get back to you, hopefully, from Minnesota.

Aloha.

Episode 24: Understanding Depression

In my last episode, The Space Between Breaths, I mentioned tWitch, but I stayed away from the topic. What can I add to the conversation? As I say in my podcast, I am not a mental health care professional with letters at the end of my name. I am just a guy who has been there. What the hell do I know?

An article/post got me typing. It featured a smiling picture of tWitch and was, "I Still Don't Think We Understand Depression" by Dr. Jen Welter.

I read the questions and advice the post posed and realized that I do have something to add, that I may even be able to make an impact. No, I am not a mental health professional, but I am a guy who has been there. I understand what I do know about depression, and I understand what I don't know about depression. Most importantly, I am learning what I need to learn about depression.

Who am I? I'm Chris, nice to meet you. Have you checked out my podcast? A lot of the answers are here if you care to check it out. I suffer from depression, among other things, and have almost taken my life twice. I was a leader and educator in my industry for 35 years. I am a storyteller/journalist, and I have answered many questions in the first 23 episodes of my podcast from a personal point of view, with what others are saying is insightful.

Now, let's get into the episode.

First, let's break down Dr. Welter's article.

[Side note: Dr. Welter, I am not trying to attack you. I am merely answering questions you pose and adding my thoughts.]

Dr. Welter wrote, "Mental Health: just because someone seems funny or healthy or strong (or all of the above) does not mean he/she does not struggle with depression/ mental health."

True, but what does that mean? She gives general examples about comedians and being the life of the party, how we use that to divert people from our center, our core.

One of my earliest podcast episodes was about my secret world. Nobody ever knew about it. I am a master of disguise, putting a façade on to face the world, the other world. Whether I was a high-school student, infantryman, chef, college student, business owner, husband, brother, son, educator or what have you, these were the identities I allowed others to see. The depressive, my secret world, was what I did not allow anybody to see until it became apparent in crisis.

I talk about how there is a part of me that wishes I was like my mother, who was bipolar with schizophrenic tendencies. When she was not doing well, it was like a neon sign, the size of a stadium, lighting up with an arrow pointing to her saying, "there is something really, really wrong here." There were even massive fireworks displays.

Me? My bad times can be interpreted as me being a piece of shit, lazy, having a bad day, when the internal secret world would slop over beyond the facade.

"Strong people," she writes, "those who claim strong shoulders, often feel like they are burdening others by sharing with others."

"Read that again," she wrote.

Yes and no is my response. There is a lot of truth to it. I often felt that way, that I was burdening others. I was the strongest of the strong, trying to help everybody--which was a sign of my depression. So yes, I talk about how not being a burden to others was one of the reasons why I hid it.

There was another reason though. I hid it because the lessons I learned inspired utter terror to keep it hidden.

Back to my mom. I was taught to hide it by people's reactions to her, and the system's reaction to her. She came from a huge family, the youngest of nine. When I was born, I was grandchild number #35 or so on her side alone. I was one of three children. There were so many times throughout her life where I was --and this is the reality and not a perception-- the only child of an only child.

On her deathbed, one of her surviving brothers came to see her who she had not seen in 35 years. It made her happy, so I just kept my mouth shut, but it made me angry as he gushed about how much he loved her.

My brother was there, the first time he had seen her in 25 years.

During my first time that I almost committed suicide, I lost close friends. They did not see "crisis." They saw me burdening them and living off of them because I could not do anything else. It was much like when I broke my ankle, but there was no physical cast for people to see and associate with me not being able to do anything.

I also believe that this is a problem with the system in general, a failure to move beyond "crisis intervention" and to "illness management." I don't blame my mother's family or my brother. I finally dealt with the anger.

Imagine, I talk about, living in Miami. I was there for Hurricane Andrew. But imagine that a Class 5 hurricane will hit every year, maybe twice a year, guaranteed, destroying everything. What do you do? You move. Stay away.

I don't blame them. It was hard, though, being the only child of an only child of a very sick parent. I never wanted to put somebody in that position. It would end up costing me everything during my next suicide plan.

"With that being said," she writes, "the next question is often, how do I know if someone is actually ok? Well, honestly, it's hard… but also, honestly no one is good all the time, no one laughs at their own jokes all the time, sometimes sunglasses are to cover tears & give the illusion of a sunny day….

Realize that one-word answers actually tell you nothing. So, ask questions that encourage sentences, thoughts, activities, actual updates.

--if at first you don't succeed, try again… and again… in another way on another day."

Again, yes and no. That's another episode.

The answer is: first, you will never know. You can ask, check in, even stop by, and you will never know. If you had stopped by with pizza and beer while I was suicidal, you would never have known. I would have laughed with you, telling stories, and everything with me was fine, A-okay.

Second, and this is an interesting thing I came across in my self-reflection, checking in on me can do more harm than good. My question in an episode is "should you check in?" The path to hell is paved with good intentions. The path deeper into my personal hell is paved with the wrong people checking in on me.

A great example is my brother. He loves me. I have no doubt about that. He is a good big brother and has always been. He also shared with me one time that he has the emotional intelligence of a shrub. He a guy's guy, characterized by Deborah Tannen's book, "You Just Don't Understand: Women and Men in Conversation." He wants to fix everything.

If you are not ready to invest the time and emotional energy necessary in communicating with me, please don't check in. Please don't try to help. Really. You do more harm than good.

"Close the distance," she writes, "a text is better than nothing, a call is better than a text, a FaceTime is better than a call, and in person is best… it's easy to hide behind an emoji, words, a voice, much harder to look into the eyes of someone you care about and lie.

Don't be so afraid of saying or doing the wrong thing that you do nothing… what you don't want to live with is the wish that you had made the call, given the hug, asked the question, or held the hand… the past is past, can't change it, so instead, let's be a little better, kinder, more proactive in the future… especially during the holidays (which some people really struggle with)."

Eh. The first thing that jumps out at me here is, "the past is past, can't be changed." I disagree. The past can be changed. There's an episode about that as well.

I'm learning a lot about changing the past these days as I do my podcast and educate myself on depression, PTSD, trauma and other mental health issues. Simply, we cannot change events of the past, but we can change our perception of those events. By changing our perception, we change the past.

I am a child of trauma. I need to nurture and allow that inner child to grow where that growth was stunted. How do I do that? First, by recognizing the signs.

I read an article recently, a meme really, about the signs of unresolved childhood trauma in an adult. Each point was something I was not expecting, and each point was like a hammer blow between the eyes. Yes, there is a podcast about it.

Then, what are the more subtle signs of depression? I read this in an Instagram post from the Real Depression Project. The one that jumped out at me the most was, "rewatching old reruns of tv shows to feel comfortable and safe." When I read that, everything clicked. I won't get into the clicks here, but it had a profound effect on the way that I view my past, the way I perceive it, and the perception is helping me to change it.

The second thing that jumped out at me about what Dr. Welter wrote was, "...much harder to look into the eyes of someone you care about [and] lie."

No, it's pretty easy. Eh, I've been doing it for the better part of 51 years now. It may have been hard at first, but now? I am the master of disguise. I've worn the facade for so long, it is second nature to me.

Another thing she wrote that jumps out at me goes back to my brother and communication styles and what has helped me. If you have the emotional intelligence of a shrub, please don't speak. Please, for the love of all that is holy, don't offer advice and try to fix things. Just hug me. That could be all that I need. It could be enough.

But also understand that that is me. That's my communication style, as revealed by multiple tests. I love, and am loved, through touch. It is what grounds me and centers me. It is what keeps me connected.

Communication, like therapy, is a two-way street. Just as there has to be a healthy therapeutic relationship established, understanding the communication style of the person you are reaching out to is of utmost importance.

The final thing that jumps out at me about that section is, "...what you don't want to live with is the wish that you had made the call..."

Something about that bothers me and I do not know what. An interview I did with Leo Flowers, host of the podcast, "Before You Kill Yourself," comes to mind (found on my website). We spoke about how it can be selfish of a person to say something like, "don't kill yourself because I love you." They miss the opportunity to really understand you by placing themselves first.

Second, it's not about you. That's another podcast. No, I didn't want anybody to live with the wish, and possibly the trauma and mental issues, of not calling. Have a ceremony, spread my ashes at South Point in Hawai'i, talk about the tragedy of a life cut short by an illness, and then get on with your friggin' life. My will allows for that. Have a party. Celebrate my life.

And know, whether you made the call, didn't make the call, stopped by and hugged me or didn't stop by to hug me, at a point, there is absolutely nothing you could do. There is a point of no return. I passed that point now twice. I can tell you with absolute certainty that there was nothing that could have stopped me except myself.

How I stopped myself is another episode, but both times had to do with me reaching out. Once to a friend and a second time to the Universe.

"And… get professional help," Dr. Welter writes. Remember, if you fear someone is a danger to themselves or others, get help."

I agree, but how? I'll be getting into that next. Most people who need it can't afford it. When they are at that point of needing intervention, when it is seen and known, they are typically in crisis. We need to do a better job of being proactive and helping people before they are in crisis.

Just as an example, I'm there now. Not suicidal, not in crisis, but the depression is kicking my ass. I've learned enough that I have not crossed into crisis mode, and won't, but I could really use help, therapy. I can't afford it. I've been out of work for months, broke my ankle, and am stranded in a foreign country. What can I do?

And what happens if I cross the border (I'm in Tijuana) and check myself into a hospital? At my nonexistent income level, that thought terrifies me far more than the depression. I know what those places are like. I knew what they were like in the 70's and 80's visiting my mother and I know they have gotten worse.

I did visit a very nice one once, but the person was paying out of pocket.

One of my mother's suicide attempts in 1999 was because she would rather die than go into the hospital again. I really can't blame her. It was during her previous hospitalization that an event occurred that brought on the madness that made the choice between hospitalization and suicide a reality.

"Getting help," she finishes up with, "is a sign of true bravery."

I completely agree. But that is not the perception. It's getting there, but it needs a lot of work. More so for men, I think.

I saw this video and wish I could remember where I saw it, but it was about being a man in America, particularly a black man. We are taught at the youngest of ages to be strong, shake it off. That is our job and our identity. That is who we are. Add in "black man" on top of it, and you add an entire level of complexity to the situation.

Then, how do we reach people? How do we explain this to them? How do we change perception and culture?

I'm seeing a lot of great stuff online. The Real Depression Project is doing fantastic things on educating people about depression and trauma. Do you follow or support them? Have you checked them out? Did you even know about them before reading or hearing it here. It really is an incredible resource.

There is a project to reduce suicide by 20% by 2025 by The America Foundation for Suicide Prevention. I think we can do 50%, if we do it right.

How do we do it right?

Well, first, let me in!

Aye, I need a job. Don't make me go back into orthodontics. Yes, I can make a lot of money there but I'd really rather not. I'd rather continue my journey as a mental health advocate. I might not be a mental health professional, but I have a hell of a resume and a background (though rusty) in communications.

Second, watch movies. I have a list of "must watch" movies for, well, everybody. Some of them are even entertaining.

1) Mindwalk. Free on YouTube. It was a movie that I was forced to watch in a science writing class in college a long time ago and it changed how I look at everything. It is an introduction into systems theory, which must be applied to everything we do. It basically says, but not in so many words, that the mental health care system really got screwed up with the invention of the first clock.

With the invention of the clock, society moved from a "prevent" mentality to a "fix what is broken" mentality. Watch it. Please.

2) The Legend of Bagger Vance. A more entertaining version of Mindwalk, watered down a bit, but just as powerful in some of the scenes.

3) No Cure for Cancer. Denis Leary's very non-PC comedy routine from 1993. It has some amazing pearls in it to take away and addresses the comedian aspect Dr. Welter spoke about.

Other notables are Good Will Hunting, Bill and Ted's Excellent Adventure, Scent of a Woman, and Patch Adams. They look at mental from a first-person perspective, real and uncensored.

Next, check out this response I received from Antony Malmo on LinkedIn when we were discussing the mental health care crisis and what to do about it, what's wrong with it. It resonated with me and should resonate with everybody. It might seem like common sense to many, but I have found that things we think of as common sense may not be as common as we think.

"Here's a back of a napkin summary of what I know," he wrote to me.

1. Human threat perception is very sensitive to fast moving, physical emergencies. (AKA predators). We did not evolve to perceive intangible, creeping calamity. (AKA climate change, societal mental health trends)

2. Science (and business) demand measurability of impact preferably delivered ASAP. The catch, measuring the effectiveness of Upstream preventative interventions in complex systems require massive data sets, serious statisticians, money and time. Downstream reactive measures are cheaper, easier and faster (albeit less effective).

3. When it comes to budget time, critical care gets priority over prevention [because] we have an emotional response to helping someone in critical need, whereas "non-urgent/non-critical" issues don't trip our amygdala. That's fine if it's a 1:1 ratio. However, in practice, [population] level prevention saves far more lives. E.g. Modern plumbing (clean drinking water + hand washing) has saved more lives than all the doctors of history. And to take it to a more cynical level, disasters make better photo ops for politicians.

Solution: Change minds. Story telling is crucial."

My initial response is he's right. I see all of the pictures of tWitch, just as I remember seeing all of the pictures of Robin Williams and other smiling celebrities who lost their lives to depression, and I see all of the calls for action.

The cynical side of me, and the infantryman, sees it all like the flag waving and praise for veterans on certain holidays and during election time: lip service while the veteran population has continued to have a suicide rate 6x more than the non-vet population. They also have a 7% jump on the non-vet population on homelessness.

Next, it reminds me of an episode of The West Wing. A very wealthy man went to the press secretary and asked how he could really, really help. What could he do? Her answer surprised him. "Build roads in Africa."

It's not sexy, she explained, but necessary. The foundation of roads makes everything else possible.

I think we need to get away from the poster children of suicide prevention (no disrespect intended to tWitch or others) and start building roads. It's not sexy. It costs a lot of money. But it makes everything else easier.

Next, Antony Molin asked for a storyteller. Well, here is a storyteller, just waiting for an audience. Trying to reach one. Let me in? Follow my podcast? Support my podcast? Share my podcast. I'll keep talking.

This next thing may make people choke so make sure you are not drinking or eating anything while reading or listening to it. I'll give you a second to finish swallowing.

...

Okay, here goes: Give me a lot of money and leave me alone to get it done.

I'm serious! I did it before, but with no money. That's how I burned out and was part of what almost brought me to kill myself. I did help save an entire industry though. Long story.

Then, when the industry people were asking me what to do next, I told them to give me a lot of money and leave me alone. Nobody took me seriously. Not that I can blame them, but I was serious. I'm a pretty smart guy, already accomplished a lot, saved many in my industry, but I saw many still struggling, wading through new technology and new concepts. Over and over, I said they were trying to jam square pegs into round holes. They were adapting, but not well.

Many finally figured it out, after 5-6 years, but it would have been a hell of a lot quicker and more efficient if they had just all chipped in, given me a lot of money, and left me alone. --and the association that turned its back on me still owes me $1,000. That's what you get for electing a board instead of continuing to be a dictator.

A very simple thing to do, that doesn't require any money, is break down my book.

As I said, I am a storyteller, not a mental health professional. I would love to have a second version of the book where, essentially, a mental health professional breaks down my stories into counseling sessions. Just tears them apart with the precision of a surgeon--or like the editor who is currently making me cry editing my first book. She is making me a better writer. You can make me a better advocate. Any takers?

This is some difficult stuff. I have many instances in the book and podcast where I say, "I don't know." Places where I am trying to figure things out. I'm stumbling a lot. Lend me your arm. I'll be Dante, you be Virgil. [Just in case, that is a reference to the first part of Dante's Divine Comedy, Inferno. Which is an apt metaphor if you think about it.] Let's share my struggles and screw ups with everybody. I'm game. Lead me through my personal levels of hell and show me how I got there.

Which leads me to my next point: share my book. Aye, I'd love to make my $2 per copy on it, but I'd like to make it available to anybody who wants it.

Giving my book away is probably not the best business decision I have ever made but that is not the point. I want to get my story out there, help people to get help. Start talking and keep talking so we don't suffer anymore tragedies like with tWitch.

Look, I'm not saying I have all of the answers. I'm not that arrogant. But I do have some. And I have directions to other answers. We cannot possibly understand tWitch unless we walk in his shoes. Or if he had a podcast about that journey.

I talk and write about my journey to break it down and dissect it. My two times almost committing suicide were very different but shared many similarities. The more I understand about depression, the more I understand that the doorway to suicide was somewhere I was going to end up eventually, and somewhere I am trying like hell not to return to.

Was tWitch like my first time, where time compressed into a single moment filled with unbearable pain? When the depression altered time and reality so the question "how can I do this to my loved ones" is altered to become "how can I NOT do this FOR my loved ones"?

I have a podcast about that.

An extreme example is what happened to my mother during a psychotic state. Her reality was that she was an instrument of Satan sent to spread disease on the earth and had infected me and her grandson. What would you do in that situation to protect the people you love? If that was your reality?

Or was it like my second time for tWitch? Was the exhaustion, over such a long period of time, so that every breath was a burden, made me feel like what I saw in friends and family who finally passed from cancer? Where I was angry at the people who loved me and wanted me to continue?

I compared that depression, that experience, to a cancer of the soul. I justified suicide by saying it was just like my loved ones who died. Time compressed and distorted reality again, so that the 5% of my life that had been depression became 100%.

I had sat with others. For a month, I sat with my best friend, my dear, sweet girl, while she battled cancer, and the end finally came after 14 years. That final month was excruciating to watch. She was in so much pain. Just let go, I wished. And she finally did, finding peace. To me, my cancer of the soul and spirit was no different. Just let me go so I can find peace.

Or was it completely different for tWitch? Is there another reason, another altered reality that allows us to override that basic instinct to survive.

I think that that is a way in, something to be talking about, something to research to better battle suicide. What are the stories? What are the stories of non-depressed people who choose doctor assisted suicide? The stories where that basic instinct for survival for any organism is overridden by something more powerful? What is that "more powerful" and how do we address it?

For me, the answer is in Mindwalk and systems theory. We have to move upstream from the "crisis" period and prevent the crisis from occurring. Some of the answers are simple, yet difficult to implement, like minimum basic mental health care and preventative care as I discuss in my Mental Health Triangle--another episode. Building the roads.

There are many stories and examples from outside of the mental health space that directly correspond to mental health care. I knew a woman who died from a cavity. Seriously. She got a cavity in her tooth and was terrified of going to the dentist. There were other issues involved, but it abscessed, the abscess spread throughout her body, and she died.

Then there is the story of a person I know closely, the biggest pain in the ass who ever lived, who is still alive and living well. He taught me everything I know about being a pain in the ass.

He was diagnosed with Hepatitis C and almost died when he finally received his liver transplant. He was down to under 5% liver function. When the treatment came out that cured Hepatitis C, he started writing his insurance company about it because the treatment was $100,000 and not covered.

The illness was still at work on his liver, he was coming to the end of the new liver's life, and he started to write to the insurance company with a very simple question. "You will pay the 2 million dollars plus for another transplant. Why not pay for the treatment that has a 95% effective rate and save all that money?"

Denied.

He kept writing. On a fixed income, he laughed off the offers of 20% off, 50% off, etc. and kept writing. When the price came down to $10,000, I jumped in. I said I would pay for it. He replied, "No, I got this." And he kept writing.

They eventually paid for the treatment and cured him. His liver regenerated as it is meant to do when not being attacked by the illness.

That story, though so common in health care, boggles my mind. It makes no logical sense. A company is more than willing to pay over two million dollars in reactionary care but not $100,000 in preventative care.

This absurdity must change. How do you fix it though? --the first thing I wrote was "how do you fix stupid" but that was a bit harsh. But it is stupid!

My final point brings me back to Mindwalk and terminology. Yes, we use mental health care and have different rules for mental health insurance. It is just like dental insurance. That's absurd.

We are not pieces. We are not a clock that needs to be fixed. We are more than the sum of our parts. The mouth, and dental care--though my example is an extreme one--is a doorway to our general health, so proper dental care is essential for proper health care.

Mental health care is the same. There are studies, tons of them, that show a direct correlation between mental health and physical health.

We need to redefine things. We need to change attitudes and perceptions. We need to stop the crisis before it becomes a crisis. We need to add our collective knowledge and attack these issues and educate others.

We need to do more.

We need to not only start talking and keep talking, but we also need to change the landscape to make the conversations more accessible and relatable.

Y'all need to watch Mindwalk.
Aloha.

Episode 25: Not Really An Episode

Let's unmask mental illness!

Why the book?

There are a bunch of reasons, but I can't help but laughing as I think about lecturing my sister, daughter and many other younger people. It got so that I was repeating myself often. I got to the point where I wanted a book of lectures.

Let's open our hymnals and turn to lecture #182...

As I plug myself into the mental health network on LinkedIn, I found myself not wanting, but needing, the same thing. I wrote it often. In response to one post or another, I found myself writing, "that is episode so and so" and then posting a link to that episode on my website. Now, I can just post "that's in the book."

I also wanted to get something out there to spread awareness. Is print dead? I don't think so. I was able to edit the transcripts to hopefully draw in more people and spread the word. As I say, I really do repost, "that is episode so and so" very often. With the physical book that I will have in my hand, which I will get once I am in a new home, I can start having fun with videos. Annoy the living hell out of people?

The book can also help me spread awareness by mailing it to various groups and associations.

I also hope to earn some income. It is not the best business decision, but the eBook version is available free to anyone that requests it. Making money is not really the point. Spreading awareness is.

I know. Now, due to my situation, I completely understand the power of a few dollars. $7 here in Tijuana, the price of the eBook on retail sites, is food for two days. I just don't want anybody having to decide between potentially getting help with my book and not buying it because they could use the $7 somewhere else.

More information can be found on my website.

When I get to somewhere that is quieter, I'll make an audio version of the book. My apartment here has too many ambient sounds that intrude and the audio publishers are very strict when it comes to that.

That has been my last week. Waiting. Holding my breath. Thinking. Writing.

As I write about, but don't really advertise because I am so bad about it, I am hoping to make this a full-time job. I have a Patreon account that has been well hidden. In my page, "Supporting the Podcast," I now write about it a bit more openly.

Patreon allows people to become patrons of the podcast and website for as little as $4.95 a month. Unlike other Patreon accounts however--again, maybe not the best lure or business decision--there is no extra content for patrons. There are a few perks, however. Again, I just want to make the information available.

Patronage will allow me to expand the podcast into something that I have in mind now for a very long time. Even before I graduated college in 1997, I envisioned a magazine and non-profit to disseminate news and information about mental health.

I need your help, though. This isn't easy and I really have no idea what I am doing. I have done it before though. Life, and the depression I am learning, took me along other paths and into the orthodontic laboratory industry.

It was not a bad life, but not really fulfilling. I felt fulfilled when the industry and many of my friends were threatened by the new technology that was changing everything. A new paradigm was unfolding. We had been so used to an industry that had not really changed since the mid 1970's. The shift threatened to kill labs and may have contributed to the deaths of people I knew.

Two people I knew took their lives.

I was overwhelmed myself but had started a Facebook group to help others learn what I was learning, really staying just one step ahead of them--and a few steps behind the big labs that could afford to invest the money and time that us small labs could not. Aye, I had always been at my best when I was overwhelmed. Long story. That's a past episode.

I believe I was one of the first small labs in the country, if not the first, to be 100% digital capable. I began speaking, spent hours and hours on the phone with other lab owners, went to a conference for dental labs where I gave a two-hour clinic, and then I formed a non-profit and started our own orthodontic lab annual conference, the first of its kind in the world.

I did it once. I can do it again. But I'll do it right this time.

The second part of this non episode is a column I wrote for the website, inspired by events on Christmas day.

Chance Encounters

This might be for my Coffee Chronicles, or this might be a part of Let's Unmask Mental Illness! Anyway…

I firmly decided not to have a Christmas. It was not a choice to be miserable, but just make it another day. There's a podcast about it, The Holiday Special. In the podcast, I talk about my aversion to Christmas and how I need to work on it.

The Universe (God if you will) works in mysterious ways. Sometimes, it's not so mysterious. It gives you a smack across the back of the head.

I'm still stranded in Tijuana. Long story. Tijuana celebrates Christmas differently. They ignore the song "Silent Night" and start setting off fireworks on Christmas Eve. In the US, think 4th of July on steroids.

The fireworks made me think of something and I reached out to Dani's original owner who I had met on a few occasions.

Alyssa had come looking for Dani, whose first name was Soledad, about a month after I adopted her. With me not speaking Spanish, and her not speaking English, I never got the entire story. It was a sad one, though, with Dani placed with her brother, then escaping, living on the streets, rescued by someone who could not take care of her, and then adopted by me.

As soon as Dani saw her, she went crazy. The bond between Dani and Alyssa was apparent. Instantly. Love.

I invited her to stop by any time. She did, then with her boyfriend, Allan, a few times. A fine young lady and a fine young man. It was supervised visits at first because, well, I am from Philly, and I have been around the block a few times. But there was something about Alyssa and the way that Dani reacted to her that made me trust her, want to trust her. The supervised visits went to unsupervised, and they took her for walks and Dani even spent the night once in the house they had rented.

Alyssa has been following me on Facebook and I mentioned in the text I sent her on Christmas Eve that I would be leaving any day and that she was more than welcome to stop by any time.

She replied to come over and enjoy Christmas Eve with her and her family. I had the urge, but the car was still packed, it was late, and I had just taken my nightly pills. There was also the push/pull of my feelings about Christmas. It's just another day. Nothing to celebrate. Only something to endure.

I replied that I couldn't possibly but thank you.

She replied, "then tomorrow." I received the text after I was in bed.

Christmas Day. Sipping my coffee. Just another day. Alyssa texted me again. That's about when the Universe slapped me across the back of the head again. Harder this time.

As I have mentioned in my podcasts, and seem to have forgotten, each morning we are given a choice: to continue on in our rut or take a chance to be happy. It is so much easier to continue on in our rut, follow the path of least resistance. It can be extremely difficult to take a chance. There was the packed car I would have to unpack, the altering of my routine, the trouble of getting Dani into the car, the fear of how she would react to a house full of people, and, really, the fear of bumping and mingling with my aversion to Christmas that I talk about in my podcast.

I'm slowly learning to ignore the baggage that surrounds me, layers me, and follow my gut...and the slaps by the Universe.

I finally texted a reply to Alyssa: "Okay, let me empty my car and take a shower." Dani and I made the 15-minute drive.

Alyssa and Allan were waiting for us as we pulled up. Dani went crazy and it took the three of us to unhook her from inside the car--I keep her leashed inside to keep her from jumping into the front seat and into my lap.

The family adopted me as soon as I walked in the door. Before I was even there. Alyssa had texted me I was family.

I was home. There was Alyssa and Allan, parents, an uncle, young kids and even a grandmother that reminded me of my own--I received a hug and a kiss. Dani was excited and happy: the vicious beast was climbing into people's laps to give kisses and get pet. She can be very overprotective, but she loves to be loved. She knew she did not have to protect me from these people. She knew that she was safe and that I was safe.

Lessons from the Universe? Lessons from a dog. Who rescued who?

I had a fantastic Christmas with people that I barely know, that are family. I struggled against the embarrassment at times as they would not allow me to do anything, getting my drinks and food. I laughed with the family, and especially the uncle and father. There was a discussion at one point about hairy chests.

Hairy chests is just one example. They were having fun. Allan was translating. They started showing off their hairy or non-hairy chests. The layers of baggage that I had wrapped around me screamed at me to smile but not join in. I told it to "piss off" and lifted my shirt to reveal the hairiest chest to a round of laughter.

At one point, I had to leave. I was exhausted. I have not been doing much and the food, exercise, and two drinks were getting to me. I needed a nap. I made my goodbyes, with them insisting I return after my nap. They did not believe me, I think, when I said I would.

I did.

It was much, much easier to shrug off the baggage and hesitation after my nap and coffee. I went prepared with a cup of coffee for after the drink and the food to stay a bit longer. Everybody, including Dani, was starting to nod off so I said my goodbyes again. I was offered a place to sleep, a ride home, anything. I was good. I wanted to return home and just be happy.

It really does come down to choice, acceptance, and learning lessons. That was my Christmas present from the Universe: a lesson.

It's not the pony I still want, but a damn good present all the same.

Aloha.

PS. I do have another place where I post stuff and write columns. You can find it in the link below.

https://thechrischronicles.com/

And now the final part of the non-episode that seems to becoming a bit of an episode. It is the first draft of an article I am writing based upon some work I did for the founder of Simply Mental Health. It is about...well, that's the point of writing an article.

Speak Up! And Turn off the Video in Video Conferencing!

I personally love video conferencing. With the pandemic, it has become a part of the way we do business. I also realize that many people do not love it. It can cause stress and anxiety and add to deteriorating mental wellness. Research supports me.

Speak up! Tell your boss. Ask to be able to turn off the video. Send them this article if you have trouble articulating how you feel.

Studies suggest that one in four to one in five people suffer from conditions that could make forced video conferencing from uncomfortable to traumatizing. It can negatively impact employees and their contributions.

Adam Nemer, former CFO of a 3+ billion-dollar health care company and current founder of Simply Mental Health was one of those people and now campaigns for the ability to turn off video.

"I had always struggled," he said, "with meeting people in the eye. It was even brought up once during a performance review, where my boss feared that it may make me seem untrustworthy. I struggled with the feedback."

He continued, "It has only been since the advent of video conferencing that I put two and two together. The feelings that I experience on a video call are the same as when I'm in a room looking in someone's eyes: anxiety and panic. It was not that I couldn't look people in the eye, it was that it brought on anxiety and panic that made me less effective in meetings, so I avoided it."

I understand. Though I like video conferencing, I encountered similar issues when I first graduated and started interviewing for positions. I was very qualified and had much to contribute, but I have a speech impediment, a stutter, and the first interview was always over the phone--a situation that made my stutter even worse. I did not get any second interviews for a long time.

There is an old school thought that does not consider reality, being human. It is how I was taught. When you meet someone, you give them a firm handshake and meet their eye. If you do not, you are thought of as less.

A weak handshake can mean a weak person. Not meeting someone in the eye can mean they are lying or untrustworthy. Imagine meeting Stephen Hawking, one of the greatest minds of our lifetime, who suffered from a physical disease that made a firm handshake and meeting the eye impossible. You would not think less of him. The same is true for 20-25% of people on video calls.

From autism to PTSD, researchers have found many reasons why turning on video and making eye contact is difficult for many.

Sustained eye contact overstimulates a certain area of the brain for those with Autism Spectrum Disorder (ASD), causing extreme stress and discomfort. Eye contact for people with PTSD can cause responses like fear, pain and anxiety. There are many other examples. Some have to do with mental health issues, some with invisible physical disorders, others with a person's personality.

"I struggled daily with making and maintaining eye contact and had no idea why," said Nemer. "It would make me panic and lose my train of thought. I was actually at my best when I looked out of windows in conference rooms. Staring off into space allowed me to collect my thoughts and be more effective as both a leader and a contributor.

Nemer finally brought the idea up to allow everybody to shut off video during conference calls and explained why. When allowed, many people sent him private messages of thanks.

Researchers at Carnegie Mellon's Tepper School of Business and University of California found that, despite contrary thought, video conferencing can reduce the effectiveness of employees at meetings.

In an article, "Speaking out of turn: How video conferencing reduces vocal synchrony and collective intelligence," they explain how verbal cues, as opposed to visual ones, increase the collective contribution of the team.

Employers benefit by taking Nemer's advice.

Don't require video for conference calls

Don't assume a 1:1 conference call is okay before learning the person's preference

Don't use negative verbal cues

"We paid a lot of money for video so let everyone turn on the camera."

"Let's see all of the brave people turn the camera on."

Speak up and let your boss know. The benefits of allowing people to turn off the video after a quick introduction are both for you and for them, along with the company. With communication and understanding comes better mental wellbeing as well as a healthier work environment.

***

And that is a wrap for this non episode, finishing it just before it is time to record it.

Check out the book and the website. Remember, if you would like a copy of the book but cannot pay for any reason, just email me and I will email you a copy of the book.

If you would like, check out the "Support the Podcast" webpage. Help me help others.

I hope everybody is having a wonderful holiday season. With the way things are going here in Tijuana, I am preparing for a new, regularly scheduled podcast. Simply, I am waiting for the deposit returned to me that the GM said I would receive on the 13th.

Aloha

Episode 26: Breaking Down Reactions

The first podcast of 2023 and, hopefully, the last from Tijuana.

Yep, still stranded in Mexico. Long story. But I'll be getting on the road before this podcast is actually posted. I hope.

I'm still scattered. I did finally unpack my car but am about to repack it from the pile I have in my living room. I still have no idea what the hell I am doing or what to do--part of that longer story.

Since my belongings are still scattered, my thoughts are still scattered.

I thought to myself, "the hell with this episode, the hell with my streak, nobody would blame me if I skipped one or two weeks with everything going on."

I decided, though, to keep talking, keep writing. Break down some of the columns I wrote and react to some things that I ran across.

For now, following the path from reactions seems to be the best way to get on the path to my authentic self, but I'll be getting into that later.

Now, let's get into the episode.

Things tug at me. Thoughts and ideas push and pull at me. Some slap me on the back of the head. I'm reacting to the slaps. One thought just slapped me on the back of the head from Chicago, wielded by an old, dear friend, Regina.

It was on a rooftop bar in Chicago in 2019 that I met with an old friend of mine from the University of Miami. It had been years since I had seen Regina, decades, but we quickly fell into our easy, comfortable relationship.

Regina has always asked me the best questions.

"Why," she asked me at one point as we discussed life, "do you call yourself a PWS (person who stutters) but also a depressive?"

I think she knew the answer when she asked the question. I didn't. I figured it out, though it took me a couple of years. It was not a matter of semantics, of wording, it was something deeper that I needed to figure out to really get on with my life. I think she knew this as well, and also knew I needed to figure it out on my own for it to cause an authentic change. She even gave me a hint, using both the stuttering and the depression.

A couple years later, I finally stumbled across the answer.

As identifying as a person who stutters, as opposed to a stutterer, it meant that I did not allow my stutter to control my life. It was something in my life, but just something that I dealt with like a bum knee or a broken ankle. Adjust and adapt.

There is no adjustments or adaptation identifying as a depressive, as opposed to a person with depression. By identifying as a depressive, I give it control over me, power. I think Regina knew this and was nudging me along.

I first wrote the following in 2014 in a piece I wrote about the death of Robin Williams when he lost the battle to depression. He did not commit suicide. He died from a disease, depression.

Depression is a disease.

Depression is real.
Depression can be treated.
You are not alone.
There is hope.

I wrote it many times. I think it was only in 2022 that it really started to sink in. Aye, what can I say? Some of the more unflattering adjectives that can be ascribed to me at times are stubborn, dense and resistant to change.

In 2022, though, my dear Regina, I think I finally shrugged free of the mantle of "depressive" and became a person who suffers from depression. I still have a long road ahead of me though. Now that I realize and understand, and accept, that I have an illness, I can begin untangling it from my authentic self.

It's a start.

The first question of many to answer is "am I suffering from depression now?" I can say with absolute honesty that I have no friggin' idea. None. I don't know.

I talk about it in previous episodes that just as it is difficult for our loved ones to see the effects of the illness, it is just as difficult for us.

It is not a broken ankle with a cast wrapped around it. That is simple. The cast a visible sign. The swelling and pain I see and feel now a visible and tangible sign that something is wrong, and I need to work on things. The ankle is healed, but I spent a long time in a cast, a long time doing nothing but sit on my ass.

I did the doctor recommended exercise bike a few times. I wore shorts--a bad idea. My legs, side by side, look ridiculous. My left one is a monster if I do say so myself. It was what I used to hobble and roll around for a few months, doing the work of two legs. My right one is scrawny, like I had not eaten for those three months.

That's depression.

I need rehab. There are parts of my psyche that are monsters. There are other parts that have not been fed and nurtured for decades. I need to balance the two.

This is where it gets confusing. Where does the depression leave off and the need for rehab begin? Has the cast come off or is it still on? The feelings and thoughts I have now? Are they the illness or are they the side effects of the illness? Am I still laid up with a broken ankle or am I stumbling through the swelling and pain of healing?

I really don't know.

I'm guessing it is a measure of both.

See, that is the thing that so many people get wrong about depression and so many other mental illnesses. There's a pill for that! Yes, I take mine regularly. Many people think since you are taking medication, it is like magic, or like aspirin for pain. Take the pill and everything is okay.

Doesn't work like that.

I talk about it in a piece I wrote a long time ago, a hint that I gave myself back in college that was published internationally. Dysthymia: The Thief of Happiness. You can find the article by following the link if you are reading the transcript or you can find it on my website under "articles."

Dysthymia is a low-grade chronic depression. You need to have it for two years before you can even be diagnosed with it. But what does that mean?

Yes, after diagnosis, you can begin treatment that will heal the damage, take a pill, but there is still the scaring of living that way for a minimum of two years. Imagine if you have a cast on your ankle for two years. My legs look ridiculous after three months. Imagine what my psyche looks like now.

Even if the depression is gone, I still need to figure out what to do about it, how to live that way. I still find myself hopping now when I don't need to, still find myself favoring my left ankle. I was told that the swelling and aches could last for a year. I need to rebuild muscle and tendons. Imagine if I had had that cast on for decades?

I guess this is where a psychologist would come in handy, the mental health version of a physical therapist.

Depression is like cancer. Long term, untreated, it is like a cancer that metastasized, sending numerous tendrils to infiltrate, wrap, and choke parts of my psyche. It is going to take a while to treat.

The important thing, though, is realizing it is there, realizing and accepting what I have been writing all these years. The important thing is taking those first steps: admitting I was powerless over depression, the Universe could restore me to sanity and help me find my authentic self, and then decide to turn my will and my life over to the care of the Universe.

Aye, I can't do this alone. I understand that. It is where the column that I wrote this week came from.

Perspective: Use it or Lose it

2022 was one of the toughest years of my life. It got downright ugly. I'll make the jokes and share the memes on Facebook because they are funny, but I'll also look back on 2022 fondly.

It was the year I was fired—twice. Completely ran out money— a few times and dipped far below the poverty level. Broke my ankle. Walked three blocks on the broken ankle with a half-trained dog in the most excruciating pain of my life. I was stranded in Mexico. Completely helpless. Had to beg. Totally fruitless six-month job search. And I've spent the end of the year waiting for management to come through on their word to return my deposit, so I have traveling money. My car has been packed since the 13th, all my life's belongings with room to spare.

And those are just the things that are at the top of the list. I could go on.

If all goes well, I'll be starting out 2023 on the roads in a snowstorm.

What a great, awesome year!

I really began to find myself this year, after 51 trips around the sun. I started a podcast and found my passion for writing again. I met some truly wonderful people that have further blessed my life. I renewed contact with old friends and severed contact with unhealthy ones. I have purpose again, and within that purpose, I have found a measure of peace and happiness that I never knew existed.

It's not a contradiction.

It's about perspective.

Yeah, the depression kicked my ass on many occasions, and still is, but I have learned so much about it, myself and how it has influenced me. By learning about it, I have shrugged free from the hold it had on me. Well, I'm getting there. I now know the paths I need to travel.

In 51 years, I have never had such an awful one, emotionally, financially and physically. In 51 years, I have never had a better one.

No, I am not one of those hippie type people. I'm definitely not the "turn the other cheek" type of person. The memes about appreciating what you have make me gag.

Through the lens of perspective, though, I find myself smiling at 2022. I really don't understand it myself.

The only thing that truly bothers me about 2022 is the way I broke my ankle. After walking away from train wrecks, car accidents, hurricanes and other natural disasters, and many disasters of my own choosing, I broke my ankle walking my dog. It is just...boring. It is prosaic, completely in contrast to everything that I am.

There are some lessons in that as well.

But I am sipping my coffee, greeting another morning. No, it is not my Hawaiian Kona, but it is not all that bad. I am looking at another day of waiting, sitting in my chair.

Live aloha. Be aloha. Be excellent to each other. Be excellent to yourself.

***

A lightbulb went off inside my head the other day. Things clicked. I'm seeing many "end of year" things. In my writers' groups, there is a lot of talk about writer's block and how to overcome it.

A very long time ago, I wrote about it.

In a short piece, "Foreword," this is the opening paragraph:

"The concept of writer's block doesn't hold much weight with me; I know that there are ways beyond that wall if I but choose to take them. Music lifts me over it, sex allows me to seep through it, letters to friends gets me around the sides, and simple determination makes me hammer myself against it until it shatters and crumbles. And yet I have not written anything for over two years."

Thinking about depression and writer's block, and looking back on my life, I realized that what I wrote was a lie. Due to the depression, my life had become writer's block. I did not write that particular piece for two years, but my attempts to write for the next couple decades were sporadic, disjointed, and never focused.

I'm still doing it, I realized. It is where a very short column came from that I posted in my writer's groups.

5 Subtle Hints of Depression for Writers

Writer's Block can be a sign of depression in and of itself.

When many think of mental illness, they think of the extreme forms. I am on a journey through my mental health in my podcast, "Let's Unmask Mental Illness," and I am learning about the subtle signs of depression. It is teaching me that depression has had a grip on me most of my life. It is teaching me about writer's block.

On the Real Depression Project on Instagram, I ran across a series of slides about the subtle signs of depression.

1) Rewatching reruns of old TV shows you used to enjoy to feel a sense of comfort and safety.

2) Neglecting chores/habits because you have no energy—all of it is used up fighting depression/faking a smile when you're with others.

3) Spending long periods of times distracting yourself/finding an escape from your inner turmoil.

4) Planning out how you'd explain your struggle to others (and even typing it out via text) but then not following through with it because you fear being a burden (or that you won't be accepted).

5) Getting lost in / fantasizing about a memory you cherish.

I delve into all of them and how they influenced me as a writer in Episode 22: Are We Okay?

At 51, I know what it takes to be a professional writer. I knew at 16. I went into orthodontics and had a very successful--but unfulfilling--career. I am realizing now that my life has been writer's block.

In short, I can react to things very well. The life of an orthodontic laboratory owner is all about reaction and daily gratification. A pile of molds come in and then a pile of retainers go out that night.

Writing is a very different animal. It is an act of creation that takes will and purpose. There is no instant, daily or maybe even yearly gratification beyond that of the act of creation.

I delve deeper into everything on my website: www.friendsofgina.com

But let's break it down. (Yes, the various 80's songs are playing in my head.) Let's dive deeper into it. I think by using that as an example, I can learn more about depression and myself.

The first one is the easiest and jumped out and smacked me. Not the back of the head slap, but a full frontal one.

"Rewatching reruns of old TV shows you used to enjoy to feel a sense of comfort and safety."

It changed in my mind, transformed into an answer to a question I have been asking myself all of my life, "what the hell is wrong with me?"

You see, all of my life, I have wanted to be a writer. I'm serious when I say, "all of my life." My first article was published when I was about eight in a Philadelphia newspaper kid's section. It was about an older man who always had a jar of candy to give out to the neighborhood kids when they came up and asked politely.

In high-school, I learned what it really meant to be a writer, what it took. The top two rules were 1) write every day and 2) read voraciously.

I did, but I am finding out now that my depression nudged me into the wrong directions. The "read voraciously" part troubled me. I did. I write about it often, asking, "what the hell was wrong with me?"

It is a necessity to read what you want to write. I always knew I wanted to be a novelist, contemporary fiction, and support that with articles on mental health. I even worked with my college advisor to alter my requirements so I could focus on that.

I never did. Oh, I read. I could have a read a library by now. Maybe a small one, but a library all the same. All the greatest works, all the newest works, every article appearing on health and mental health, and even the scientific periodicals. I didn't. I kept returning to the same fantasy fiction books that I read over and over again, a genre that I enjoyed reading but had no intention of writing.

Over and over throughout my life, especially as I picked up an old, tattered book to reread again or replace with a shiny new one, I'd ask myself, "what the hell is wrong with me?!? I know better!"

And then I would dive into Pern, or Middle Earth, or some other fantasy world.

The guilt built over the years. A few years back, maybe four, I couldn't read anything anymore. There was no escape for me. Every time I reached for a fantasy book, I felt the lashes of "should have." Every time I finally reached for something that would help me with my journey to be a writer, I felt the lashes of "could have."

It was the depression. "Rewatching reruns of old TV shows you used to enjoy to feel a sense of comfort and safety." I found safety, security and escape in those old fantasy books. I never put it together until I read that quote on the Real Depression Project. It was a subtle sign of depression I never realized until a month ago.

The next slide from the Real Depression Project was just as revealing to me.

"Neglecting chores/habits because you have no energy—all of it is used up fighting depression/faking a smile when you're with others."

Exhaustion I could understand. It was the extreme exhaustion that eventually led me to want to take my life. I was just so damn tired, soul wearied and aged far beyond my 49 years. It still bothers me in a way when I hear, "50 is still young."

No, it wasn't. You don't understand. 50 felt like 250 and I could feel every single one of those 250 years, like I was stretched far beyond a human lifespan.

Yes, I understood the extreme exhaustion of major depression very well, but what about simple weariness? The tiredness of coming home from work and not being able to or not wanting to do anything? I never put that together with the depression.

Writing is a chore, a habit that you must get into if you want to be a writer. I wrote about it often. Yes, "should have, could have and would have" are no-no's in therapy, but if you have a goal, they become essential. If you want to be an Olympic Athlete, you can't just sit on the sofa and eat Oreo's all day. You need to train. Writing is the same way.

Day after day, year after year, decade after decade, I was just weary. Not that soul weary exhaustion. Just tired. So, I wouldn't write. I'd read my fantasy fiction, play computer games, watch tv and hated myself for it. I had the time! I just never did anything with it. I neglected my chores and habits that I knew would make me feel more fulfilled.

The third slide, "Spending long periods of times distracting yourself/finding an escape from your inner turmoil," goes with the second.

No, I was too tired to write, to think, but I had the time. Even when I was buried in work, which I am pretty sure I did on purpose, I still had time. I could have made that time.

It was only six years ago that I finally started sleeping well, and that was with pharmaceutical help. The turmoil of the day began intruding into night. When I was not doing anything, when my mind was at rest, that's when it would really get going.

I had started having panic attacks. The panic attacks intruded into my sleep. I would wake up heaving, on the floor, panting and gasping. It got so I couldn't sleep, was afraid to fall asleep. I was completely defenseless when I was asleep.

Awake, I could escape. I could read into all hours of the night. I could work until I was exhausted. I conquered the world, demons, and old gods thousands of times with computer games. I watched all of the old movies so many times I got sick of them.

When my mom was dying, when I was told that there was no way she would survive this time (another long story as she was dying for 10 years), I couldn't even find peace in sleep. I would later be told by my wife that she was afraid to touch me in my sleep, that I always jerked and spasmed. Then, there were the panic attacks.

Down in Florida for my mom's final days, I rented a house with my brother. When he saw me afraid to fall asleep, he gave me a quarter of a pill. .25 milligrams of Clonazepam did what nothing else had ever been able to do. It doesn't knock me out. It's not that kind of pill. It allows me to turn off my mind and sleep peacefully.

After my mom passed, and I returned home, my doctor gave me a prescription. I was amazed at the difference it made. My wife was amazed. I began to sleep peacefully every night.

Clonazepam is addictive--I want to add that because it is important. I've been on it ever since. I peaked at 1.5 milligrams and never had to go beyond it. Am I addicted? Damn right I am. I don't care.

I did wean myself off of it once. After the multi-billion-dollar settlement against the drug companies, Clonazepam was getting harder and harder to get. I used the step-down method, a half milligram at a time for a week. Each step was mildly awful. Withdrawal. I managed it. The doctor then tried me on just about everything else. Nothing else worked. I finally convinced him to put me back on the Clonazepam.

A peaceful night sleep--now--is well worth the potential side effects of long-term use. I'll try again when I get other things figured out.

One of my routes around writer's block was letters to friends which brings us to the next slide from the Real Depression Project.

"Planning out how you'd explain your struggle to others (and even typing it out via text) but then not following through with it because you fear being a burden (or that you won't be accepted)."

Want to see my computer file on it? Aye, I'm a writer. Emails, no texts. I have an entire file filled with emails to friends, family and people who I do not even know anymore. All unsent.

I attempted to write a book about everything a few times. I could make a book of the "introductions" to the book. I never actually got very far into the actual book. There are dozens of them. I have written plainly and clothed it in metaphors. I tried from every angle imaginable. Nothing I wrote ever gave me something solid to hold onto and write the rest of the book.

To a writer, that translates to about a year or two of concentrated effort on books and articles. The attempt to explain the struggle became the struggle. It also drove me into a very informal style of writing. Emails are easy, less formal even than columns. My writing skills deteriorated to the point where I didn't think I could write anymore, not anything formal like an article or a book.

I would make feeble attempts through my website, but even my Coffee Chronicles got lost somewhere in the digital universe and I lost the rights to it. I did finally revive it as The Chris Chronicles.

It was only on my journey to self-destruction that I really started writing again. Facebook posts became columns that became a book. It's not ironic at all. Think about the last part of the slide: "... but then not following through with it because you fear being a burden (or that you won't be accepted)."

Who really gives a shit about being a burden or not being accepted when you are planning on ending your life? Hell, I even lost all my anxiety. All. Nada. Nothing. I have a phobia when it comes to flying. It has never stopped me, but I am gripped by terror during take-off and landing. I flew to both Alaska and Hawai'i with no issues at all. I was at peace. If the plane went down? I didn't care.

Trying to explain my struggle has now become my purpose. Hence, this podcast.

Then, the final slide, "Getting lost in / fantasizing about a memory you cherish."

This was my specialty. It is still how I spend time, particularly during the ten minutes or so that it takes me to fall asleep at night or for a siesta.

I have rebuilt my life from the ground up paying attention to every detail. It is in the details where I lose myself and fall asleep. A memory becomes a "what could have been if." I wrap myself in these illusions and fall asleep.

Fantasies become my reality when I close my eyes. I have a lot of material. I am also extremely creative with an imagination that may be unmatched.

Nowadays, I am trying to retrain my mind and thoughts. I try to move away from fantasies, though I do indulge in them from time to time. I step away from "what could have been if" and towards something scarier for me, "what could be."

I now fantasize about balance and hope, about this podcast and books I am working on. I fantasize about a new life in Minnesota these days. I push towards a path where fantasies can become dreams that can become realities.

It's hard, so damn hard. It really is. Depression, unknowingly, became engrained into every facet of my life, even my dreams and fantasies. The need to escape has to be pushed aside for the desire to live, to find my authentic self.

Small steps, baby steps, maybe even falling backwards at times. One day at a time.

And that is a wrap. Be kind to yourself. Realize and learn that your struggles may have more to do with deeper issues than you imagine. Take steps forward. You may be standing in place like I did and not even know it.

Aloha.

Episode 27: The Problem with Absolutes

Nope, still in Tijuana as I write this. I may even record and post it from here, early, but I'll be getting on the road soon.

My last podcast had me thinking about things, breaking down the subtle signs of depression. A column that I just wrote, "Lessons Learned from a Bar Fight," was a mixture of the podcast and reactions to posts I am seeing. That led me to Robin Williams in Good Will Hunting.

All that led to this podcast. It is about something I have been saying for years in various forums and various lectures on many different topics. "Don't screw up like I did."

Learn from my mistakes. Please. If you do, it makes my mistakes more bearable, gives them purpose. I wish I had learned more from other's mistakes but that has not been my way.

I also want to introduce you to this incredible woman that I met, though I do not know her real name. You'll need to keep an open mind.

Now, let's get into the episode.

First, before sitting down with Mr. Williams, this is the column I wrote with a few tweaks.

Lessons Learned from a Bar Fight

From posts I am seeing, I imagine that many people were disappointed by other people in 2022. I am reading a knee jerk reaction, about how if we don't have expectations, we will never be disappointed. All of the memes and posts are making me facepalm. Often.

Umm, no. Don't do that. It is all about a bar fight in SW Philly.

A very long time ago, probably when I was in high-school, I had been disappointed by a close friend and was going to cut them from my life. I was talking about it with my stepfather, and he told me of a story of a bar fight he was involved in during his younger years.

He was at a bar with two of his friends and they got into it with four other guys. At the start of the fight, his one friend ran and a 3 on 4 turned into a 2 on 4. --he never did tell me who won as it wasn't the point, but he smiled that cocky smile of his.

Rich explained that he remained friends with the guy who ran, completely surprising me. He said that the guy that ran was a nice guy, had good qualities, but Rich learned that he would not trust him in a bar fight. He just accepted it.

It is not a black and white situation. There is a lot of gray involved.

Each person that we meet brings something into our lives and takes away, positives and negatives. We have to evaluate each relationship and see if the positives outweigh the negatives. This determines if the person should be in our lives and how far we let them in.

It confused me. It was so at odds with something I learned before. I attribute the story to my grandfather, but I don't think it could have been him as I was more of a baby when he died but...

"If you can count your friends on one hand when you die," he said to me, holding up a hand missing two and a half fingers from a work accident, "consider yourself lucky."

My life became either/or, black or white, friend or enemy. Absolutes. That's what you get for taking life lessons from a violent alcoholic.

I am a child of trauma. There is an article here based upon the effects of childhood trauma on an adult. It can really be summed up, though, by a scene in Good Will Hunting.

Robin Williams is talking to the math professor about Will's friends. The math professor is saying something to the extent that they are gorillas and holding Will back. Williams yells back that any one of those friends would take a baseball bat to someone's head for Will and that is what Will needed.

I remember cheering during that scene. I remember reflecting on that scene for years to come. I remember thinking about that scene from the perspective of my stepfather's story.

My best friend in high school was Dave Pearce, may he rest in peace. From 8th grade to 11th grade, he was the Ben Affleck to my Matt Damon. Dave would, and did, do anything to protect me. He was all that you could ask for from a best friend and saw me through many difficult situations. He had my back, we'd wrestle and throw parties (sorry Mrs. Pearce), and he held me when I cried.

It was sometime in 11th or 12th grade that he found a new best friend, though. Drugs. We battled, fought, I had a few interventions, but his new best friend was far too powerful.

We got an apartment together after high school. Things went from bad to worse. What had been all positives, the ultimate best friend, went to being mostly negatives. For my safety, I had to cut him from my life and move back in with my parents. I would eventually move to Miami. It was one of the most difficult things I had ever done.

We were both screwed up kids in our own ways. I could just have easily found myself on his path but found other ways to screw up my life. He was such an incredible person, though, filled with love and loyalty, and I mourned his passing long, long before he passed away from an overdose. I never hated Dave. I hated the disease that stole him away from me.

But I was alone. I had also read the wrong books, learned the wrong lessons.

Dave epitomized that black and white scenario of friendship. It was us against the world. He was also the one who introduced me to a new world of heroes and villains, with the gift of the book, "The White Dragon," by Anne McCaffery.

Long before I met Dave in eighth grade, that black and white world got technicolor thrown onto it when I started reading fantasy books. Everything I read was about ultimate things: ultimate good versus ultimate evil. Heroes and villains. It all lacks, well, the gray of being human.

I still remember a book I read in 4th or 5th grade that I had to get special permission as it was in the older student section of the school library. The Wolf King, by Joseph Wharton Lippincott. --yes, that Mr. Wharton. He was not only an author but he had a business school named after him. Out of print, I'm still looking for a copy of it that I can afford. Any help?

The book is much like Jack London's Call of the Wild. A wolf cub had to grow up by himself. In this one scene, almost into adulthood, he is being harassed and harried by a group of hounds. He gets cornered in a cabin. Triggered, tired of running, he turns on the pack of hounds. The wolf arises and he tears them apart.

Not too long after reading it, I turned on the pack that was harassing and harrying me. I got tired of being tortured and teased because of my stutter. I took them all on.

No wolf king arose.

I got my ass kicked.

That became my world, though, influenced by fantasy books and stories like that attributed to my grandfather. It really screwed me up and destroyed every relationship I formed. People couldn't be my friend, they had to be my best friend willing to take a baseball bat to someone's head for me. Girlfriends had to love me unconditionally or else I did not recognize it as love, but as someone I was better off without. There was no such thing as acquaintances or casual relationships.

I would pour all of myself into everything I did, offer people everything that I was and had, and if that was not returned, then they were cut out of my life.

That's not healthy. It's unhealthy. A bad way to live. It led to a very lonely existence. It was about a total lack of boundaries. It is about that gray spectrum. Casual can lead to closer bonds. May or may not, but the potential is there. I never looked at it that way. It had to be all in or nothing. Immediately.

Then my stepfather told me his story.

Aye, I get it. 2022 was one of the most difficult years of my life, if not the most. Even now, writing this, I struggle. Do I go with my grandfather's story or my stepfather's? Do I go back to the old me, standing alone so no one is able to disappoint me? Me against the world? Or do I look upon it with soft eyes and accept people as people with imperfections? Do I look upon myself and make myself harder to make myself better, or do I look upon myself with soft eyes and forgive myself for being human with human imperfections and frailties?

I've learned in my most difficult times, when I'm struggling with what to do and how to react, to reach out to my better angel, Mike, Papa Bear. I've pretty much learned to just do what he says when I can't let go of the anger. There are quite a few people and organizations I'd like to blast in a public forum, but Mike wouldn't approve.

But isn't 2022 the point? I'd say we all had a string of bad years. We have been traumatized and beat up. People aren't doing well. Mental health is deteriorating. The way people act and react may be completely out of character. Them disappointing us may be the best they can do.

I understand that as well. For a long time, I was the caregiver. At my lowest point in 2022, when I was begging for money, old friends reached out to me, not knowing my situation, and asked for help. They were in awful situations. Ugly. The old me would have helped. The current me was unable to do anything except wish them the best of luck and offer advice. One would reach back out to me. The other I never heard from again.

Never have expectations and you will never be disappointed.

That's an answer, but the wrong answer, I think. I think we need to be understanding and compassionate to others--and ourselves, not judge without knowing more. Then, if the negatives truly outweigh the positives, wish them the best and be on our way. We still need to remain open to possibilities though.

Aye, ya know, I'm still Philly. This isn't about rainbows shooting out of my ass, turning the other cheek, and putting on a robe and flip flops to follow the Dali Lama. There's still that one prick where one month said I saved his lab and the next month said I was too much of a risk for 60-day terms. Him, I wouldn't...

Okay, Papa Bear, I know.

I've been disappointed by many, both those I know and those I don't know. Hell, I was stood up on New Year's Eve without a word. That hurt. When I am already hurting. But I don't know her situation. I don't know how she interpreted what I may have said or done. No, I don't think I'll let her in any further, even if she does ever text me back, but I also know it cannot allow me to continue reaching out for opportunities. As I have said, I have met some truly wonderful people here who have enriched my life.

2022 was also the year I disappointed others. I don't want you to walk in my shoes to understand me. I would not want to put anybody through that. I've had a lot going on and have done the best I can.

It is really not about the others. It is about offering aloha to ourselves. Loving ourselves, being compassionate to ourselves, being merciful to ourselves. It is about not closing the door on opportunities.

It is about learning lessons from the right places and looking upon things with soft eyes. In this instance, it is about looking with soft eyes on a bar fight in Philadelphia.

Aloha.

***

I wonder what Mr. Williams, aka Sean Maguire, would say about this? In the movie, in his South Boston way, much like the Philly way, he talks about, and yells to the math professor, that it is a defense mechanism.

We isolate and make out group of friends small --if any-- to protect ourselves. I've done this all my life.

Now that I think about it, it really hit me when I was planning for my wedding. Who do I ask to be my best man? Who do I ask to be a part of my wedding party?

Think about it. It's the time to think about it. If you are unmarried, who is the best friend that will stand at your side? Who is the small circle of closest friends that will be in your wedding party?

At the time, it was my cat. Pretty. But that would have been kind of ridiculous. I had not been in touch with Dave in a long, long time and had not reconnected with Papa Bear yet.

My situation was simple because I think my soon to be wife was in the same situation as I was. We kept it simple because it had to be. Her maids of honor were her sister and daughter. My best men were by brother and brother-by-law--as he put it.

But then look upon the wedding. Who is invited? We decided to keep things small. Who do you invite to share in your joy? For me, it was mostly family and co-workers. For her, it was mostly co-workers and their plus ones.

I think it was about that time that I began to change, began listening to my stepfather's advice. I had been taught love and acceptance by my girlfriend/fiancé/wife/ex-wife. I reached out to Mike, Papa Bear, and renewed our relationship. Through Facebook, I reached out to many people from the old days.

I began to open myself again. I began being open to possibilities and potential, getting away from absolutes. I began being accepting of other people and began accepting myself. I learned not everybody is ideal for every situation. I learned that I am not ideal for every situation.

I still screwed up. By that time, I had made work my addiction, and made my family, old and new, my addiction. It left very little time to cultivate new possibilities.

I made a little bit of time. I cultivated and found relationships with my neighbors in Springfield and found an awesome group of loving and caring people. I had the incredible pleasure and pride of meeting their children and watching them grow into adults.

I reached out, and despite my mind screaming at me not to do it, I joined my high school reunion committee. Again, I found this amazing group of people, this amazing group of humans. Not perfect, but wonderful.

Reconnection was the theme of the new century.

Then, I went out and formed a national association for my industry and met many people. That is really when the unhealthy coping mechanisms began to show themselves, the lack of boundaries. I was already living the co-dependent's dream and the manageable addiction became unmanageable and I was swept into a deep ocean where I drowned. I think I understood Dave better.

It is about a bar fight, and it is also about setting healthy boundaries.

It is not about having no expectations.

It is about learning how to say, "no," and being accepting of when others say, "no" to you. It was not until the last few years that I am learning that particular lesson. It is about learning how to be disappointed and not falling into the absolute paradigm. It is about a balance sheet.

I have been talking about this for a long time, as taught to me by my stepfather. I've altered and adapted what he taught me and explained it to others. It's funny, but it is talking about being human by taking the humanity of it.

Rich was, and is, a big one for making lists. I think it is a main component of counseling as well. When faced with a tough decision, make a list. Pros and cons. I am sure you have all heard of this. Personally, I've never done a written list as I did it, though I should have.

Should I move to Philadelphia or Minnesota?

The same, I found, can be done for people. You can even assign values. Seriously. "Makes me smile" is plus 50. Bad drug habit is a negative 1,000. Being a perfectionist--which annoys the hell out of me, though I have been accused of it as well--is a negative 100.

Standing me up with no explanation is a negative 200. Being a family member is automatic plus 200 whether I want it to be or not.

The number you come up with puts the person on a spectrum, a chart if you will. Where do they fall? Except in rare, rare cases, it will not always be on the positive or negative extreme. It will be somewhere in the middle.

Pick your "acceptance." It can be anywhere along the spectrum, though I would suggest it not be too close to the extremes. Where the person falls, to use the wedding example, will determine whether they are your best man, part of the wedding party, part of the guest list, part of the "almost list if I could afford it," or part of the "not worth a stamp" list.

Mental illness, depression and defense mechanisms, want to force us into extremes for our own protection.

Thinking about it now, and remembering what I spoke about in a previous podcast, makes me realize something ironic. Deciding to end my life gave me the freedom to save my life.

I spoke about it before in regard to anxiety. When you truly make the commitment to commit suicide, as I did, the anxiety vanishes. What the hell is there to be anxious about?

When I truly made the commitment to commit suicide, what the hell is the point of having defense mechanisms.

The Suicide Therapy to prevent suicide? I very strongly do not recommend this. Learn from my mistakes and accomplishments instead. But seriously. When you truly make the commitment to take your life, there is no longer any need for anything.

2020 was my journey towards self-destruction. It really started in 2019, but let's just jump ahead. One last hurrah, I told myself, aka "Scent of a Woman," before I ended my life.

The path I meant to go down was completely at odds with the path I went. I am not quite sure what happened. I was alone and isolating, on purpose. As I traveled, there would be debauchery involved. But then this interesting thing happened. I began connecting.

There was still some debauchery, but even that led me to meet some incredible people that I connected with and am still in contact with. I found teachers. Absolutes were gone, out the window, and meaningless. Instead of hardening myself to what I was about to do, I opened myself to what could happen. Just as I opened myself to the United States and any road that presented itself as I drove close to 40,000 miles, I opened myself to the humans who populate it.

Okay, okay. It was a secret but, now, for this episode, I am revealing the secret. Many might find the secret not to their liking, even repulsive, but it is what I did. It is also the natural evolution of this podcast. Keep an open mind.

I am not making excuses as I still find the idea attractive, and it bears a lot of weight into my current mode of thinking and this podcast. I will not apologize.

As my marriage and business partnership were crumbling, and with the simple fact that I had not had simple human intimate contact in years, I stumbled across certain websites.

Yes, this is difficult to write, to reveal. And there is a part of me that demands I state the simple truth, that I never once cheated on my wife. I never even thought about it. I simply closed myself off to those types of feelings and buried them. In isolating myself, I closed myself off to one of the things that could help heal me: touch. Not sex, as that didn't really work all that well anyway, but touch.

When I separated, I started going to the strip clubs again where I met a wonderful young woman who gave me the idea to explore what is called "alternative dating" websites.

I checked them out and became a member.

Mutually beneficial relationships.

Did I mention it is hard writing about this? It is not that I am embarrassed. It is more that the people who know me might not approve or understand. But it is time to open up about it because the idea of mutually beneficial relationships changed my life and potentially saved my life.

...I almost just deleted all of this, but I am going to keep going because it is important.

I would go on to use the idea in business lectures, cajoling businesses into sponsoring my nonprofit association. Mutually beneficial relationships. I just never explained where the concept came from. The concept pops up often now in my personal philosophy and ideas about mental wellness. Are you in mutually beneficial relationships? It is not about sex. It is about everything from your business relationships to your friendships to your intimate relationships.

Yes, the websites can be exactly what you think. In fact, I'd guess that 90% of the woman on there are exactly what you think. Escorts. There is a deeper level, though.

When my friend introduced me to the website, she knew me. Knew who I was and what I needed. She knew it was not just about sex for me. She explained that a close friend of hers had been involved in a relationship from the site for years. I dove deeper in looking for that 10%. It turned out to be a lot like dating.

I learned a lot from another person I met on another site, an escort site. Kate was an incredible teacher. I included a podcast that she did, below, when she was invited to be a guest on the podcast and discuss her role as an escort/companion.

One little lie, she explained, leads to a whole bunch of truth. The money exchanged create a boundary and expectations, which was really ideal for someone like me, who had no idea what boundaries were and had very little experience in communicating my expectations and needs. It was baby steps, first grade, towards educating myself.

Kate was one of the college professors I met.

Companions like Kate offer, and prefer, longer dates. Our initial meet surprised the hell out of me. No money. Just a meet for breakfast and coffee, and she was in her gym clothes. She was very particular in who she met, and she wanted to get to know me more before we went out on our date, which included dinner and some really great conversation.

A little lie for a lot of truth.

The lie is the money. The truth is real. Because of the boundaries and up-front expectations we had set, I could tell her anything. She explained that many of her clients just want to talk. I did not believe her either, but it made sense and why would she lie?

When I began my journey across America, I had planned on taking my profile down from the website. Someone I had met, though, suggested I keep it up and just change the location. Meet women for coffee. I did.

It was expensive cups of coffee, but I did meet some exceptional women, along with some duds. Like I said, it really is just like dating. I even met some women that had far more money that I did, who were on the site just because of the boundaries and expectations. They were tired of meeting the duds on the regular dating sites.

Yeah, I am still shying away from a lot of it. I think that is enough truth for today. I will, however, be listening to Kate's interview again. You should listen to it. There is so much relationship wisdom in it. Maybe that is my next podcast?

Aloha

Kate Interview:

http://itsjustbanter.com/2020/06/09/episode-678-2/

Episode 28: Rectifying a Disservice

Well, I'm a mess right now. I'm in the middle of a cross country move and it's hard to focus on a four-thousand-word script for the podcast let alone record it. Instead of skipping, I wanted to do something that I know I can do and something that I need to do.

After 27 episodes, I keep referring to two of them most often. This week will be a repeat of Episode 5: The Mental Health Triangle, with a special introduction--though I am not sure if I can record it and add. I'll see.

This is all a journey. As such, I am evolving and noticing things from previous episodes and the way I think about things. I realize that I have been doing a disservice to those struggling with bipolar disorder.

In a video I posted, I talk about not being afraid of mental illness. In my podcasts, though, I talk about how bipolar disorder scares the living hell out of me. My mom had it, so it triggers me. The thing to keep in keep in mind, that I need to keep in mind, is it is from way back when, when it was still called Manic Depression.

If I combine my thoughts on Manic Depression with Episode 5, it reveals a different picture and a different perspective.

With my mom, we are talking 1970's and 1980's here. She was an extreme example but also never treated properly. Back then, the thought, that was even expressed by a doctor, was, "give up your kids and go live on a farm so you are away from all stressors and triggers."

Meds were her only form of treatment. There was the lithium until it began damaging her organs and then a cocktail that I don't think they ever got right. As far as I know, there was no talk therapy and there was no self-help.

I always wonder what could have been. My mom was a mental giant, with an IQ far surpassing genius level. It was only until much, much later in her life that her social worker set her up with a volunteer job. I saw such a huge increase in her quality of life. What would it have been like if she had been engaged in the world, working, living, getting proper therapy and had access to the meds and therapies available now.

Yes, I talk about myself and what I know: Major Depression, PTSD, Anxiety Disorder and Childhood Trauma. I know very little about Bipolar Disorder. What I do know about it is a warped perception, the point of view of a child living with someone who was not under proper care.

Just as the Business Production Triangle I talk about in Episode 5 can be applied to any business, I feel that my Mental Health Triangle can be applied to any mental illness. Even if you or someone you know is suffering from one of the more severe forms of a mental illness, know that there is hope. There are treatment options. We are witnessing a renaissance in mental health medications and therapies that offer far more than what I, and my mom, experienced.

I just read an article about a new medication for bipolar disorder that offers a lot of hope.

So, with my apologies, let's return to episode 5...

Episode 5: The Mental Health Triangle

Episode 29: Let's Have a Chat

The return to Philadelphia was as expected: hectic, crazy but exciting. I'm sticking with Plan A and reposting Episode 17: The Tangled Path to Communication, with a special introduction.

It's appropriate. And, I found, necessary. I'll be answering the same questions many, many times. I don't mind, but it would really help if you read the damn book. Or listened to the podcast.

The answers to many questions can be summed up as, "That's episode 14. That's 7. Hell, that's episode 1."

Like I said, I understand you not understanding. For many, it is very difficult to wrap your mind around such a distortion of reality that is mental illness. But the simple fact is that when I left home in July of 2020, it was for a grand adventure. The ultimate goal was to finish the journey and then find a nice quiet place to kill myself.

I was in the midst of a massive depressive episode that I hid very, very well. I was, and maybe still am, a highly functioning depressive--there is an entire episode about that.

I'm working on things. Things are going well. I hope to never be where I was emotionally and mentally ever again and I am doing the things I need to ensure that.

But that is where I was. Where my head was. The place where I was influenced everything that I did. It is why I gave everything away, spent all my money, ruined my credit, and really had a damn good time. Without having to worry about tomorrow, I had a freedom and sanity that I had never experienced.

Then, tomorrow became a possibility and that's when things got very difficult. I struggled and then crashed in Texas and then made my way to Tijuana where I really began healing. Then, I broke my ankle.

I'm in a good spot now. A great spot, though you may not know by looking at it. I'll share where I am typing this and recording this another time.

But I do want to get back to talking about it, and listening, communicating with someone struggling. As I talk about in episode 17, the path to a person's personal hell may be paved with the best of intentions. Sometimes, the best you can do for a person is not to try to help.

I also wanted to talk about the other side of things, of the people struggling who are reaching out. Just as we need to understand that people may not understand us and may have no idea or understanding of where we are at, we cannot possibly know where the people are at that we are reaching out to.

Maybe we have found someone who does understand. Maybe we have found that net of people who love and care about us that we can reach out to. Maybe we reach out...and they are not there. Or it seems like they are not there.

They are. It must come down to faith.

Our struggle puts us into a very vulnerable and perhaps selfish place, a place that is super focused on us and where we are at. We reach out to no reply, or not the reply that we have come to expect.

The cascade of thoughts is bound to occur. That we are a burden, became too much of a burden, that they have discarded us, that our net lost strands and knots and some of the safety.

It may not be the case.

Perhaps, the people we are reaching out to are struggling as well. We need to push beyond our tiny space, expand into the wider net, and have trust and faith.

It is all about communicating.

And with that, Episode 17.

Episode 17: The Tangled Path to Listening

Episode 30: A Momentary Lapse of Balance

Like LL Cool J said in "Momma Said Knock you Out," don't call it a comeback!

It's been a while longer than I wanted, but I'm back with a new episode. I need to post a new episode. I'm not really there yet to post one, as I am still unsettled and things are chaotic, but I know a part of being unsettled is that I am losing balance. I am hoping the episode will help me regain at least a little bit of it.

It was nothing I did not expect. The entire transcontinental move and then settling back into the Philadelphia area with next to nothing meant I was going to slam into all of my triggers. I knew I was going to have to push aside the side of me, this, that kept me balanced as I focused on building balance--if that makes sense.

The thing I was not expecting was how okay I was going to be with everything. I was terrified of moving back here. It was like walking into a room barefoot with loaded mousetraps strewn about the floor. Would I be okay, or would I run for refuge in the closet?

There were a few trips to the closet, but it turns out I was okay. Overwhelmed, I did a little bit of backsliding, found some refuge in working too much, but even that was okay. I'm still feeling overwhelmed. I'm still feeling the pull to work too much, escape in that. But the big question was answered.

I'm okay.

I was able to bring with me the lessons I learned while I was away, lessons about balance and boundaries. Lessons about the net and positivity. Lessons about how it is okay about standing still in certain parts of my life without feeling stuck, that it is only a momentary situation that I will move past.

Now, let's get into the episode.

The drive did not start off well. I left Tijuana, made it across the border, and drove a few hours into California. With the sun rising, I made my first stop at a rest area to take some pictures and stretch my legs.

I got back into the car...and it wouldn't start. Nothing. Nada. Dead in the water--or on the highway. A guy pulled up next to me with my hood popped and I asked him for a jump. He nodded and walked around to look at things.

"I'm a mechanic," he said. "Want some advice?"

"Sure," I replied.

"Your next stop has to be an auto parts store. That battery is dead and needs to be replaced. You won't make it very far. You can have it checked out, clean the connectors, check the cables, but the battery is bulging. That means it's shot."

He got my car started and I changed my GPS from Austin to AutoZone.

That's really where my story changes, where I had an inkling that things were different. The old me would have been pissed off, maybe kicked the car, definitely cursed Murphy and Murphy's law, and maybe whined a little bit about the unfairness of the Universe. Aye, I was broke and starting a cross country trip. The last thing I needed was to replace my car battery.

That's not what happened. I just shrugged and accepted it. I owned it. It was not about the universe being unfair or Murphy's Law. It was completely about me not having my car checked out before I left, not spending the extra time and money to make sure the car was in tip top shape for the journey as I had always done. It had sat in Tijuana pretty much unused for about nine months. What the hell did I expect?

So, after a stop at AutoZone, and $220, I was back on my way. It was a great day for a drive, the music was playing, and I was completely back in my comfort zone. I had a long drive through a desert to look forward to. Instead of being miserable, I just accepted what I had done wrong, and was able to look forward to the trip, something I knew I would enjoy.

While hoping the tires would hold up.

No, the beginning of the journey had not started off well. But it had in a way.

Practice what you preach. I preach regularly about attitude. I really do believe that a healthier lifestyle begins and ends with the right attitude. For many years, decades, I had had a pretty shitty attitude. Murphy's Law, the universe was against me, life was more unfair to me than others, etc. My life had reflected that. I had learned things and was finally putting them into practice. I was learning it made a difference.

Tijuana had been a refuge of sorts, an oasis. As one friend put it, it was fantasy land. It was like what my mom was told a very long time ago, to give up her kids, and life in general, and go and live on a farm where there were not any triggers.

My world in Tijuana had become very small, even more so after I broke my ankle. It was a tiny, safe place, living in an apartment complex that was open on the inside with a courtyard. I couldn't do anything so didn't do anything. Beyond crutching my way around the corner for groceries, I could sit in my chair and indulge my fantasies.

Yeah, there was the entire lack of funds things, but I was okay. I settled into a routine where I could play at a job search and switching careers, be a writer and concentrate on my book and podcast. All my triggers, life, existed outside of the oasis. I found simpler routines, simpler ways of doing things, simpler ways of existing. I found a certain kind of freedom and health completely restricted inside of an oasis that was about a square quarter mile.

I knew that things were happening in the outside world, and that I would eventually have to engage in it, but, for a while, I could exist completely inside of the moment. The question became: could I carry it with me outside of the oasis?

At a rest stop in California, I had the idea that I could. I was still carrying a part of the oasis with me, as long drives are my sanctuary and peace, but I was heading to something. First: Austin. Friends and house sitting for a few days after an 18-hour drive through sunshine with the music playing.

Then, there would be another 24-hour drive back to Philadelphia, the place I had run away from. There would be bills to pay, a company to get started, a home to find and settle into, and more complex routines and a much more complicated life.

Could I take the lessons I had learned about balance and boundaries and build an oasis, a refuge, while I reintegrated into life? Could I find peace while being at rest?

I made it back to Philly, where I immediately slammed into all of my triggers. There was a lack of funds, struggling to find a home, the pull towards my drug of choice, co-dependency, and the pull towards my other escapes from the world.

I was Dorothy again, "Lions and tiger and bears oh my!"

I can really get into that, my sense of humor slamming into Philly: "Lions and tiger and bears oh my! Lions and tiger and bears oh my!" Me in my Irish cap, skipping along a golden, cobbled street. Then stumbling to an abrupt end where the cobblestone street had been stolen. --Some guy actually did steal a few blocks of a cobblestone street here. A golden one would be gone in no time.

Anyway...

Instead of being terrified, though, with the lions and tigers crouching along my path and the bears whuffing not too far from off the tree line, a new theme entered the composition. There was a harmony to the discord. There was, well, Will Smith.

Yeah, I watched the clip of the movie a half dozen times at least, about the field, about looking upon it with soft eyes as opposed to a dragon to slay. Instead of a turbulent storm, I found myself drifting into a harbor, typing up my Subaru Outback filled with most of my life's belongings inside, and disembarking into my new reality. I got to work.

There were things to do, lots of things to do. There were pressures from outside and within.

Aye, right now, as I type this, there is the thought in the back of my mind to run away. First, a pitstop in Austin. Then, a run down to Tijuana. I even have the justifications for it. I can justify anything. Hell, I even just got a reminder that my many, many American Airline miles are about to expire, and I have to do something with them.

But, I'm not. The stuff in Austin can wait. I'll visit my friends and oasis in Tijuana when it is okay to do so.

For now, I am looking upon things with soft eyes.

Dragons popped up all over the new landscape. Big, terrible things, gouging the earth with their massive claws, crouched, prepared for battle. I looked upon them with soft eyes...and they disappeared.

No, there are no dragons to slay. But there is work to be done.

The first choice, the toughest choice, was this. The podcast. I was able to stumble through a couple of repeat episodes while I was in Austin. When I returned to Philly, though, I knew I would have to put away the laptop for a while. I just still haven't learned the trick of sitting down in a coffee shop, or garage, and allowing my mind to unfold and fly through the wilderness of thoughts and ideas.

The laptop became, as it had to be, a thing of work and work projects. I had investors to consider and a business to build. The birthing of Axiom Orthodontic Studios became my goal that I had to focus on. Without the other things in place, like a home, I had to allow myself to stumble away from balance and fully into that realm of existence.

I had to stumble back into the thing that had dominated my life for a long, long time. I had to start working again.

But isn't that what balance is all about? Isn't that what I am all about? It is not about existing on a farm, in an oasis. It is about creating a harmony in balance among all of the things going on around me, among all of the things I need to get done.

In creation, there is chaos.

I needed a place to set up my coffee maker.

I needed to relearn how to use QuickBooks.

When I was in Tijuana, I got into a very weird sleep schedule. I'd go to bed around 9-10, wake up between 4 and 5, write, and then nap for a few hours around 8. I swore I was just on east coast time. I'd get back into a normal sleeping habit once I was back.

Nope.

For over a month now, I would open the laptop and go directly to the work partition. Do not pass GO, collect the $200, and get your ass to work. Aye, you try building a business from scratch. The coffee flowed and I got done what I needed to get done.

Building the business is much like life I have found. Or at least it is that way for me. You need the foundation in place, a strong foundation. The devil is in the details. The imps and demons are in the feedback that forces me to go back and adjust the foundation. Tinker here, nudge there, rip up and start over in places.

It's done. I did just write, "for the most part," but I deleted it. No, it's done. The foundation is in place, and it is a strong foundation. There is just a little bit of waiting and some fine tuning to do on the structure built upon the foundation.

My home is the same. I found a nice little place in Ridley Park, outside of Philly, in an old Victorian home. It is not as grand as I once had, nor as secluded as I had in Tijuana, but the foundation is in place. Rent is paid, the coffee maker is set up, I have a bed, and I even added a few odds and ends, the necessities that I need to be comfortable.

Like with the business, I write "It is done" and want to add, "for the most part." But, like with the business, that's not true. It is done, the foundation is built, and now I just have some fine tuning to do with the structure I built on the foundation. In my case, it means hitting the "purchase" button on the things I picked out on Amazon when I get my next check.

Now what the hell do I do?

The undertow is so damn strong. The old Chris is rising up and screaming, "It's not done! It's not finished! Everything needs to be in place before you even attempt any more steps forward! That business needs to up, running, and turning a profit in record time!"

That's exactly what enfolded me and consumed me yesterday. On a Sunday, I did what I promised I would not do anymore: I worked. But the video needed to be made? I had to tinker with the website a little bit more.

That's when Bryan stepped in. He gives me the gentlest kicks in the ass I have ever received. He is a friend, that I am supposedly not allowed to call a friend. My brother, Mr. Business, says he is a business partner and that is it.

He keeps nudging me in the oddest ways, ways that are unexpected. See, he knows me, knows my past and knows all about this podcast. He knows my journey and probably understands it better than most.

He is also my lead business partner, the one who got the other investors on board that persuaded me to return to Philly. The business needs to be self-sustaining soon, quicker than most start-ups. This is what he does, this is what he depends upon and is expecting from me. He, of all people, should appreciate the time and effort I put into the business on a Sunday, the time and effort of waking up at 4 AM and starting work.

"So," he asked me yesterday, "get to work on the new podcast yet? It's important."

He's right. He knows that he is right. I know that he is right.

I told the old Chris to go scratch his ass this morning, grab some coffee, and leave me the hell alone. I ignored the Axiom partition of my laptop, opened up the podcast portion, and got back to work on this.

One of my goals for the day is to find the cords I need to hook up the microphone. After some more coffee, after another nap, after I get some work done on Axiom. It will get done. This will be recorded and uploaded.

Thanks, Bryan.

I've been unbalanced, only making brief forays into the things that will balance me. It hasn't been enough, and I have been feeling the effects. By only making brief forays, by allowing myself to drift too far into my old ways, I've been feeling the gathering pressure towards unhealthy things.

I've been looking at my airline miles often, wondering about a quick drive, escape, down to Austin, feeling the pull that makes the "fine tunings" into necessities. I've been sitting at night wondering what to do with myself, lost. When I am not lost.

I am exactly where I need to be.

Yeah, I have work to do.

As discussed, and agreed upon by Bryan when I accepted his offer, work now has to become the Monday through Friday, 9-5, that I have on my website and in my "terms and conditions." It is all about sales now and processing orders. There is not a single person I can reach out to at 4 to 5 AM.

I need to dive back into my groups, the mental health groups and others on social media. It is where a lot of my ideas come from for this podcast. The smallest comments or posts trigger something or another and the next thing I know, I have a few thousand words for the podcast.

I need to get back into Instagram. It was always a fun way to start my day when I was in Tijuana. I follow a few people that post videos of themselves doing things they love to do. There is a dancer and choreographer in South Korea, a dancer in England, a skateboarder somewhere or another and a motorcycle wanderer based in Sweden. I always enjoyed starting my day by watching their latest posts. I got away from that somehow.

I need to figure out what to do with myself between 7 PM and bedtime, always my witching hours.

I need to get back on that journey towards balance and integrating the lessons I learned in my oasis into my new life.

Yeah, there is an entire other podcast here. I feel as though as I am just wading into the surf and not diving in.

There was an epic battle last night, Friday night. It took place in a very comfortable chair in my office as I sipped coffee. Without even realizing it, the dragons had come out. I tried looking upon them with soft eyes, but they didn't go away.

It was Friday night, the end of the official work week! 7 PM. The apartment is done, the work stuff was done until Monday. What the hell do I do with myself? How do I live?

I sat in my chair and thought about things. I had money in my pocket. I crave human interaction and companionship. There were places to go that were only short drives. How the hell do I do this living thing? It was so much easier in Tijuana, in my oasis. In my fantasy land, where I was restricted with where I could go and no money in my pocket.

Mind if I switch metaphors? Those dragons that I could not get to go away became sea serpents. Sitting in my nice comfy chair, I was standing shoulder deep in the surf on a bad day with a very strong undertow. Battle was joined as I sipped my coffee.

I remember these days from long ago. Just about ten miles away in another apartment in Havertown. Wait. Just wait. Hold off the undertow until midnight or 1 AM. That's it.

I'd lose most of those battles.

I sipped more coffee as I considered it.

I know that one of the most important things I learned, that I am still trying to integrate into my life, is patience. I know and realize that those sea serpents are not only ready for battle, but I am ready for the battle for something to do. I want them to pull me under and drag me far out to sea. It was so easy back then to allow the undertow to drag me out, let go and join in battle. Indulge in my unhealthy escapes.

That's where I screwed up my life.

Yes, I laugh about how the Universe got tired of screwing around with me so broke my ankle on purpose to force me to learn patience.

Patience is key. It is kind of necessary when you have a broken ankle and no money. But what about when you have money in your pocket and are mobile? That's what I sat in my chair and considered.

It is so easy now to not exercise patience and restraint, to be impatient. To indulge in those unhealthy escapes, lie to myself, justify it, and say it is only to pass the time until the right thing comes along. What I have learned, though, is that the right things are blocked from coming along by the unhealthy things.

Bryan talked to me about it. Even in recovery, it is still so damn hard to get off the roller coaster. --sorry, I need to introduce another metaphor. Most of the healthy people and groups of people don't want to have anything to do with the roller coaster. If the roller coaster is all that you know, though, it is hard to get off, difficult to learn more and healthier ways to live. Staying on the roller coaster is the path of least resistance.

Now I'm about to channel Al Pacino in "Scent of a Woman." I'll paraphrase as I don't want to look up the exact words.

"I knew, without exception, the right paths to take. I never took them. It was hard. Too damn hard. Now, Charlie is at a crossroads..."

I am at the crossroads. I know the right path to take. I choose patience.

It really was an epic battle. I guess you had to be there.

I sipped my coffee, ignored the undertow and sea serpents, played around on my phone for a bit, and then went to bed. I guess you can make forward progress when sitting in a comfortable chair.

I know tonight will be easier. A little bit at least. You see, that is something else I have learned. Getting started down the right path is difficult as hell, even when it is clear and visible. The early going can be a real pain in the ass. Once I do get started, though, once I make it past that initial stretch, it gets easier. Maybe I'll work on my book tonight? It is a project I have been meaning to dive back into.

So, Bryan and Mr. Pacino, this podcast is for you.

With that, it's a wrap for this episode.

Aloha.

Episode 31: The Illusion of Absence

Rob Thomas did it again. I really need to talk to him about that. Anybody know how I can get in touch with him? I like his solo work and his album, "The Great Unknown," has been something I have been playing a lot recently.

Certain lyrics just come out and grab me. If they have the right music behind them, it creates a theme in my mind, a starting point for me to wander down my own paths. Some of Rob's songs have created guard rails and direction signs on those paths.

With other conversations I have been having, and things I have been thinking about, that's been happening again. A song and the lyrics create the structure to an answer to a very basic question: why do we stay in bad relationships?

The relationships can be with people or things. "Bad relationships" is a spectrum, not a black or white thing. It can be an extreme, like staying in an abusive relationship, or it can be a not so abusive relationship, like why I still follow the University of Miami football program.

We have choices. But Rob gives me a hint at the answer in, "Absence of Affection."

"In the absence of affection, we'll take anything and call it love..."

Now, let's get into the episode.

It's the absence of affection that drew me to many places that I shouldn't have gone throughout my life. It was absence of affection that kept me in places and situations I should not have stayed.

I've heard the horror stories. The physical and mental abuse. I don't have any of those stories. I did brush up against one a long time ago, but it was only a faint brush. No, my people, places and situations were more mild, more mundane. They were unhealthy all the same. Places I should not have stayed. So why did I?

Rob hints at the answer in his song, "The Absence of Affection."

The Great Unknown is the album title and that points at the answer as well. I got comfortable in the known, set up house and set up shop. I settled in and bought myself a nice, comfy chair and set up my coffee maker. It got to the point where I would not even look out the windows into the great unknown.

The unknown can be a scary place. It so much safer to stay in the known, so much easier, comfortable. I can fully understand and appreciate why a person will stay in a relationship where they are being beaten and abused.

I know the other side as well, the frustration and anger with a friend or loved one who stays there. I know my friends and family know the frustration. But I have also learned that the known can be such a powerful force to hold a person in place.

Someone pointed out to me that I very rarely talk about my marriage in these podcasts. I guess that it is time to do it. I will not bash her or the marriage, or even the institution of marriage. It was just a situation where I should not have stayed in, simple as that. I stayed and I own that.

I still feel the pull towards something like that, as I sit in my home at night, alone, there is the pull to be together with somebody. There is the pull to be a part of something. It is about the absence of affection. It is about the illusion of the absence of affection, but I'll be getting into that later.

To my friends and family: stop it! Seriously. Stop it.

With my ex-wife or others, they hate it when I sound apologetic for people they perceive treated me badly. They can get pretty vicious about it. That alone can circle back into the "illusion" of the "the illusion of the absence of affection."

But just stop it. She was not a bad person; she was just the way she was and I was the way I was. I accepted it and I own it. The ending of our marriage was one of the most amicable splits that I have ever had. Hell, it was more friendly than when I asked my business partner for a divorce about the same time. He stopped talking to me. Tracy and I, after a few days, still slept in the same bed for months while we tried to sell the house.

But our marriage ended long before I asked her for a divorce. Years before. We both knew it. It wasn't healthy for either of us. Why did she stay in it? Why did I stay in it? It was probably something that should never have been. I'm not going to go back that far though. I think I already covered it in other episodes, about the red flags that I saw and ignored, the orange cones I drove through until I ended up in a ditch.

But I remember specifically driving over railroad tracks. We're in the car going to the last and final home that we would eventually buy, after looking at about 80-90 of them. I remember the pressures inside of my head. Maybe it was the railroad tracks on Route 1 going to Chadds Ford that shook the thoughts loose and made them rise up to the top of my head.

"What the hell are you doing? You are going to look at a house that you cannot afford, in an area where the taxes are insane, for a "turnkey" house that may be turnkey for her but is not for you. You don't need to buy a new house. You need to get a divorce."

But I looked at my lovely, beautiful wife, smiling, thought of vows I had spoken about forever and for better or for worse, smothered the thoughts, and went and bought the house.

Friends and family: stop it. Just stop it. I know. But aye, the co-dependency was in full swing, there was the illusion of affection beyond in the great unknown, and I was comfortable.

"Okay," I said to her before we signed the final papers, "we really can't afford the house. To be able to afford it, we need to live house poor for at least a few years while we catch up on our bills. Then, we'll be okay."

She agreed.

Then, we bought the house, poured tons of money into the turnkey home, and went on a few very expensive vacations.

The pressures began to build. The patch I had put on the emptiness inside of me began to tatter and fray. Everything began forcing me to look out into the great unknown from my nice comfy chair. The depression began to build and pull me further into the emptiness.

I didn't know what the hell to do so I grabbed on to the known and comfortable. The terror of falling into that vast emptiness made me grab onto any lifeline that I could find.

We all know the story of the guy hanging on the crumbling cliff face, so he grabs at a tuft of grass or a slight branch that would never support his weight for long. But he grabs anyway. I grabbed. Then, I fell into the emptiness.

What I did not see at the time were the strong heavy ropes, the ladders and slings, hell, the hammocks and life vests that were all around me with the rescue helicopters circling overhead.

I fell deeper into the depression, into an unhealthy marriage, and an unhealthy business partnership.

A soundtrack entered the emptiness. No, not Rob Thomas, though his older album, his first solo work, Something to Be, was somewhere in the background.

This is where irony really comes into play. It truly breaks my heart, but my daughter does not speak to me. He birthday just passed. I was around for quite a few of them and she was my daughter, and I was her father. For one of my birthdays, or maybe Christmas, she bought me tickets to see a band that I had started listening to. The X Ambassadors.

As I have mentioned in past episodes, I hate being that kid with the mix tape. The scene from the movie, Almost Famous, where Kate gives her brother the album and says, "listen to the words," makes me squirm.

But it is what it is.

I went to the concert with my wife, with the tickets my daughter had bought me, and the X Ambassadors slammed into my mind. They shattered the illusion of being comfortable. They made me look at my beautiful wife, with the soundtrack and theme of their concert enveloping me, and I knew the marriage was over and I had to ask her for a divorce.

It would still take a couple years.

Aye, I had made vows. I had built a life. Things were not terrible. There was no abuse, no cheating that I know of, and there were not even any arguments. That was part of the problem. There should have been a lot of arguments. But there was...nothing. I conditioned myself to be comfortable with that.

In the absence of affection, we'll take anything and call it love.

I would still mouth the words, peck her on the cheek before I left for work, kiss her when I got home with her shying away from me because I stank of cigarette smoke, but did I still mean them? Yes, I did.

And that was a part of the problem. I got the feeling that she didn't. I got the feeling that I was beyond invisible, that I was an annoyance.

Then, the depression really started to hammer me, and it hammered my thoughts and feelings into those weird shapes that only have one end.

What the hell was I sticking around for? We had gone to counseling a few times and that was pointless. Neither of us were going to change into the person we had hoped for when we got married and were just drifting further and further apart. I tell people that it might have been easier if there had been abuse, cheating or throw down fights. But it just...was.

In the absence of affection, we'll take anything and make ourselves comfortable there. I became invisible, even to myself. I did not exist. Other people existed in my place. The masks I wore, the costumes, became my identity. I was a husband, father, son-in-law, brother-in-law, business partner, son, uncle, brother, cousin and a few other things. I wasn't Chris anymore. It all took effort and exhausted me. With no Chris, no identity, there was nothing to recharge my batteries or refill the tank.

By not being seen, I was disappearing.

Is that one of the reasons why people stay in unhealthy relationships? There is the great unknown and, even if there is something awful going on, at least you are being seen? At least there is the tuft of grass.

But then there was the X Ambassadors with their song Renegade. They were not yelling at me or screaming at me, even though the concert was pretty loud. It was just a simple statement. Let go.

I finally did.

My wife made it easier. I was struggling, battling the depression and the exhaustion. My identities were becoming heavier and heavier. I started to do something about it. I set things in motion to sell my business. I knew it was going to be hard, though. A tough year. I kept grasping at new tufts of grass as the ones I was hanging by pulled free.

I found a buyer for my half of the business I had built, the baby I had cared for and grown that had so much potential and so many possibilities. I told my business partner I was divorcing him. He stopped talking to me. I had to tighten my belt.

I went to Tracy. A final tuft of grass. The slimmest of branches. I didn't want to. I was already invisible. It would mean becoming visible again, vulnerable. But hadn't I been there for her when she quit her job and switched careers? Didn't I offer to pay all the bills while she rebuilt something? So, I asked.

"It's going to be a tough year. Very little money. I'm going to need your help with my share of bills." I didn't add that the 50/50 split of the bills had been absurd for years.

She looked at me, saw me, and quickly replied. "Why should I help a failing business?"

Then, she went on vacation. Two of them. I went and wiped out my 401k.

I not only let go, but I also configured myself for maximum velocity towards the bottom. Straight as an arrow, arms tucked to my side, eyes wide with the wind ripping tears from my face. I was not only headed towards the bottom, but I welcomed it. Wanted it to hit faster and harder.

The X Ambassadors would create the soundtrack, or theme, of the descent. A descent into the void, into darkness and depression. I didn't care. A lot of their songs became interwoven in the darkness. They released many singles and I just kept adding them to my playlist. Many of them meant something to me.

If "Renegades" was the opening song to the soundtrack of my fall, then their song "Hold Me Down" was the closing theme.

It was on their second full album. After I asked for a divorce, I started taking vacations because I didn't give a shit about money or anything else anymore. I was in Chicago to see them again, alone this time. There is a story about the entire experience in my book. Disconnected: An Odyssey Through Covid America.

"Hold Me Down" is a song about a guy who sees someone. The person is invisible, but he sees her, and he'll be there for her to help hold her down, help keep her from flying apart. I had been that guy for a long time, holding everybody else down. Now, I was that person who needed holding down. I was standing alone in the middle of a crowd of people, listening to the band that had crafted the soundtrack to my descent, my crisis.

Tears welled up inside of me. I crushed them out and had another drink. After the song was over, I was able to get back to enjoying the show.

It was not only the X Ambassadors that were telling me to let go, but it was also friends and family. They were all relived when I asked Tracy for a divorce, but, like I said, that took time. In between the concert and the actual asking, I started looking around me at their relationships, at my friendships that I had built over a lifetime. I even began looking at my daughter's relationship with her new boyfriend that she would eventually move in with and then marry.

I began seeing something that was so very different than what I had with Tracy. I saw friendships and connections. I saw healthy boundaries. I saw balanced relationships. What really struck me was the friendships that I had ignored since marrying Tracy, that I began exploring again. I was welcomed back.

That is when it really hit me. My life partner was not my friend. Maybe we began that way, or maybe it was just that first flush of the relationship and getting to know each other. But after that first flush, after the usual acceptance of everything that is overshadowed by that first flush, the honeymoon period, I realized there was no sustainability.

I knew it. I saw it. But I was so damn comfortable. It was nice and safe going home to somebody every night. There were also the other unhealthy situations in my life that compounded the problem and forced me into a very tightly, focused world. I was a co-dependent and a workaholic. It gave me a tunnel vision to see, and only see, a very beautiful and lovely wife, who was accomplished and extraordinary.

Were we ever truly friends?

I don't think so. Looking back, I began asking very simple questions of myself and others: "why is water wet?" What is friendship? What is love? What is balance and mutually beneficial relationships? What are healthy boundaries?

But it was so damn safe and comfortable, and there was the age thing. I had built a life. My relationship with my business partner and my wife spanned my 30's and 40's.

I had started my life over a few times. As I talk about, it was easy when I was young but grew harder as I got older. Now, I was looking at the end of my 40's, with 50 around the corner. I was also looking at an exhaustion that seeped deep inside of my core, into everything that I had and was. There was nothing left, nothing to pour into a rebuilding or reshaping.

So, I let go, not with the intent to fly, but with every intent of hitting bottom. I welcomed it, welcomed a passing into the next world, into the end of exhaustion. Yes, the plan was to commit suicide after one last adventure.

There was nobody to hold me down. That was okay now.

I had the best time of my life. That free fall was glorious. Rob Thomas, the X Ambassadors, and a hundred other artists created a playlist for me as I reveled in the open road and freedom, at the absence of masks and identities.

And that is about when all of you people that love and care about me, my friends and family, really began to piss me off. Even chance, wonderful encounters began to intrude and piss me off.

Justine, this fantastic lady I met when I first got separated, really annoyed the living hell out of me.

I had a plan! It was a good plan! I was finally free of the unhealthy relationships. The exhaustion was not replaced by anything like hope, but the contact and interactions I had with people began to point towards other things beyond "The End." They started to point towards the next chapter. They started to point towards things I could learn, things that could help me establish boundaries and healthy relationships.

They started to point towards the wider field. They started to point towards what was wrong about the line from the Rob Thomas song. "In the absence of affection, we'll take anything and call it love."

That's about when Sara entered my life. She taught me the idea of being intimate with myself and caused me to look without tunnel vision towards the bottom, and to open my damn eyes to the wider field, the wider world.

I'm gloriously free falling, reveling in it, and then I see a net below me. Not the rocky bottom I wanted.

Shit.

You may have seen it at the beginning of the podcast. I know it now but did not know it then.

The tunnel vision and the depression caused me to see only one thing while making me miss the wider truth. There was never, ever, an absence of affection. There was never, ever, a time where I was not seen, when I was invisible. There was never, ever, a lack of options.

Now that I think about it, as I type this, it is like the old joke.

***

Floodwaters came and a man was trapped inside of his house. A boat came by, to rescue the man, and the man replied, "I'm staying. God will save me."

The flood waters continued to rise, and another boat came by. The man replied, "I'm staying. God will save me."

The flood waters rose even more, and the man climbed onto the roof of his house. A helicopter came by. The man called out, "I'm fine. God will save me."

The flood waters continued to rise, the man was swept away, and he drowned. He appeared before God and prostrated himself.

"God," he said, "I do not understand. I am a good and pious man. I lived a good life in your service. Why didn't you save me?"

God replied, "I sent you two boats and helicopter. What else did you want Me to do?"

***

Yes, God speaks with a Philly accent.

But that is what I missed, and what I think a lot of people miss. I was holding onto the tufts of grass and the slimmest branches. They pull free and I grab onto another. Did I mention there is another X Ambassadors song about Indiana Jones?

The depression, and all of my other issues, created this tunnel vision. I wanted to be seen and loved by this one person. I needed this one person to complete me and validate me. So, I held on, exhausting myself reaching for tufts of grass and the slimmest of branches.

What I failed to notice were the helicopters circling. It is so damn hard to see them at times. I needed help to open my damn eyes. Friends, family, loved ones and acquaintances were all there, probably facepalming. There are support groups and associations just like the one I created.

Probably the biggest thing in the air, dangling a nice comfy hammock with a cup of coffee in a holder, was the Goodyear Blimp. It was being piloted by me, with a cup of coffee and a cigarette hanging out my mouth, shaking my head and facepalming. Probably saying my favorite Scottish expression.

The blimp was all lit up. Sparkling, blinking colors with the word "SELF" rolling across it.

There was never any reason to fall.

I forgot. I couldn't see.

But I guess that is sadly the way of things. It is so much like addiction. You need to hit rock bottom. Some of us need to find the cellars beneath the bottom. I've been there as well, waiting, my heart breaking, for a loved one to find that bottom.

It's a scary proposition. I know what the bottom means. You need to let them hit it, and the impact means one of two things.

236

Either they will start getting the help they need, or they will die. The death, though, can be a lingering thing.

When I was stranded in Mexico, I received a phone call. It was from a young lady I had met and had not spoken to in a couple years. I was surprised she still had my phone number. I didn't have hers anymore.

She was in tears. It turned out that she had gotten married, and the guy had become physically, mentally and emotionally abusive. She told me of her terror, her broken nose and broken arm. She needed help. Just a little money, enough to get her home, away from him.

I couldn't help. I didn't have anything. I would have sent her a bus ticket if I did. I was down to nothing myself, was begging myself. The only thing I could do was tell her, beg her, to go to a shelter. I had no idea where she was, but I knew that help, a helicopter, a rope ladder, was only a phone call away. She hung up on me.

I hope she found something and did not return to her husband.

Why do we stay in unhealthy relationships? There are a lot of reasons. As I said many times, we can justify anything. It's usually bullshit.

For me, it was a lack of a sense of self, and a fear of the great unknown. It was all of my issues and insecurities creating tunnel vision. It was a lack of view of the field and the net of people that surround me and care for me. It was the depression, the anxiety disorder, the PTSD, the co-dependency.

Lions and tigers and bears, oh my!

It was forgetting the people that had my back. It was not thinking I was worthy for people to have my back. It was a lack of aloha.

With that, the episode is a wrap.

Be kind to yourself. Be merciful to yourself. If you are struggling, stop squinting your eyes, open them, and see the net of relationships all around you. Start there.

Aloha.

Episode 32: Something to Be

With the last episode, Rob Thomas got back into my head, so he'll be joining us again this week. I really do need to find a way to get in touch with him. We'll also be joined by one of my favorite writers, LE Modesitt Jr.

Thomas' first solo effort, vastly underrated in my opinion, is the title of this podcast. Something to Be. It is also the answer to a question. Modesitt helps answer the question as well.

I've been struggling. Starting a new business is like a vortex for me, pulling me in. I'm a workaholic. It would be sort of like a recently recovering alcoholic buying a bar. Too much temptation. Far too much temptation.

There are 100,000 things to do when starting a business and I want to get them all done all at once. I need to get them all done all at once. I think anybody in my profession has to be borderline something or another, if not fully across the border. OCD, control freak, perfectionist, something. It has the tendency to not leave room for much else. In my case, the pressure of not having room for anything else creates a pressure in my skull.

The pressure can immobilize me, even when I have extra time to do whatever I want. Not doing anything creates a feedback loop, a distortion, that creates even more pressure. It is one of the things that led to my fiery burnout years ago.

A very long time ago on the podcast, I talked about getting into an episode about professional burnout. It was in one of my first few episodes. Well, I'm finally getting around to it.

Now, let's get into the episode.

First off, to any of my investors or business accounts that might listen to this, I'm okay. Really. It's not the "I'm okay" when I'm really not from previous episodes, it's an authentic "I'm okay."

But that is one of the things that is creating pressure on me.

It was very easy to be me, something to be, all of me, when I was not a business owner. As I spoke about in the previous episode, it was easy to be an author and a mental health advocate when I was unemployed in Tijuana. Not only did I have the time to do it, but there was no fear of having the stigma attached to me.

The stigma is very real. When I first started this podcast, I burst out of the closet in a big way, talking about depression, suicide,

PTSD, anxiety disorder and all kinds of things that scare the living hell out of people. Hell, I had the trumpet line like you see in the old medieval movies announcing me.

When I first began coming out about it, I immediately started running into odd stares and people shifting away from me. Me being me, it just led to me adding another line of trumpeters and telling them to up the volume and put some swing into it.

Aye, I was planning on killing myself. What the hell did I care? There is a certain amount of freedom, a huge amount, in not giving a shit anymore. When I shifted away from the plan to kill myself and into the role of a mental health advocate, I still didn't give a shit. That was the entire point: to talk about these things and be open about things to encourage others to do the same. To live life out loud instead of quietly in desperation.

There are a lot of misconceptions about mental illness. There is a lot of stigma attached.

The fear really started to worm its way into me when I was living in Tijuana. At 51, I was unemployed for the largest stretch of my life. I have a killer resume. I was considered one of the top people in my field. I couldn't find work.

Did it have anything to do with my LinkedIn profile and the posts about mental health? Aye, it's a real enough question.

I did hear that one of my investors pulled out, maybe two, when they researched my posts on Facebook. I think the mental illness posts scared them away.

"Don't worry about it," Bryan said, my main investor and business manager, "I got this covered. You be you." Now, he gets after me for not doing weekly podcasts because he knows it a part of my healing journey.

He's got 26 years sobriety and is very open about it. I'm not quite falling off the wagon and then running to catch back up. It is more like I fall off, get something caught on the bumper, and get drug along for a mile or two before I clamber back up.

The last thing that is going to happen is burning out again and seeing the wagon far away in the distance. I've learned too much. And I have help. I guess Bryan is my sponsor.

I need to figure out, though, why I burned out in the first place. There were many things going on. Professional burnout played a heavy role in what happened to me. How did I get there and how do I not go back there? More importantly now, how do I be me, all of me, the best version of me?

Well, it started out the other night, Friday night. The 100,000 things to do when starting a business have been whittled down to a much more manageable 8,549. I knew I was there, and it was time to start putting the plan into place that Bryan and I spoke about when I first moved back up here. Work, the business, is Monday through Friday, wake-up until about 3PM. That's my 50 hours or so. After 3 and weekends is all about the other parts of me, the balance.

I swore that when I woke up on Saturday, I would not touch anything to do with work.

So, of course, when I woke up on Saturday, I did a little bit of work, catching up on some emails. I felt myself bouncing along behind the wagon, being drug, as I signed the last email, and then I clambered back onto the wagon.

Aye, what can I say? It's a work in progress.

But then I closed out of the email, with other work things tickling my mind, pushed them away, recentered, and finally opened up the file my editor sent me a long time ago. I got back to work on my book.

It was a glorious morning, just reading, writing and editing.

Then, I bumped along behind the wagon again as I made my way to Staples when they opened to pick up a few things for the business.

Did I mention it's a work in progress?

I worked on the book for a bit more and then really started thinking about this podcast. I haven't been doing too much with it. That was expected. This really takes a lot of effort. I've always said it is like having a part time job that doesn't pay anything. The emotional effort is huge as well. I pour myself into this. The only way to do it right is to be completely and totally vulnerable.

To do the podcast, I need to get metaphorically naked. I didn't have a problem with that in Tijuana. Here, in Philly, starting a business? I can feel a pressure against it. That pressure combines with the time and energy investment. Do I make this my last podcast?

That's about when Rob Thomas came in and urged me up on stage to do some karaoke.

Hey man
I don't want to hear about love no more
I don't want to talk about how I feel
I don't want to be me no more

But I do. Rob is urging me through the next lines and then the chorus...

I've been looking for something
Something I've never seen
We're all looking for something
Something to be

Each podcast is about 4,000 words or so. That's easy. I can give you 4,000 words on any topic at any time. Go ahead: get me started on a tangent. You'll shut me up after about 50,000 words. Or try to.

But there is more to it. For one thing, there is the entire getting naked and being vulnerable part. To do that, I need to shut out everybody and everything. I need to maintain a detachment to all things, like a LinkedIn profile.

The real time and effort comes from research, looking for triggers. Rob can't be there to help me all the time. Something needs to trigger the podcast. It's not really hard; it is just about exploring myself and the web. LinkedIn actually. There is always a lot of information on there in certain groups, non-orthodontic related. I find triggers, inspiration, in posts and articles. I don't even have to think about how it relates to myself. The right one just wraps itself inside of my head and begins squeezing out thoughts and ideas.

I've been moving away from those posts and groups as I concentrated on my business. I now have a ton of article and video ideas on orthodontics. Aye, it was what I had to do.

And that's how I got into trouble before.

My business partner sucked, but I was doing okay. He was an employee, but I had managed to get everything under control with my own employee work and fiduciary duties. I thought I could finally start being a writer again.

I remember it clearly, though I forget exactly when it happened. About ten years after starting the business, I dove off a high cliff aiming directly towards the wagon that could take me to where I could be something. Be me.

I had good aim. Damn good aim. I was heading right for it. That's about when the technological tsunami hit my industry. Instead of hitting the wagon, I hit the wave and was carried away. I was soon doing my employee work and the business management work, but I was also learning technology. Fast. I pretty much had to teach myself how to be a mechanical engineer with an expertise in 3D printing and software.

Long story, but I rode that wave into professional burnout. It was a hell of a ride, a rush, exciting...until it wasn't anymore. The tsunami wave finally crashed and left me on a beach, exhausted and hurting.

LE Modesitt Jr is sitting in the audience. After I get done my turn at karaoke, he takes out his ear plugs, and says, "You forgot about Lerris."

I have to nod in agreement.

As I've said many times, I'll take my truths anywhere I can find them. Many of my truths did not come from holy books or books of wisdom. They come from the oddest places, like the movie, "Bill and Ted's Excellent Adventure."

Be excellent to each other!

Mr. Modesitt is a fantasy fiction author. I picked up his first book a very long time ago. It's remains one of my favorites, The Fires of Paratime. In his Recluse Saga though, with Lerris the main character of the first couple books, I found a lot of truths.

Talk about attention to detail. I think you can actually use Mr. Modesitt's books to learn trades like carpentry and metal work. I found a lot of truths in there. I would later put it together that his magic system in the universe is based upon systems theory, one of my soapbox issues. But I could dive deep into Recluse and lose myself and find pieces of myself. I'd forget though.

"What did Lerris learn," Mr. Modesitt asks. "One of the first lessons he learned from Justin?"

Rob and I pull up chairs to sit with him. I need to explain it all to Rob who may or may not have read the books, but you need a little background for any of this to make sense.

Long story short, Lerris is a young mage who is exiled to go find himself. He meets with an older mage, who later turns out to be his uncle, after an encounter with a chaos wizard that he barely escapes from. The older mage, Justin, takes Lerris under his wing and starts teaching him order magic.

The chaos wizard--I forget his name--is looking for someone exactly like Lerris, a young, inexperienced mage who has power but cannot protect himself. Chaos wizards extend their lives by taking over the bodies of others with power and transferring their identities into them.

--this really does all relate to the podcast and professional burnout.

Justin explains that the only way he can teach Lerris how to defend himself is by showing him.

Justin enters Lerris' mind. Lerris' mind is fogged. Swirling fog is all that he sees and knows. He gets lost. Justin is taking over his mind and body. Lerris is losing himself.

Then, he remembers what Justin had tried to explain to him.

"I am me," he starts thinking. "I am Lerris!"

By concentrating on his identity, who he was, he was able to shatter the fog and really do a number on Justin--who was really a good guy trying to teach.

Yeah, it's easy for me to get lost in that fog. It's even easier for me to get comfortable in it. That's where the pressures puts me. I forget who I am and embrace it. I lose myself in fantasy fiction books, strip clubs, and other assorted unhealthy coping mechanisms. The easiest thing for me to get lost in is work.

Aye, it is fun starting a business. Building the foundation is much like the lessons taught about other trades in Mr. Modesitt's books. It is easy to get lost in the details. Details and feedback from potential customers lead to other projects.

Feedback from business people and other lab owners also has my Philly attitude up. I'm being challenged. Battle! --like in the John Travolta film, Michael.

My deal with Bryan and the other investors was a very simple one. The investment money has to carry me and the business until it becomes self-sufficient, can sustain both the business and my salary. With the investors that pulled out, I was told that is impossible. A start up, I've been told, will never be self-sufficient until maybe after the first year. I'm planning on doing it in months.

Other lab owners have my back up, the infantry really combining with the Philly. The plan was to just build a small, little business, operated and run by myself, to make money while I work on my personal projects. I'm pursuing ideas I had years ago when the technological shift occurred in my industry. I'm stepping on toes.

Some who got my old accounts have their panties in a twist about me approaching them. That pisses me off. Another challenge. Another battle. I was there long before you. Hell, I taught many of you how to get there. My small, little business unfolded in my mind to become a national lab. It's not that hard to do it with what I know and what I can put together, how to approach offices and staff, how to educate them on how to integrate the new technology to improve their bottom line and open new avenues of revenue. I have over 35 years experience and expertise at this. Hell, parts of my plan intersect with the "Mental Health Advocate" label.

I'm stepping on your toes? Bullshit. This is my stage. I own it. Your toes are on the stage because I allowed it while taking a sabbatical. I'm back now, to rock it...

John Travolta is smiling his Michael battle smile. Rob Thomas and LE Modesitt Jr are facepalming and shaking their heads.

I've been looking for something
Something I've never seen
We're all looking for something
Something to be

Who am I? What do I want to be? How do I get there? How do I fight the forces of the vortex pulling me in, down, to the label of "workaholic" that burned me out?

It is so damn easy, and it is so damn hard. It is like last night, Saturday night, and not allowing myself to allow the repulsion from the vortex to tumble me into a bar or other unhealthy coping mechanism. It was about sitting down and working on this podcast. Working on the book a little bit. Then, I did what I rarely am able to do. I watched a movie before going to bed.

The pressures of so many things are building. I pushed them aside yesterday and did something that brings me so much joy: I spent time with my 2 1/2-year-old nephew.

Before my burnout and after I separated from my wife, Thursday night became strip club night. The atmosphere, dancing, touch and illusion of intimacy was a balm for me. An escape. My new work schedule, and my new sleep schedule, makes it impossible. Friday or Saturday night instead?

Thursday night is now Anne and Michael night. Anne, my sister, makes dinner. She wants to try to impress me or something. We ordered out a few times. I didn't like it. So, I asked for what I really wanted: something simple.

Last Thursday was one of my favorites: Hamburger Helper Beef Stroganoff. This past Thursday was another one of my favorites: Salisbury Steak with mash potatoes and corn.

Thursday is also nephew time. I haven't had a two-year-old nephew in 20 years. There are differences between Michael and Joseph, but the pure joy is very much the same. He has this belly laugh and smile that is infectious. He has this awe and wonder about everything. He has this very weird fixation on my table that makes me laugh because he always asks about it, where it is.

I know from previous experience that the clock is ticking with Michael. "Uncle Chris" is huge right now. In a few years, though, I'll start getting smaller as he grows into video games and friendships. It's okay. I understand. I expect it and want it for him, to explore the world that will become increasingly larger. By six or so, I'll be relegated to a secondary position as opposed to the primary that I now play. I'm okay with that but I need to take advantage of it now.

So, I stop by on Thursdays, have dinner, play, and then help get him ready for bed. He wants me to sit by him on Anne's bed while she wipes him down and changes him. Then, we pick out a book to read, I read it to him, I get my kisses and hugs, and then Anne puts him down.

I hang out for a little while longer while he gets out of bed and opens his door a half dozen times.

"Go back to bed, Michael! I love you."

I smile with Anne and shrug. He's two. Then, we go outside, have another cigarette, and I make my way home. Always smiling. Yeah, Thursday night is now Anne and Michael night. For as long as he'll let me. It recharges me in ways that other things cannot.

An uncle to a two-year-old is something to be.

Then, I get home. About 8 or so. I fight the vortex and the repulsion against the vortex. Pressure builds. I can't go to bed yet. What do I do? Who am I?

I am not a tv watcher. I just can't.

I am a writer, a podcaster, an author and blogger. I am a mental health advocate. I am a mentor to children who stutter and their parents. That is who I am, something to be, something to strive for so the balance between work life and personal life makes the pressure go away.

I need to start moving back towards that. It's things that I learned while traveling and then living in Tijuana. I fell into the other extreme, a fantasy land of being who I was without the balance necessary of a work life, an income.

I have the tools necessary to move forward. Slow steps, baby steps.

Is this my last podcast? No, not by a long shot. Instead of unplugging from it, I need to fully plug back into it, get back to incorporating it into my weekly routine.

Something to be. While supporting myself.

It's a work in progress.

As it will be for a long time, perhaps the rest of my life. Another step I really need to pursue is socializing. I need to develop personal relationships with, well, people. I need the interactions that I seem to deny myself while wearing the personas of business owner, writer and podcaster. Everybody thinking I want to date makes it difficult.

Anybody want a cup of coffee? Let's just meet and chit chat, talk story.

And, with that, it's a wrap for episode 32. Episode 33 will be along next week, on schedule. There are a few bumps coming up in the schedule as I have to balance some business and personal trips, but weekly podcaster is something I have to be.

Aloha.

Episode 33: A Wishy-Washy Pause

Well, I missed the scheduled Episode 33. By over a month. Which is telling me something. I know I was saying in the last episode that I wanted and needed to continue to do the podcast, and I do want to, but it is time to pause for a while.

I know, I know: I was just saying...

But, as a friend mentioned, sometimes you need to unplug from things to concentrate on other things. This is something that I really enjoy, but I need to unplug for a while to plug back into life, a healthy life. Getting off this damn rollercoaster is proving to be more difficult than I thought.

Now, let's get into the episode.

I really am doing okay. I am also not doing okay. It is hard to explain but I am going to give it a shot.

Physically, mentally, emotionally and spiritually, I am feeling great. I am feeling better than I probably ever have. I feel good about moving back here, starting up a new kind of orthodontic lab, and the joy I get from spending time with my nephew is enormous.

As I just wrote a friend, and spoke about in the past few podcasts, I had to take some steps backwards. I was expecting it. As positive as I am feeling about my new business venture, I knew I was facing a Herculean task. I was up for it. I wanted the challenge.

Everybody says that startups do not make money in the first year, maybe even the first two. I knew I could do it in six months. Had to do it in six months. To get there, I'd need to dive into "workaholism," as a therapist put it--love that word. I dove in, played in the waves, got swept out by the undertow, and laughed the entire time.

I'm back on the beach now, staring at the roller coaster.

I am not doing okay because of the overpowering shadow of that roller coaster, the pull to jump back on. I want to jump back on, need to. It is the easy and comfortable, and the path to it is the path of least resistance. I know if I just allow myself, I'll be swept up on to it, enjoying every second of the movement. I'll enjoy riding it again.

Until I don't.

The roller coaster was my life up until a few years back. You should be able to talk to anybody in a 12-step program and they'll be able to explain the roller coaster to you. I've spoken about it before.

Any kind of addict, from booze to drugs to workaholism, knows the roller coaster well. Even if they kick the habit, they tend to still live the life of an addict. For people with an addiction to booze, it's called being a dry drunk. For me, it's called being Christopher Gajewski.

Somewhere along the way, many, many years ago, I got my wires crossed. The workaholism, escapism, co-dependency and all manners of unhealthy coping mechanisms became ingrained into my life and my daily routines. So, though I think that I have kicked the habits, I am still acting like I haven't.

Case in point: my gym membership. I got one. I'm paying for it. But I haven't used it a single time yet. I just don't have time--or at least that is what I tell myself.

I'm pretty sure I am standing in the shadow of the roller coaster now, and not actually on it. My daily habits have improved, I take "me" time, I'm building better boundaries...

But I know I need to do better, need to do more, to put the roller coaster firmly behind me and get out from underneath its shadow. I need to take the path of greater resistance away from it. That takes time and effort. It takes time commitments to healthier things like the gym and yoga. I need to search out and find healthier social activities.

It's not enough to avoid the unhealthy activities. I need to be actively pursuing the healthier ones.

This podcast is a healthy activity for me, but it is also time consuming. I feel a pull towards it that it is something I MUST be doing. With my limited time now, even backing away from the workaholism to a certain degree, I feel it pulling me away from the things I should be doing to gain more self-actualization.

How did I do about explaining it?

So, I think it is best if I unplug for a while. A month, maybe two, maybe three. I need to put this firmly on a back burner, fully unplug, so I can pursue other things that will make this a healthier pursuit. Does that make any sense?

I suck at time management. I always have. Because of it, and everything else, even when I do have free time, I get stuck. I look and think through my "to do" list and end up not doing anything. Or I get pulled towards something that does not have to be done immediately to avoid doing something that should have been done a long time ago.

So, what will I be up to? When will the podcast be back?

The second question is easier to answer. The podcast will be back when it is time to start doing it again. It will be back after I move away from the shadow of that roller coaster and can commit the time and resources to do it right.

What will I be up to? That's my to-do list.

First, I am finishing my books. They have been on the back burner for too long. I spent the day on one yesterday and am now ready to get it published. Self-publishing can be a pain the ass, so I'll have to work through it.

I screwed up the first time I published it. I just got it done, without doing it right. This time, I need to put in the time and effort to do it right, exercise patience to really go over the first copy, and then I need to market and sell it right.

I want to do an expanded copy of this book and do that right this time.

Then, I need to make audio versions of both of the books, something that I really want to do that will take a major time commitment.

I want to practice what I have been preaching and get into the foundational stuff I talked about in this podcast, in the mental health triangle. The self-care. Did I mention I need to start going to the gym and yoga class?

I want to catch a couple Phillies games.

I need to go for a long drive before work makes it impossible.

I have all of the pieces in place. Now, I need to start putting them together.

The demons aren't even outside of my apartment anymore. They got bored and wandered off. Maybe there is one or two still hanging around for the right opportunity. But I'm just sitting in my apartment that I feel safe in, on the floor, with all of the puzzle pieces spread out before me.

How do they fit together?

Some pieces of the puzzle are still a mystery to me. They are there, but are they a part of the old puzzle or the new one?

I have some clicking and figuring to do.

When I get the puzzle finished and framed, and can comfortably fit this podcast back into it, I will.

Until then, be kind to each other. More importantly, be kind to yourself. Be merciful to yourself.

Aloha

Afterword: This is not a Wrap

When I first proposed writing a book about depression, someone mentioned that it needs to have a conclusion, a happy ending.

There is no conclusion, no happy ending. I am as happy as I can get at this point. The suicidal thoughts are gone. I am working and learning, wandering along my mental health journey as best as I am able. I'm stumbling often, but even when I fall on my face, end up with my nose in the mud, I seem to be finding things that will help me.

Yes, at some point in time, all of this, and many more episodes, will be distilled into a book. The working title of the book is "An Odyssey Into Depression." I am hoping that by the time I get to it, I will be employing the entirety of the Mental Health Triangle. I am hoping that the word "into" will change to "through."

There is hope.

I think I am on the correct path.

Until then, you are welcome to follow along with me on my journey. I will keep talking. I hope you start talking and continue as well.

Mental health is something we should all be talking about.

Aloha.